CULTURAL POLITICS

From *The Avengers* to *Miami Vice*

CULTURAL POLITICS

Further titles in preparation

From The Avengers
to Miami Vice
form and ideology in television series

David Buxton

MANCHESTER UNIVERSITY PRESS
MANCHESTER and NEW YORK

distributed exclusively in the USA and Canada by ST. MARTIN'S PRESS

Published by Manchester University Press
Oxford Road, Manchester M13 9PL, UK
and Room 400, 175 Fifth Avenue,
New York, NY 10010, USA

Distributed exclusively in the USA and Canada
by St. Martin's Press, Inc.
175 Fifth Avenue, New York, NY 10010, USA

British Library cataloguing in publication data
Buxton, David
    From the Avengers to Miami Vice: form and ideology in
    television series. – (Cultural politics)
    1. Great Britain. Television programmes. Sociopolitical
    aspects
    I. Title   II. Series
    302.2′345′0941

Library of Congress cataloging in publication data
Buxton, David, 1955–
    From the Avengers to Miami vice : form and ideology in television
    series / David Buxton.
        p. cm. — (Cultural politics)
        ISBN 0-7190-2993-7. — ISBN 0-7190-2994-5 (pbk.)
        1. Television serials—History and criticism. 2. Television and
    politics. 3. Popular culture. I. Title. II. Series.
    PN1992.8.S4B89   1990
    791.45′75—dc20   89-36672

ISBN 0 7190 2993 7 hardback
      0 7190 2994 5 paperback

Photoset in Linotron Joanna
by Northern Phototypesetting Company, Bolton

Printed in Great Britain
by Bell & Bain Limited, Glasgow

Contents

Acknowledgements

I am especially grateful to Andrew Benjamin who brought the Cultural Politics series to my attention, read a first draft and made many valuable comments and suggestions. I am also grateful to Rhonda Garelick for commenting on parts of a first draft.

This book began life as a research paper for a Centre Nationale de la Recherche Scientifique project on television series directed by Michelle Mattelart whom I thank for asking me to contribute. Alan Sinfield showed enthusiasm for the project at an early stage and made several helpful suggestions.

Finally, my thanks go to my wife, Marie-Agnès, fellow writer, for sharing the word-processor more than equitably during the writing of the manuscript.

D.B.
Paris, June 1989

For my parents

Theoretical underpinnings

What is there to be said about a television series? What, if anything, will viewers of the twenty-first century make of *The Untouchables* or *Miami Vice*? Will certain series, or individual episodes, be rehabilitated for their intrinsic artistic merits in the same way that French new-wave critics discovered overlooked qualities in the western or *série noire* film? To pose this sort of question from the outset is to realise the extent to which any attempt to treat the series specifically rather than generically implies a retreat back into the minefield of subjective impressions: as the forced irony of newspaper criticism shows, judgements seem somehow irrelevant in the case of the series, whose directly industrial nature ('produced in series') resists the *auteur* theory on which most film criticism depends. Everything in commercial culture conspires against the obvious, that its forms have a history, as freeze-frames of the present, time-capsules of dead ideologies. Only by situating series in ideological terms can we lend a semblance of dignity to those once proud figures that now haunt the late night re-runs and seem destined to do so for a long time to come.

The fact remains that, compared to serials (continuing narratives, usually in a 'soap opera' mode), very little has been written about series (the use of recurring characters in discrete episodes) outside anecdotal material for fans.[1] The development of cultural studies as a university discipline seems to have passed them by, while the interest of academics in 'television studies' has largely been limited to the question of 'effects' (especially those of violence), audience reception and news bias. Given the sheer number of people who watch the same series on a world scale, the lack of work on their content at first sight seems surprising. Something more is involved than the traditional contempt of the academy for popular culture. The aim of this chapter is briefly to discuss the reasons for this lack in terms of theoretical difficulties, and then to construct an object of analysis, in other words, to find a way of approaching series that allows progress to be made towards understanding their meaning and social importance. This means artificially delimiting an object which, for too long, has remained at the level of television as a whole, a purely technical object that makes it almost impossible to advance beyond ahistorical generalities. It should be pointed out from the outset that the focus of this book is on the analysis of particular series and that the purpose of the discussion that follows – necessarily somewhat polemical in character – is not so much to engage with other approaches (this would require a book in itself), but rather to indicate the book's theoretical options. Although the validity of these options stands or falls on the strength of the analyses, it seems only fair to readers to make the theoretical framework explicit and to outline, as simply as possible, the way in which I have worked through the problem.

It is no exaggeration to say that almost all work hitherto on the meaning (as opposed to the political economy) of popular cultural forms that goes beyond mere textual exegesis has oscillated between two classical positions broadly within the Marxist or critical tradition. For Horkheimer and Adorno,[2] the social meaning of the cultural product under capitalism was entirely determined by its commodity status, which functioned to produce a homogenous, uncritical consciousness. For Walter Benjamin,[3] on the other hand, the technology of the mass media (mechanical reproduction on a vast scale) produced a collective meaning, opening up the possibility for cultural struggle over this meaning, even within the framework of the capitalist cultural industries.

There are problems with both these positions. For all their force, Horkheimer and Adorno's strictures – particularly applicable to television series – against commercial culture can and have been used to justify an elite culture, uncompromisingly leading a shadowy existence on the fringes of the market. Their generalised rejection of commercial culture remains deservedly influential, but in closing off further discussion, it is liable to degenerate into a moralistic denunciation of 'low' culture, now almost entirely integrated into the commodity system. Benjamin's position, on the other hand, while avoiding the trap of economic reductionism, can easily lead to an exaggerated optimism attached to symbolic readings which evacuate the relations of production: at its worst, it can slide into forms of technological determinism of which McLuhan[4] was the most influential recent representative.

The sheer vigour of rhythm and blues-based pop music in the 1960s spearheaded a more general legitimacy of 'pop' culture and made the blanket, moralistic denunciation of commercial or 'mass' culture prevalent in the 1950s increasingly untenable, a form of wilful anti-modernism. Rock critics like Greil Marcus[5] insisted on the active role of rock music consumers in imposing their own idea of community on a mass cultural product. The position of Benjamin, as processed and distorted through McLuhan's 'retribalisation into a global village' seemed to apply, if not to television, at least to rock music which, integrated into identifiable subcultures, thus became a positive example of cultural struggle.[6] It was not that Benjamin had got the better of Adorno: rather, the opposition between these two poles was reproduced within the terrain of electronically amplified music. While rock was valorised as an authentic form of popular expression, 'commercial' pop represented and reflected the soporific consciousness condemned by Adorno. Meanwhile, in opposition to fears of manipulation on a mass scale, a new generation of academic sociologists in the United States argued that the meaning of a cultural product was not 'objective' but the result of an 'interaction' between producers and autonomous consumers.[7]

This short detour through rock music is important in that it helps us understand at least in part why television series have attracted little attention within cultural studies. The Adorno/Benjamin axis was not only introduced within a popular cultural form but also between forms: thus, for the 1960s counter-culture, rock and television were invested with oppositions between 'active' and 'passive' consumption, 'true' and 'false' needs.[8] The American music critic Ralph Gleason argued that 'radio and pop music belong to youth. Television belongs to their parents.'[9] Countercultural guru Charles Reich evoked the horrific spectacle of 'minds closed to new ideas and feelings, their bodies slumped in front of the television', in sharp contrast to the 'total participation' of rock audiences, 'feeling the music with all their senses'.[10] Finally, an article in IT (London) affirmed that 'while their parents continue to be lured by need-creating advertisements on TV, the first generation that grew up on TV is rapidly turning to music, art and literature, not only consuming it but creating it'.[11]

And yet rock, no less so than television, was a product in the market-place and a highly profitable one at that. Its supposed superiority lay in its being the 'authentic' expression of youth, charged with positive ideological virtues: the question of quality, either political or aesthetic, was circumvented by arguments for its sociological importance. Television series, however, were decidedly not the stuff of which heroic social myths were made, despite the efforts of McLuhan, relayed by media professionals, to valorise the participatory virtues of the television medium. Viewed in terms of (slumped) bodies massed, and hours accumulated, in front of the screen, series appeared to be of overwhelming importance, but only very rarely did this translate into anything beyond the small change of public discussion. The flat rejection of television by the 1960s counterculture (and later by the punks) remain rare examples of ideological engagement with television, however negative. The lack of public response in political terms seemed to constitute *prima facie* evidence both for the pacifying effect of television and for the essential passivity of the television viewer. For critics on the left, this posed a problem: the stigmatising of television series also amounted to a stigmatising of the very mass audience in whom hopes for political change were placed. In these circumstances, the attractions of asserting the 'activeness' of the viewer, however removed from any political engagement with television, have finally proved too strong. In the most sustained treatment of 'television culture' so far produced (in reality more of a catalogue of different approaches), John Fiske has extended the arguments of interactionist sociologists to television series in his insistence on meaning's being the result of a negotiation between producers and consumers:

Meanings and pleasures circulate within (the cultural economy) without any real distinction between producers and consumers . . . Its commodities, which we call 'texts', are not containers or conveyors of meaning and pleasure, but rather *provokers*. . . The production of meaning/pleasure is finally the responsibility of the consumer . . . Television is the plurality of its reading practices, the democracy of its pleasures . . . It promotes and provokes a network of resistances to its own power whose attempt to homogenise and hegemonise breaks down on the instability and multiplicity of its meanings and pleasure[12]

The credibility of this interactionist approach depends to a large extent on *a priori* assertions about the viewing process at a very general level. The apparently unacceptable alternative to this 'viewer-centred approach' to meaning is to treat viewers as 'cultural dopes', to use Fiske's term, to imply that they are incapable of 'resistance' to the proposed meaning. As common-sensical as this humanism sounds, it is nonetheless a tautology: the viewer is constituted as an 'active', freely-resisting subject while television is defined in its very essence as a 'provoker' of a 'meaning/pleasure' which is left to the viewer's discretion.[13] Meaning is therefore dispersed among the different individual reactions ('pleasures') to the manifest content which can be duly gathered as empirical evidence of 'resistance' to some ideal reading of bourgeois ideology. Two interrelated points can be briefly made here: the (ideological) meaning of a series cannot be limited to the level of *conscious* reaction and second, meaning cannot be isolated from the wider social context, nor therefore can it be evaluated in terms of 'effects', whether they be of indoctrination or resistance. The uncovering of left-wing voters who also watch *Dallas* only disproves the most caricatural theories of audience manipulation. Renouncing the very possibility of an analysis of content, the viewer-centred approach simply thrusts the burden of interpretation back on to the viewer. It is hard not to conclude that the loss of nerve involved in the reduction of analysis to qualitative audience research – who wants this 'knowledge' and why? – reflects the disarray provoked by the collapse of interpretative approaches based on structuralism and semiology.

Any attempt to analyse the content of television series must confront this disarray. Little structuralist analysis of series was actually carried out, partly because television represented a highly illegitimate object of research in a field still fighting to establish its legitimacy, but ultimately for reasons pertaining to the inherent weaknesses in the structuralist approach such as it was applied to film and advertisements during the 1960s and 1970s. And yet, structuralism – the search for a hidden grammar of meaning based on the analogy that language is 'structured' by grammatical rules – seemed tailor-made for avoiding the questions of taste and quality which had dogged attempts to incorporate a 'low' cultural form like television into academic discourse. In the influential analysis of 'bourgeois myths' by Roland Barthes,[14] it was implicitly held that all 'texts' were of equal value: the task of the analyst was to reveal, beneath the appearance of obvious discourse, the hidden contradictions of the dominant ideology. A more 'scientific' form of structuralism, semiology, was especially influential in film studies. More rigorously based on the linguistic model, semiology considered verbal expression and filmic expression to be virtually assimilable. In retrospect, its success is easily understood. Only towards the end of the 1960s were film studies integrated into university programmes: teachers, most of whom came from literary disciplines, were only too happy to find a field previously dominated by tentative cultural and stylistic appraisal promoted into an advance guard of scientific rigour. The strict, highly reductionist analogy between film and language which replaced subjective references and intuitions with rational analysis nevertheless had the disadvantage of transforming film studies into a colony of linguistics.

Unable to analyse the changing dynamics of film signification, semiology was destined to remain forever at the level of descriptive theory, an increasingly sophisticated form of taxonomy without causal explanation. The attempt to formalise a universal grammar of film meant that every specific film analysis aspired to a generalised theoretical statement relating to all films: each new analysis could only confirm or modify the original taxonomy. As Jean Mitry argued shortly before his death in 1988, 'if semiology is able to say *how* (*a film*) *means*, it is incapable of saying *why it means* . . . Operative when it is a question of analysing a particular film, semiology fails when it has to draw codifications, laws and rules applicable to all films. Its systematisations are always *a posteriori*.'[15] In the 1986 preface to a new French edition of his classic *Praxis du Cinéma*, Noël Burch ruefully confessed:

The main reason for the embarrassment I feel about this book today is easily found: it is called *formalism* or worse *musicalism*. It is called above all *the flight from meaning*. This book is shot through with a paradox: on the one hand, a neurotic rejection of "content" . . .; on the other, an equally neurotic perseverance in the quest for abstract, quasi-musical figures called "structures".[16]

Although the original concern of Barthes was to 'demythologise' the concreteness of everyday life, seen as a giant sign system, structuralism in its various guises rapidly tended to theoreticism and formalism. Texts were chosen in terms of their adaptation to theory, their meaning dense and well constituted in advance. This, and the need for legitimacy, led structuralist film analysis to privilege classic films, 'films which stood out from the others . . . In other words, formalism was coupled with elitism.'[17] The difficulties in introducing the structuralist method into the stony ground of television series are readily visible in Fiske's 'model' of an episode of a popular series from the 1970s, *Hart to Hart*', which related the adventures of a wealthy husband and wife team of private detectives. Invoking Lévi-Strauss, Fiske sees cultural contradictions as binary oppositions, large abstract generalisations like good and evil which are metaphorically transformed into concrete representations. In the episode in question, the Harts are posing as passengers on a cruise ship on which a villainous couple have committed a jewel robbery. For Fiske, the 'deep structure of *Hart to Hart*' can be expressed in the following list of binary oppositions:

good : evil
hero : villain　　　　　　　　　　　　　　　　　　　　　ABSTRACT
metaphorically transfromed into concrete representations
　　American : non-American
　　middle-class: lower-class
　　attractive : unattractive
　　light (cabin) : dark (cabin)

softened, individualised (cabin) : hard, impersonal (cabin)
close couple : separated couple
humorous: humourless
close-up : extreme close-up   CONCRETE
The opposed values are then given the narrative consequences of successful :
unsuccessful. Alongside this is another deep structure:
masculine : feminine
active : passive
thinking : object of look
controller: controlled[18]

Something has gone wrong here. A method which has supposedly revolutionised the human sciences has come up with a very thin broth indeed, so much so that it is difficult to see what has been gained in the process. Admittedly, Fiske's model is presumably meant as no more than a summary illustration of the possibilities of structuralism, but the oppositions remain at the level of simple description (the light and dark cabins) or are so general as to apply to any genre from any historical period (masculine – feminine). Fixed and atemporal, such a listing of binary oppositions cannot begin to explain the *singularity* of *Hart to Hart*, why it appeared on the scene at the time it did. It is little wonder then that the viewer-centred approach has arrived to compensate for what is essentially static description. Viewer-centredness and this form of structuralism are concordant only to the extent that the proposed meaning is limited to a smorgasbord of rather obvious binary oppositions from which viewers can presumably pick and choose. But theoretically, this is a formalistic dead end: whereas in the structuralist problematic, the reader/viewer is positioned by the text, the viewer-centred approach implies a subject who is independent of the text. Logically, the two approaches are contradictory and cannot coexist within the same theory of meaning. The problem here is that in themselves, 'television series' *do not constitute a theoretical object*: given to appearances, they can only be described and categorised, their essential truths extracted in the form of theoretical *a prioris* which become conclusions rather than premises. For this reason, it will be necessary to return to the theory of Lévi-Strauss, to see whether it will sanction a different approach.

The structural law of the myth

Structuralists analysis consisting of the listing of a large number of binary oppositions derives not from Lévi-Strauss but from a seminal article on the James Bond novels by Umberto Eco, the first attempt to introduce structuralist categories into the study of modern popular culture. According to Eco, the novels of Ian Fleming are constructed around a series of fixed oppositions which allow for a limited number of changes and interactions:

a) Bond : M
b) Bond : villain
c) villain : woman
d) woman: Bond
e) Free World : Soviet Union
f) Great Britain : non Anglo-Saxon world
g) duty : sacrifice
h) cupidity: ideal
i) love : death
j) chance : planning
k) luxury : discomfort
l) excess : moderation
m) perversion : innocence
n) loyalty : disloyalty[19]

These purely descriptive binary oppositions are combined with a plot analysis derived from Vladimir Propp's formalist analysis of Russian fairy-tales.[20] Writing in the 1920s, Propp argued that 'all fairytales are of one type in regard to their structure' and Eco likewise contends that the Bond formula is merely a variant of the archetypal structure of all narrative. For Propp, this universal structure consists of thirty-two basic plot functions performed by seven basic protagonists. For his part, Eco identifies nine basic moves in the Bond stories, present in all the novels but in differently ordered sequences:

a) M gives a task to Bond
b) The villain appears to Bond (perhaps in vicarious form)
c) Bond gives a first check to the villain or vice versa
d) 'The girl' shows herself to Bond
e) Bond possesses 'the girl' or begins her seduction
f) The villain captures Bond and 'the girl'
g) The villain tortures Bond and sometimes 'the girl'
h) Bond kills the villain or helps at his killing
i) Bond, convalescing, possesses 'the girl' whom he then loses[21]

What are we to make of this? In a carefully argued critique of Propp, Lévi-Strauss[22] shows that his model suffers from a dual, paradoxical weakness. On the one hand, Propp's 'functions' (the villain learns something about his victim; the hero leaves home; the villain is defeated; etc.) are insufficiently abstract because they are still formulated – albeit very generally – in storytelling categories. In other words, narratives are simply rewritten in terms of another, meta-narrative. On the other hand, Propp's functions are too abstract, to the point of being meaningless. To paraphrase Lévi-Strauss, Propp's formalism wipes out its object: there is finally only one story and there is no way of distinguishing between different narratives. The consequences of this are nicely expressed by Fredric Jameson: 'the observation that the sequence in the fairy tale is "thus and not otherwise", even if true, confronts us with something as final and enigmatic, and as ultimately "meaningless" as the constants of modern science, for example, pi or the velocity of light'.[23] Like Eco's binary oppositions, Propp's functions oscillate between formal statements so general as to apply to all narratives ('the initial misfortune is set right') and a simple restitution of the content of particular narratives ('a member of the family leaves home'). No theoretical development or synthesis is possible. Fiske, for example, informs us that he tested Propp's structure on an episode of Bionic Woman and found an 'astonishingly precise conformity', concluding that 'in general, (Propp's) structure underlies the typical television narrative with remarkable consistence'.[24] Presumably, all that is left for students to do now is forever to confirm the conformity of series to 'Propp's constant'.

Analysis based on identifying the permutations of a basic narrative works only too well in the case of television series, typified by what Todd Gitlin[25] calls 'recombinant thinking', a creativity of least resistance which proliferates variations from basic models. Gitlin sees the recombinant style as the result of conflicting pressures for novelty and constancy, the product of a television system organised around the principle of attracting mass audiences so as to maximise profit. An assembly-line demand for scripts and an unwillingness to take any risks means that inevitably a limited number of basic plots are continually repeated in slightly different guises. Far from being a genial insight of intellectuals, recombinant thinking is, as Gitlin's richly documented study shows, part and parcel of the common sense of series production. According to producer Aaron Spelling, 'there are only seven original plots'.[26] Also quoted by Gitlin, TV agent Jerry Katzman declares: 'the subject matter of all these TV movies you can list. There's only ten or fifteen story lines that they'll use.'[27] Given the narrow range of stories considered commercially acceptable, any analysis of the content of series must also concentrate on what makes them different over time, inversing the tendency of structuralism to reduce surface differences into similar ahistorical structures.

For Lévi-Strauss,[28] myth cannot be analysed at the level of language. Just as language itself is made up of constituent units (phonemes, morphemes, sememes), myths are also composed of what Lévi-Strauss calls *mythemes*. These mythemes consist of the relations or more exactly *bundles of relations* which appear diachronically (sometimes at remote intervals) in the myth. To illustrate this, Lévi-Strauss uses the example of archaeologists from another planet discovering, on an Earth from which all human life has long disappeared, an orchestra score and eventually deciphering it by reading it diachronically along one axis (left to right) and synchronically along the other (top to bottom). Only the synchronic reading would reveal the underlying rules of harmony without which the composition could not exist. Applying this method to the Oedipus myth, Lévi-Strauss organises various narrative fragments into four columns. The first and second columns group relations whose common feature refers respectively to the overrating and the underrating of blood relations. In other words, blood relations are either more intimate or less intimate than they should be. The third column is concerned with monsters and their destruction: the overcoming of monsters by humans is interpreted by Lévi-Strauss as a denial of the autochtonous origin of man. The fourth column, which groups the proper names whose meaning suggests a difficulty in walking straight and standing upright, represents the persistence of the autochtonous origin of man. Sketchy as it is, Lévi-Strauss's analysis has the merit of confronting the essential *unnaturalness* of the myth, giving us a corner of the eye view of a mentality now lost to us. If we are to see the myth in materialist terms, as part of the social practices of Greek society, we must recognise that *nothing of the myth remains*, or rather, nothing but its traces. The meaning which the ancient Greeks unconsciously 'recognised' in the myth and which made it 'worth the telling' has been lost forever. Any attempt to recover its meaning can only be the partial, speculative reconstruction of a mentality that is ultimately too strange for us to comprehend fully.

The Oedipus myth makes sense in a world torn between the observation that each human is born of the union of a man and a woman, and the cosmological explanation that mankind is autochtonous, born of the earth like plants. The contradiction cannot be solved directly: instead, the original problem – born from one or born from two? – is related to another problem; born from different or born from the same? The tensions of kinship as the cornerstone of social relations are structurally related to the mystery of origins in ways we can only guess at today (one of the Sphinx's riddles about the nature of man involves the analogous comparison of day and night – both of feminine gender – to two sisters who engender each other). Lévi-Strauss concludes: 'although experience contradicts theory, social life validates cosmology by its similarity of structure. Hence cosmology is true.'[29]

Accounting for the multiple versions of the same myth (for example, in earlier, Homeric versions, the story does not end in tragedy), Lévi-Strauss argues that a theoretically infinite number of variants can be created from the logical possibilities of mediating fundamental oppositions. But here, he is susceptible to the very criticisms he himself makes of Propp: the fact that mythemes are permutable does not mean that they are arbitrary. His 'structural law of the myth' which reduces all myths to the same structure is in itself an enigmatic, meaningless constant. Clearly, the problem of determination arises. What causes variations of the myth? How can its specific content be explained?

Lévi-Strauss is fundamentally ambiguous on this point. His contention that the function of myth is to supply a logical model for resolving a contradiction, an impossible task so long as the contradiction is a real one, would seem to place the structural analysis of myth firmly within a social and political context. But elsewhere,[30] he collapses the structure of myth into the inner workings of the cerebral cortex, a form of biological reductionism so radical as to annihilate the basis of materialism itself: matter becomes an explanatory principle of the mind.

The question of determination is a crucial one: if we are to explain the specificity of Sophocles' tragic versions of the myth (c. 430, 401 BC) in materialist, rather than universalist, transhistorical terms, we must be able to relate them to the political and ideological context of Greek society of the time. As Jean-Pierre Vernant asks:

If tragedy draws its subject matter from a form of universal dream . . . why then was tragedy born in the Greek world at the turn of the 6th and the 5th centuries BC? Why was it completely unknown in other civilisations? Why, in Greece itself, did the tragic vein dry up and give way to philosophical reflection which replaced . . . the contradictions on which tragedy constructed its dramatic universe?[31]

The emergence of the City of Athens in the sixth century BC, the abolition of slavery for debt and the establishment of equal rights for all citizens supposed the corresponding emergence of abstract social relations, free of personal or family ties. The political order became detached from cosmology to become the object of discussion and debate. Vernant argues convincingly that in Sophocles' tragic versions, situated at the frontier of human responsibility and divine destiny, the traditional myth is used as a framework to call into question an enigmatic, inconsistent model of human nature, oscillating between the equal of the gods and the equal of the beasts (both without an incest taboo). Knowledge of human nature defined in cosmological terms (the riddle of the Sphinx) is 'tragic', that is, useless if humans cannot escape their destiny. Sophocles' play can therefore be seen as a *strategic intervention* to affirm that human nature consists in the ability to question, to refuse the ambiguous language of the divine oracle and the equation of the march of Time with Destiny.

Lévi-Strauss's analysis, which lacks a political dimension able to account for the shifting versions of the myth, is therefore radically incomplete. This is not a question of detail, for no modern explanation can ever hope to come to terms with the richness of Greek cosmology. It is rather one of principle: the emergence of a class society, composed of free citizens and slaves, cannot be without influence on the positioning of the figure of the tyrant king, no longer part of cosmology but a potential political threat to the democratic order of the City. To be fair, Lévi-Strauss's interpretation was meant only as a demonstration of the possibilities of structuralist analysis. But this did not stop others from seizing on a ready-to-wear methodology, applicable – often in travestied form – to all manner of texts, translating narratives into *descriptive* lists of binary oppositions. Two essential points need to be made here. First, the results of Lévi-Strauss's 'method' are merely a starting point for further analysis: the oppositions need to be *related to one another* and *interpreted*. Second, the oppositions must be *contextualised* in terms of the social system in which the myth appears: in other words, the myth must be related to something other than itself if we are to propose an *explanation* of its content.

A structural absence

Whatever its shortcomings, especially for 'myths' in class societies, Lévi-Strauss's model does, however, enable significant advances to be made. Drawing on the insight of structuralist linguistics that meaning stems from the relations between components which have no fixed identity in themselves, Lévi-Strauss takes us beyond the surface level of the narrative, showing that the meaning (or the structure that makes the narrative

possible) is constituted by the *condensation* of the relations generated by
the narrative into several basic oppositions. It is the interrelation of these
oppositions and the *displacement* of one set onto the other(s) that gives the
underlying meaning of the myth.[32] Rather than seeing the binary opposition structure as a biological constant, we should see it as a formal
condition for a shared, social meaning: just as language depends on the
formal difference between what is uttered and what is not, themes from
social life can only be identified and (de)valorised by being placed in
relation to what they are not. As Lévi-Strauss argues, a myth is meaningful
to the extent that it engages with the fundamental contradictions of a
society and offers a 'solution' or mediation.

But the structural analysis of myth cannot be simply applied to the
modern literary work, film or television series, even if, in a very formal
sense, the existence of social meaning demands a 'structure' or interpretative grid. The structure is never immanently present in the text.
Arguing the contrary, implicit in structuralism, would deny the very
possibility of social determination. The text must be related to
something other than its own structure: in other words, we must explain
how it comes to be *structured*.

Unwilling to confront the question of determination, structuralism is
forever limited to a *positive* analysis, unable to explain why the myth is
'thus and not otherwise', why 'bourgeois ideology' is manifested in one
form and not another. As Pierre Macherey argues: 'Better than anyone
else, Lévi-Strauss is able to say what is *in* a myth. But . . . *he cannot see what is
not there, and without which the myth would not exist.*'[33] If the myth functions as
an imaginary resolution of a real contradiction, this is because it has
selected a contradiction which *it is able to resolve*. Its content, therefore, is
also structured by contradictions which *it is forced to ignore, which cannot be
resolved* within the structure it gives itself. This form of determination,
called by Macherey a *structured absence*, necessarily relates the myth to its
social and economic context. A text exists as much by *what it cannot say*, by
what necessarily produces fissures and strains within it, destroying its
internal harmony.

Applied to modern societies, the term 'myth' is a metaphor, not a
concept. The 'demystification' of 'bourgeois myth' in the Barthesian
sense consists in its *designation* as myth: it can describe (the advertisement
as 'disguised' myth) but cannot *explain* why specific cultural forms, figures
and themes exist, except in essentialist terms of reflection or adequation
to the economic system in which they function. For this reason, we shall
adopt Macherey's term *ideological project* which suggests the determined

relation between a text and its social and economic context. Given the inseparable connection in the television series between an (unconscious) ideological project and a (conscious) commercial strategy – the series being consubstantially an economic and an ideological form – the term ideological *strategy* will also be used.

Macherey illustrates his argument in a brilliant, extended analysis of the works of Jules Verne[34] which, given the extent to which it has influenced my own approach, is worth summarising. Briefly defined, Verne's ideological project is to show that it is the conquest of nature that defines the history of the second half of the nineteenth century. The future is contained in the present: humankind will one day know all there is to know about the planet and rule over it as lord and master. Nature is in advance: the conditions of a harmonious future relationship take the form of an absolute identification with it. Between humankind, the machine and Nature, a series of identities is established based on their fundamental complementarity. But the translation of these thematic elements into a narrative form, characterised by the absence of fundamental social conflict that would disturb the realisation of human destiny, leads to an extraordinary contradiction. The voyage of discovery follows in the traces of another lone voyager who has already anticipated the future in the past. The future is thus but a retracing of the past.

This is strikingly evident in the novel The Mysterious Island. Verne assembles the elements which translate his ideological project: the island (nature in a perfect, pristine state), a society in microcosm (a 'family' of representative individuals), and science (the engineer). But what are Verne's protagonists to do once the island has been explored and its features named? 'We shall transform this island into a little America! We shall build towns, railways, telegraphs . . . .'

At this point, a line of fissure develops between the ideological project and the intrigue. The social relations of industry and science evacuated, there is no discordance between the project and its realisation, no internal conflict that might propel the narrative. As the story advances, the original protagonists are no longer the conquerors of nature but the objects of an action from outside. The island is not deserted but inhabited by a 'mysterious force': far from being nature in its virgin state, the island is an artificial base for the scientific experiments of Captain Nemo. Verne's initial project – to recount the reality of science in fiction – has been subsumed by fiction. The centre of the narrative shifts to Nemo who, for all his 'revolutionary' advancement of science, is deemed to be mistaken in thinking that the past can be revived and in fighting against 'the necessity of progress'.

The reduction of science to the brilliance of individuals and the inability to confront the relations of force in industrial capitalism runs like an enormous fault line through the work. Instead of recounting the conquest of nature, Verne paradoxically shows that the elements assembled to translate his project are historically bygone. Unable to represent the future, Verne returns to the past, to that mythical theatre of pure bourgeois individualism: the island of Robinson Crusoe. The conquest of nature is reduced to the story of past colonisation, a past which already contains the present. These limits in no way betray artistic weakness on Verne's part: rather, they represent the *real limits* of the ideological project he sought to illustrate.

Three formal elements can be derived from Macherey's argument, which will prove crucial for our analysis of series. These are: 1) an ideological project or strategy which the narrative attempts to illustrate; 2) an assemblage which brings together and organises the concrete elements needed to realise the project; and 3) the narrative itself which involves setting the assemblage in motion. It is in the interrelation of these formal elements that the major strains and tensions of a text occur. The more a text attempts to remain faithful to its original project, the more it is forced to renounce narrative development, or strain to return to its point of departure in an unconvincing closure: the more it embraces narrative complexity and movement, the more it is forced to contend with its inability completely to cover over the cracks that open up between the assemblage and the narrative. Under the circumstances, given the ideological and commercial importance of television as a mass medium, it is scarcely surprising that series should contain so few basic narratives. This reflects the very real difficulties involved in producing series that resolve real contradictions in ways that are ideologically acceptable to a mass audience.

The question of determination can now be addressed. Except in empiricist forms of analysis, television series are not 'things': because the economic and ideological instances of society are purely theoretical constructs, the relations between them cannot be discussed in terms of 'effects' or ultimate causes. Nor is it enough to see determination as the setting of boundaries or limits: however much this avoids the pitfalls of mechanical causality or reflection theory, it remains a *negative* explanation. As Raymond Williams[35] argues, determination also exists in the positive sense of the exertion of pressures throughout the whole social process. For too long, cultural studies has depended on falsely sophisticated formalisms like 'the relative autonomy of the superstructures' to avoid these very real theoretical problems.

How are relations of determination to be established between a series and its social and economic context, given the generic similarity of television narratives? The answer lies in concentrating analysis not at the level of narrative, as in structuralism, but at the level of the *assemblage*. Each episode of a series refers back to a limited number of premises, an assemblage of elements which functions as a machine for producing a *series* of logically consistent narrative variants. This consistency within different narratives suggests a coherent strategy which the assemblage seeks to illustrate and it is here that relations of determination can be established. The carefully designed assemblage of a series is never arbitrary: it is in the theoretical movement away from total arbitrariness that an explanation begins to take shape. This means analysing a series not in terms of simple correspondence ('reflection') to external social and economic factors but in terms of a *strategy* which determines the choice of an assemblage from all possible absences, a strategy itself determined by the need to address specific contradictions which evolve over time. The ambition of this book is not to provide a general historical study of series but rather to attempt to show (however modestly) how each series discussed relates to its time.

The role of criticism

We now have a theoretical object in the dual sense of the word. An object constructed in theory (the series as ideological strategy) and an object or goal for our study (to analyse series in terms of this underlying strategy). What follows does not pretend to be a detailed analysis: the brief for this book stipulated a broad coverage and the time has not yet come when particular series can be given academic monograph treatment. Nor does the preceding discussion pretend to give rise to a formula or method that can be mechanically applied. My aim is to establish television criticism as a form of interpretative explanation and to this end, I have preferred to 'argue out' the analysis rather than resort to positivist-style lists and schemas. Generally speaking, I have sought to condense the contents of a series *as a whole* into a limited number of ideologemes,[36] recurring themes attached to different narrative situations (although to avoid overwhelming the reader in repetitive detail, I have limited the illustrative examples in each case). I have then attempted to outline the strategy of a series by reading 'in between' these ideologemes, to map out the ground on which the strategy establishes itself. For each series discussed, I have watched (and in some cases re- and re-watched) between ten and sixty episodes, according to availability and personal inclination: inevitably, only a fraction of my material has been used here.

A series cannot exist as a negativity. Economist explanations of the 'largest possible audience, lowest common denominator' type tell us everything a series needs to be successful and yet nothing at all. By virtue of the fact that it must rally a mass, trans-class, trans-gender audience around a positive project – at once economic and ideological – which is neither reducible to, nor explicitly against, dominant class interests, the series cannot be seen in monolithic terms as the 'perfect' expression of a dominant ideology. If such were the case, it could conceivably continue to generate narratives indefinitely from the same (slightly updated) assemblage. Series are not only commercially vulnerable but also ideologically vulnerable as previously convincing strategies and resolutions fall apart under the weight of their own internal tensions or are unable to resolve new anxieties of the viewing public. Following Pierre Macherey, I have tried to pay special attention to the tensions and strains arising from the failure to close over problems completely. These problems can be brought about by the tension between the strategy and its assemblage, or by the tension between the assemblage and the need to generate a series of narratives. The series often gestures to what it cannot say, or is unwilling to confront further, in throwaway lines and verbal slips, in other words, in scenes which fill out, but are incidental to, the main narrative. Because they are ultimately related to a reality external to themselves, the resolutions proposed are highly unstable: to paraphrase Macherey,[37] series are always 'in a critical state' and are thus open to an ideologically informed criticism which refuses fiction's pretence of arbitrariness. Rather than the application of a 'method', criticism demands an attempt at distance, the tracking down of the premises of what appears to be 'just a story'.

It should now be clear that questions relating to the political economy of series have been left aside. The series is fundamentally a commercial form of fiction (the need to guarantee audiences on a regular basis) and, for clear economic reasons, an American one (a large domestic market), raising the issues of cultural imperialism and alternative forms of television which are too vast to be dealt with here.[38] The option taken up in this book is that, alongside these problems, the criticism of series also has an important role to play in the search for new forms of television fiction.[39] I have, however, scrupulously avoided evaluating series in terms of simple political categories: it seems almost fatuous to suggest that, while none of the series criticised here can be described as 'progressive' in the ordinary political sense, partisan dismissal on this ground is beside the point in view of these series' genuine popularity, not only in the United States but also in many other countries. In fact, it is the very popularity of certain series that makes their criticism imperative: the ability to address sharp ideological contradictions – as opposed to the seamless resolution of caricatural oppositions – in a relevant, convincing way requires complex political evaluation and whatever eventual judgement one cares to make of the strategies presented here, the historical contradictions they attempt to resolve are real ones which cannot be ignored or blithely explained away. In this sense, discussion of the difficulties and limitations of series should not be interpreted as an exposure of weakness from some ideological higher ground. No ideological project, regardless of political tendency, is sufficiently coherent to survive the ordeal of figuration totally intact: the absence of difficulties is also a sign that the terms of conflict have been pitched at a very simple-minded level, precisely to conjure away real problems.

So where is the viewer in all of this? In a review of audience-centred approaches to television literacy, David Buckingham concludes that many critical approaches presume that meanings are somehow contained within texts and can be recovered by a process of analysis to be imposed against the differential readings spontaneously produced by viewers.[40] Here, it is not just a question of (trivially) affirming that different viewers have different reactions to the same text but arguing that the viewer's 'reading' is a constituent element, or even the ultimate seat, of meaning. The political thrust of interpretation thus becomes extremely problematic: the intellectual's analysis is worth no more than the viewer's own 'reading', or rather the viewer is seen to be quite capable of 'demystifying' television for him or herself without the aid of (elitist) academics with their fancy (French) theories. But what is the epistemological status of these viewer reactions? The directed, ideological nature of television is evacuated in favour of the viewer's own alignment between the televisual and the real, as if an easily readable television series and the wider social consciousness existed in separate, autonomous realms, as if the viewer's reaction were not also historically and socially determined within ideology. Television criticism must begin from the fact that it is the ability of a series' assemblage coherently to translate a satisfying ideological project that gives 'pleasure', that only a humanist criticism demands that something always be 'left over'. Mysteriously promoting the act of viewing into a form of 'resistance', as does John Fiske in his neo-populist revamping of uses and gratifications theory,[41] is downright incongruous given that no one is actually forced to watch a particular television programme. To a large extent, the very need to address this question reflects the degree to which television criticism (as opposed to literary criticism) is still tarred with the brush of 'effects theory'. In 'demystification' approaches, the mere identification of a hidden, essentialist 'bourgeois ideology' is sufficient to 'resist' its social function of assuring the audience's adhesion to an equally essentialist dominant order, a direct link between television's content and its political effects being more or less assumed. But while large sections of the viewing public may find the resolutions proposed by a particular series gratifying and convincing, a large number clearly do not. The relative success or failure of an ideological strategy also requires complex analysis that extends beyond any one television series, whose relation with concrete political action is necessarily oblique: a series' exaggerated, apocalyptic rendition of urban crime, for example, may help contribute to an 'imaginary' climate in which an extension of that state's disciplinary apparatus becomes a justifiable, even desirable, response to a real problem. It is in this wider social sense that the 'meaning' of a series cannot be said to be 'contained within' the television text.

Addressed to a mass audience of different political shades and class determinations, the series is objectively ambiguous. The defence of what are ultimately narrow class interests is displaced on to generalised popular values like the family, friendship, security, sexual and racial equality, worthy values which command a wide consensus. As Fredric Jameson argues, 'all ideology in the strongest sense . . . is in its very nature utopian'.[42] It is not enough to argue that the fictional presentation of these values is 'progressive', or that the friendship between the black and white protagonists in Miami Vice, for example, does not reflect the reality of race relations in the United States. The point here is that the utopian resolution of racial tension is strategically harnessed to the fight against a moral decadence that threatens both urban dwellers and business interests. If anything is to be said about a series, it is not because it is incomplete and in need of explanation, but because its closure can be shown to be not a closure at all. The task of the critic becomes clear: to show that the strains and contradictions of a television series can be publicly engaged with at the very level it refuses to acknowledge – its own ideological premises.

Questions relating to reception theory and empirical audience studies have therefore been excluded from the object of analysis, although I readily admit that data on the social class, age, sex and political attitudes of specific audiences, along with cross-cultural comparisons, would usefully complement the style of criticism I have in mind. The origins of my approach in literary criticism and anthropology,[43] a consequence of the lack of sustained work on television series proper, has also meant largely avoiding the consideration of visual style, although I would argue for the logical priority of the type of ideological analysis attempted here over formal aesthetic devices which pose problems of a different nature. For methodological (and personal taste) reasons, I have eliminated soap operas (in the broad sense, which includes *Dallas*) and serials from my choice: series with continuing story lines demand a different approach which pays more attention to narrative development. My choice has further been limited by the series actually shown on French television, excluding consideration of certain series that a British viewer might consider primordial: unavoidably, it is from within a (rather detached) French cultural context that the 'international' series discussed here have been analysed, although I have tried to see these series in terms of the way they present themselves rather than through external themes, paying attention to their British or American origins.[44] What follows is a selection of the most influential and representative 'action' series present on the international market from the 1950s up to the present. Three thematic genres have been used to organise the analysis: the 'human nature' series, the 'pop' series, and the 'police' series.

The human nature series

The emergence of the series form

Although the series as we know it today was the 'natural' product of commercial television, it was by no means the 'natural' form of television fiction. Even in the ultra-commercial world of American television, the play was the dominant form of television drama in the mid-1950s when it was thought, by both screenwriters and network directors, that the particular advantage of television over the theatre and the cinema was that it allowed the exploration of 'emotions' because of the small screen's natural affinity with the close-up. Since the content of early series was strongly influenced by economic contingencies, it is worthwhile briefly relating the circumstances in which the series emerged as a television form.[1]

Virtually all television fiction in the early 1950s went out live. Radio was the major inspiration, either in the form of soap opera/family sagas or detective plays. Early 'episodic fictions' (*Martin Kane, Private Eye; Mr District Attorney; Man Against Crime*) were poor things (flimsy sets being less than ideal locations for fistfights), little more than writing by numbers. *Man Against Crime*, sponsored by Camel cigarettes and produced by the advertising agency William Esty, used as many as fifty freelance writers. These writers had to comply with an exacting series of instructions: bankers and businessmen were not useful characters because political reasons (McCarthyism) precluded them from being suspects; doctors (strategic allies for the tobacco lobby) were to be shown only in the most positive terms; disreputable characters were not to smoke; a plot had to include at least one 'attractive woman', preferably with a 'passing romance' with the hero, Ralph Bellamy; one of the five sets had to be Bellamy's 'fashionable' Manhattan appartment; the end of each episode had to include a search-for-the-missing-clue sequence, more or less prolonged according to how much air time remained.

Given that the live play seemed to be the natural form of television fiction, it soon seemed preferable to develop a tighter structure, more adapted to theatrical representation. A division of labour was established between filmed and live television: the twenty-five-minute film (too expensive to be generalised) was used for outdoor drama and physical action while live theatre was used for indoor drama and psychological, rather than physical, confrontation.

Especially written for the constraints of live production and with a minimum of sets and costume changes, television plays explored what appeared to be a 'natural' subject for television: human emotion and human nature, which could be graphically represented in close-ups. Often called the 'golden age of television', this period (1952–56) saw the influence of Actors' Studio techniques whose moody, physical style seemed particularly adapted to close-ups and sparse sets. By 1955, there were no less than thirteen 'playhouse' programmes on American television, sponsored by major corporations like Philco, Goodyear, Kraft, US Steel, Revlon, Motorola and others. Initially willing to attach their corporate image to 'prestige' productions, sponsors soon complained of the discrepancy between the upbeat, optimistic nature of their advertising messages and the tense, problem-laden world of psychological drama.

In 1955, Philco was the first to switch to Hollywood-produced film series. Rather than abstract themes like corporate 'prestige', sponsors began to prefer identification with attractively presented actors on a continuing basis, all the more that the latter, mostly screen unknowns, were usually willing to do commercials as well. The boycott of the television networks by Hollywood film companies came to an end in 1955 when Warner, realising the new medium's advertising potential, agreed to produce 'film series' for ABC in the 1955–56 season with a ten-minute advertising segment for forthcoming Warner productions inserted into each sixty-minute film. Three series were shot, based on old Warner films – Casablanca, King's Row and Cheyenne – with a view to amortising existing sets and old footage. Cheyenne was so successful that it ran for seven seasons and gave rise to numerous spin-offs like Maverick, Colt 45, Lawman, Wyatt Earp and Gunsmoke.

As film studios came to terms with the historical decline of the cinema, the 'film series' quickly came to be seen as a desirable alternative to B-films. In effect, the cheaply-shot budget film (usually a Western) depended on a regular, undiscriminating cinema-going public and bore the brunt of competition from television. The Western was an ideal genre for series: not only could existing sets be used but old footage of crowds, herds and bar-room scenes could be inserted to cut costs.

Whereas the average B-film cost between $300,000 and $600,000, the average episode of *Cheyenne* cost $75,000 and could be shot in a mere five days. Furthermore, earnings from syndicated re-runs and overseas sales were pure profit. By the end of 1957, over a hundred television series were in production, almost all in Hollywood studios.

The shift of American television's centre of gravity from New York to Hollywood accelerated the dominance of series which could use and re-use existing studio facilities, unlike plays which required a special set to be constructed each time. To keep up with the incessant demands of programmers to fill the expanding new schedules, it made sense to use the same actors and locations on a regular basis. Series could also make a more rational use of 'guest' actors whereas live performances immobilised even small-part actors for rehearsal and shooting times. A formula was established whereby each episode contained a limited number of regular actors plus several 'guest stars'.

The second advantage of series was their greater facility for screenwriters, an important consideration in the industrialisation of series production. Whereas for the single play, the craft of the writer consists in the (difficult) construction of a coherent, simultaneous development of both story and character, episodes in a series can be put together in the rearrangement of the logical possibilities already manifest in the preconceived characterisations. The use of preconceived characters facilitated an enormous increase in the productivity of television writing, a necessary development if series were to continue weekly throughout an entire season.

Above all, the series was a way of resolving the problem of continuity which was to be acute, once grouped advertising spots in the middle of programmes replaced sponsorship in which content was entirely subordinate to corporate image. Direct sponsorship corresponded to the early stage of television during which networks lacked the financial control to impose their own programming. Once this control was secured (in alliance with production companies), and advertisers were no longer allowed to read scripts in advance, the television networks had to be able to guarantee advertisers regular audiences for the same weekly slot. By the 1958–59 season, nine of the ten most popular programmes were series with regular characters. Live broadcasts dwindled from 80 per cent of all network programmes in 1953 to 33 per cent in 1960.

The series was an ideal form for the rationalised mass production of television narratives, walking an ideological tightrope between the

demand for 'exciting entertainment' (which necessarily invoved legiti-
mised violence) and widespread fears, derived from a simplified
behaviourism, over the new medium's potential power to undermine
traditional networks of social cohesion. Between the competing
demands for action and moral pedagogy, there was little room for
manoeuvre. The (good) recurring characters were not transformable
and their moral determinations were immediately visible. Conflict
within this static formation was necessarily catalysed by adaptable
(usually bad) 'guest' characters intervening from outside. The Western,
which dominated television programming after the mid-1950s, had a vast
literary genre on which to draw – writers like Zane Grey, Owen Wisler,
Frank Gruber and Max Brand wrote thousands of novels between them –
but scenarists could also plunder novels from other literary genres: the
series *Wagon Train*, for example, featured thinly disguised adaptations of
Pride and Prejudice and *Great Expectations*. Formally, the series was able to
establish a tightly controlled ideological assemblage to which virtually
any 'external' story could be adapted.

Populism and human nature

The series had to create not only a popular form of entertainment but
also a political consensus for the solutions proposed. Two ideological
devices were capable of anchoring this consensus: one, philosophical,
relating to the exploration of 'human nature' and the other, political,
based on the populist attack on abuses of power.

The concept of a fixed human nature enabled at once a justification for
existing institutions, seen as the expression of, or the adequation to, a
commonly shared nature; and an explanation or apology for the 'evils of
society'. The inevitability of evil, touchstone of popular theories of
human nature, provided a basis for the moral evaluation of human
actions as well as a justification of institutions of repression. The drama
anthology *Alfred Hitchcock Presents* was not a series but a collection of short
dramas grouped around the same themes and the same presenter, a
formula which was to be repeated in *The Twilight Zone* (Rod Serling) and
The Outer Limits. In the episode 'Revenge' (1955), directed by Hitchcock
himself, Elsa Spann is raped – although this is not made clear for reasons
of delicacy – and reduced to a zombie-like state. The police have nothing
to go on. Elsa identifies a man in the street as her assailant: her husband
then proceeds to beat him to death with a spanner. In the next town, she
identifies another man. . . . The ideological strategy in this anthology was

invariable: to translate the homology between huvan law and divine law (disguised as 'destiny') and the adequation of both to 'human nature' into specific situations involving 'ordinary' people. Elsa Spann's doctor has prescribed 'sea and sun' following a 'small breakdown'. Fortunately, Carl's company is very 'understanding' and transfers him to California for six months. The Spanns are vulnerable: not only are they outside any local social network (symbolised by the precariousness of their caravan existence) that might protect them, but Mrs Spann has an overly generous vision of human nature, one that excludes the possibility of evil:

Carl: No reason (why you shouldn't be all right). It's just that I don't know any of the people around here.
Elsa: . . . They're friendly and kind and generous if you expect them to be, and most of them would be very quick to help someone that they thought was in trouble. A sprinkling of sourpusses, but only slight. In short, they would be like most people everywhere, very nice.
Carl: Practising nine hours a day since the age of ten might make you a great ballerina, sweetheart, but it's cut you off from the rest of the world.
Elsa: You're much too cynical. I can't believe that your world is any more real than mine, and I know that my world is much the nicer.
Carl: . . . What are you going to do all day in this lovely, imaginary world?

Carl, an engineer, has a better sense of reality, one that a woman, in a 'woman's world', cannot understand. Elsa is last seen sunbathing in front of the caravan: common sense, expressed in the gaze of a Mrs Fergusson (and the camera) down Elsa's dancer's legs out on to the empty street, deems this to be unwise, the flirtation with danger reinforced by Mrs Fergusson's frown. It is not, therefore, purely by chance that Elsa suffers a terrible destiny. Talking of her nervous breakdown to Mrs Fergusson, she explains: 'I was dancing my first part as a ballerina and Carl and I were married at the same time. I guess that it was just a case of too much happiness at one time. Does that sound foolish?' The strangeness of the explanation is evident to Elsa herself. A fissure has opened up here between human law and divine (or moral) law which Elsa's explanation cannot entirely satisfy. Nothing in human law exists to punish a woman who puts her artistic career ahead of marriage and raising a family yet, in terms of the text's ideology, the two are incompatible and it is destiny that punishes Elsa in the form of a depression and rape. This interpretation is underlined by the fact that Elsa is lacking in elementary wifely skills: 'Between you and me, I don't know how to bake a cake either.'
As the first half of the episode makes clear, Elsa is made ideologically vulnerable by her inability to understand human nature, an inability

derived from her own distortion of a woman's role: she is therefore fated to make herself physically vulnerable by sunbathing (alone) in a swimsuit in California where, unlike the more traditional Mid-West, a naturally good human nature has been distorted by the influence of the city. The second part goes on to explore the discrepancy between divine and human law and the inappropriateness of employing 'natural law' to make up this discrepancy. Much to Carl's disgust, the police are unable to make an immediate arrest, telling him that they cannot arrest everyone wearing a grey suit. An ideological closure is supplied by Hitchcock himself: 'Well, they were a pathetic couple. . . . Naturally, Elsa's husband was caught, indicted, tried, convicted, sentenced and paid his debts to society for taking the law into his own hands. You see, crime doesn't pay, not even on television.'

A similar theme is at work in another episode, also directed by Hitchcock, entitled 'Lamb to the Slaughter'. A policeman (whom we later learned was one for 'playing around with the ladies') announces to his wife (visibly pregnant) that he is leaving her for another woman. Beyond human law, he is nevertheless punished by (divine) destiny when his wife bashes his head with a frozen leg of lamb which she then proceeds to roast. Although the police are suspicious of the circumstances surrounding the murder, they cannot bring themselves to suspect the wife and are happy enough to accept her offer of a roast lamb dinner. Human law, the imperfect translation of divine law, must nevertheless be clearly separated from natural law (or revenge): Hitchcock's postscript assures us that the wife (who seems amused by it all) was eventually caught trying the same trick on her second husband but this time she had forgotten to plug in the freezer. The integral connection between human and divine law is even clearer in an episode involving a thief who kills a monk while stripping a monastery of its treasures: the abbot agrees to pardon his crime on condition that he spend the rest of his life in prayer in a monastery cell. Most of the episodes finish with this type of 'twist', whereby a wrongdoer escapes human law only to be punished by a higher, divine law or destiny.

The second major ideological device of the period, intrinsically related to theories of 'human nature', was the specifically American ideology of populism.[2] The rapid success of the American television industry cannot be explained by economic factors alone: the ideology of populism, which was able to address social issues, distribute rights and wrongs while transcending class oppositions, was an important contributing factor in the winning over of a veritable mass audience and helped put television fiction on a sure ideological footing. The moral stigmatisation of the greed of individual members of the political and economic elite contained inherent melodrama, as well as integrating into the nation everyone who met elementary guidelines.

Populism is fundamentally characterised by a lack of class-consciousness and can be found in both left- and right-wing forms. The question of income distribution and economic privilege can be raised, but the nation is divided not into classes but into an overwhelming majority of 'plain people' (imbued with most of the desirable qualities of 'human nature') and a handful of very un-plain, sophisticated, scheming conspirators, often but not always 'born with silver spoons in their mouths' (representing a perversion of human nature). Everyone else, be they businessmen, farmers, workers, employees, is in basic agreement about what is right and wrong. Populism depends on a theory of human nature to the extent that the influence of different social and economic backgrounds is discarded in favour of a general moral evaluation of human behaviour, applicable to all. Exploitation therefore arises from an unnatural appetite for wealth and power, an appetite far in excess of rational self-interest. Social problems require greater moral sensitivity, rather than (complicated) theories or big government. As the historic leader of rural populism, William Jennings Bryan argued: 'what this country needs is not more brains but more heart'.

This distinction between a 'natural' and an 'artificial' human nature was also transferred on to the social environment. The simple, rural or small-town existence was valorised over the 'artificial' city. Nature was the grand work of God, the only clue to His real intentions, distorted by the perversions, vices and naked greed of the city (one popular drama series of the early 1960s was called The Naked City and related the stories of different individuals caught up in its tentacles). Natural social relations were expressed in the close-knit ties between family members and between equals, characteristic of an idealised rural world: social classes, where they existed, were an artificial invention of the big city like New York, locus of big business, big government and big vice. This made the Western, then, a natural moral theatre where essential truths about the human condition could be expressed without the distorting influences of the city.

The foundation of society

The Western is a very loose genre, covering a vast temporal and spatial territory, ranging from the beginning of the nineteenth century to just before the First World War, from the Appalachians, the Sierras, the Montana Rockies, the Arizona desert, the dry Texas flatlands to the Californian valleys. The common element linking this disparate chronology and geography was the idea of the frontier, whose existence was as much psychological as historical and geographical. In very general terms, the Western genre addresses a burning American contradiction: between the values of competition and free enterprise and their inegalitarian consequences, and the egalitarian humanism which formed the core of the revolutionary Constitution. This tension, endemic to republicanism, is displaced on to an imaginary past before the development of industrial capitalism, on to conflicts involving inalienable values outside commodity relations (the community, the family, the sanctity of white women). The frontier was an ideological meeting point between barbary and civilisation. In 1893, the historian Frederick Jackson Turner declared, in what was to become the received historical wisdom, that the American character (throughout the country) had been influenced by the colonisation of the West and that this influence was part of the manifest destiny of the pioneers. For Turner, beyond the limits of civilisation, existed the Wild Lands of nature: each time that civilisation came into contact with nature, society and human nature were regenerated.[3] The concept of the frontier ploughed the mythical fields of a rural utopia, a vast, harmonious Garden of the World, an idyllic vision which sprung from the theoretical social equality incarnated in the Constitution. The presence of unlimited natural resources in the interior of the continent supposedly allowed this theoretical equality to be realised.

The only obstacle to the realisation of this utopia, setting aside the 'primitive' resistance of the Indians, was the moral weakness of certain pioneers, the effraction of natural and divine law. As André Glucksmann argues,[4] the Western takes us back to the very foundation of society, that privileged moment in which nature is humanised, the law is instituted and a rudimentary division of labour imposed. The virtues of independent peasants – the descendants of the yeoman class which formed the backbone of both the English and the American revolutions – are affirmed in an imaginary theatre wherein property rights exist outside of relations of exploitation. Fundamental bourgeois values are collapsed into natural moral values. From the outset, the Western genre was closely associated with a strong, unifying moral vision. The actor Tom Mix declared: 'I have adopted a simple philosophy which has always served me well – to remain clean in body and mind, not to eat too much, . . . to keep fit, to walk tall, to be loyal, to protect the weak against the strong.'[5]

Early film Westerns were an extension of the patriotism and militarism associated with the emergence of the United States as an imperialist power. The conquest of the West and the defeat of the original Indian inhabitants – displayed into posing a sexual threat to white women, preferably virgins – were confidently affirmed. In the 1930s and 1940s, influenced by the New Deal, the focus of Westerns began to shift to the conflict between free settlers and vested interests employing illegal means to seize land, the unacceptable, monopolistic form of capitalism represented by the railroad companies. By the 1950s, the portrayal of the conflict with the Indians had become politically contentious and squared badly with the civilising pretentions of America's presence in less developed countries.

Television had a clearly understood political and ideological role to play: the integration of an ethnically disparate America into a national culture. The sociologist Daniel Bell has remarked on the slowness with which the United States was constituted as a 'national society', the media system succeeding in constituting a cohesion beyond the means of the church, the party system, the educational system and the governing elites. According to Bell,

a society lacking clearly defined national institutions and a governing class conscious of the fact was amalgamated thanks to the means of mass communication. To the extent that it is possible to establish a date for a social revolution, we can perhaps mark the 7th of March 1955 as a milestone. That night, one American in two was able to see Mary Martin playing the role of Peter Pan in front of the cameras. Never before in all history was one individual seen and heard at the same time by so many people. It was this that Adam Smith had called the *Great Society*, but great to a point he could never have imagined.[6]

This functionalist explanation is far too mechanical: as we have argued, a series cannot rally a mass, trans-class audience around a technology alone. The ability to transcend political cleavages lies not in the simple avoidance or negation of political issues but in the affirmation of a consensus, often produced by the settlement of past political conflict. The political values of the New Deal, in which the contradictions of a previous stage of capitalism were successfully resolved, allied to the proto-republican morality of American populism, were to prove essential in the early years of American television. It was by reworking the conflicts of an earlier stage of capitalism within the political framework of the New Deal – the alliance between the law (or an embryonic state apparatus) and ordinary citizens in the protection of the weak against the strong (capitalism in monopoly form) – that the television Western was able to become an 'adult' form of mass entertainment. In effect, the adult series (primordial for the expansion of television into the middle classes) could not be composed from the simplistic, abstract opposition between good and bad, characteristic of juvenile series like The Lone Ranger and Captain Video. More to the point, the Western could not exist *as a series* at such a simple, non-political level: a certain degree of sophistication, albeit very relative, was necessary if the terms of conflict were not to be exhausted after a few episodes. In other words, the series demanded a minimal political and cultural frame of reference from which narrative tensions could be generated and reorganised.

Confident in its transposition of New Deal ideology on to a mythical terrain where fundamental free enterprise values could be triumphantly demonstrated, the Western had become, by the 1950s, virtually synonomous with American culture, an ideal framework for the transmission of a commonly held moral code. In a November 1953 acceptance speech for a 'civil rights award', President Eisenhower observed:

I was raised in a little town of which most of you have never heard, but in the West it's a famous place! It's called Abilene, Kansas. We had as Marshal for a long time a man named Wild Bill Hickok. If you don't know him, *read your Westerns more*. Now that town had a code and I was raised as a boy to prize that code.'

He went on to specify this code, 'a basic ideal of the nation', as 'facing up to one's enemies in a free society'.[7]

Within several years, through the new medium of television, Americans had taken their President at his word: 'watch your Westerns more'. No less than 120 Western series existed on the television screens between 1948 and 1972. The 1957 season saw the arrival of twenty-eight new Western series, the 1959 season, another thirty-two. By this time, a third of all night-time network hours were occupied by Westerns.[8]

Television Westerns differed in several crucial respects from the film Western. Production costs precluded any extended emphasis on the imagery of the outdoors: external shots had to be reduced to a single fixed location like a ranch, trading post or town. Following in the fashion of television plays, the series had to relate compact stories involving a limited number of characters. Westerns were, in effect, a disguised form of 'realist drama' in which contemporary social problems could be treated on the surer terrain of a romanticised Western setting. This displacement of contemporary anxieties and the pedagogical function of 'Bonanzaland' was aptly expressed by John Cawelti:

The Cartwright ranch is surrounded by a world of chicanery, violence and treachery in almost the way the harmonious American middle-class suburb is threatened by the explosive forces of the expanding society. But the cohesiveness, mutual loyalty and homogenous adjustment of the Cartwright family always turn out to be capable of throwing back, or blunting the edge of, the invading forces.[9]

The second major aspect of the television Western was its concentration in the post-Civil War period so that the genocide of the Indians and the searing, still-divisive wounds of the Civil War could be avoided. This period, which saw increasing conflict between small landowners and big capitalists, was also a more relevant terrain for New Deal values, seen as the very teleology of the American Dream. The 1870s was the temporal setting for *Bonanza*, *The High Chaparrel*, *Gunsmoke*, *Laredo*, *Laramie*, *The Big Valley* and a host of other series, ranging geographically from Virginia, Arizona, Texas and Kansas to California.

Although a more 'entertaining' vehicle for social moralising than the television play, The Western nevertheless had to keep a tight rein on the violence intrinsic to its need for physical conflict. At least one successful series, *The Outlaws*, was abruptly cancelled in 1961 following widespread complaints about its excessive violence. For this reason, the Western tended towards a sub-genre of soap opera: the two most long-running series, *Gunsmoke* (1955–75) and *Bonanza* (1959–71), owed their success to their suitability for 'family viewing'.

Gunsmoke, which began as a radio serial in 1952, was the most popular television series by 1958. Influenced by the pseudo-documentary approach of *Dragnet* with its emphasis on understated, 'realistic' dialogue, it privileged characterisation over action. The minimalist Western setting was a pretext for the exploration of more general, timeless 'psychological' themes pertaining to human nature. In this sense, it was important for characters to show 'adult' human weakness and self-doubt at the same time that the virtues of civic responsibility were affirmed. The principal characters were a social microcosm in themselves: the dour, upright Marshal Dillon, his flamboyant wife Kitty, also the owner of the town's saloon (a husband-and-wife partnership of duty and pleasure, harmoniously combined within the family unit), the loyal, stout-hearted but none-too-bright sidekick Chester (the manual worker) and the resident intellectual and physician, Doc (the professional worker).

In *Bonanza*, the highest rated of all series between 1964 and 1967, the blood-family unit is the natural core of an embryonic society, a patriarchal unit for the three Cartwright sons are the product of three different marriages. Ben Cartwright is three-times a widower. The basic 'good-ness' of the Cartwright family permeates through all its members, despite their radically different personalities, aptitudes and physiques: even the rascally, dandyish. Little Joe eventually makes good. A solid, complementary bloc, the family is able to overcome hostility from out-side through its coherence and range of skills. 'Outside' is very much the operative word: the series' ideology forbids any serious interpersonal rivalry within the Cartwright family and also, more importantly, between the Cartwright family and the townspeople of Virginia City, good 'plain people' whose embryonic capitalist society is relatively harmonious. The instructions for writers of *Bonanza* episodes are explicit on this point: 'The townspeople must not turn against the Cartwrights . . . (who) are too intelligent in their behaviour, too respected and too prominent to have such a thing happen.'[10] The series' ideological bases are rock solid but cannot, in themselves, generate the conflict necessary to any narra-tive. To this end, conflict must always come from 'outside' and a strong demarcation of an 'inside' and an 'outside' is essential to the underlying ideological strategy: on this point, Cawelti's vision of a beseiged subur-bia, a 'Bonanzaland', to use McLuhan's term, is extremely perceptive. Conflict is triggered by 'visitors' or 'bad elements' who refuse to mind their own business. The cardinal principle of keeping one's nose out of other people's affairs, the very basis of the series' reconciliation of indivi-dualism and social harmony, surfaces insistently in virtually every epi-sode, often explicitly voiced as a fundamental principle of social life. This is so important to the series' ideology as to be written into the guidelines for scenarists: 'The Cartwrights are not do-gooders. A problem should never become a Cartwright problem merely by them pushing their way into it.'[11] The Cartwrights become strangely passive heroes, dependent on outsiders disturbing the organic harmony of the ranch and city to show their mettle. The threat to social order is always, first and foremost, a personal threat to the Cartwrights.

If the Cartwrights are forced to wait for black sheep to turn up, it is because the city has assembled all the necessary elements for 'free' capi-talist development (the family; proud and independent individuals; a strong moral code; the absence of a landed property class). There is no social project: the townspeople (a conspicuously diverse representation of ethnic groups) have only to wait for the seeds to bear fruit and to weed out the bad elements which inevitably exist in every social group. In 'The Day of the Dragon' (1961), which deals with a crooked politician's cam-paign to whip up anti-Chinese hysteria in Virginia City, Ben Cartwright is careful to specify that the Civic Protection League – some of whose members have been involved in anti-Chinese assaults – is generally made up of 'civilised people'. The attempt to explain racism in terms of the self-interested efforts of a dishonest demagogue, Ridley, who is running for mayor, squares oddly with the series' conception of the townspeople as plain, morally wise people: after all, a demagogue needs willing sheep to follow him. Fired by the rhetoric of Ridley, ready to lynch young Jimmy Chung who has been unjustly accused of the murder of a young white woman, the townspeople nevertheless dump Ridley from one moment to another once lectured to by the Cartwrights. Clearly, plain people, although basically good, have a tendency to be misled, to be open to manipulation, to follow the crowd: only remarkable individuals of superior moral strength can keep them on the straight and narrow. The inside: outside structure of the series is doubled up by the inside:outside relationship between the Cartwrights, who own – and crucially work on – the Ponderosa Ranch just outside Virginia City, and the townspeople. The Cartwrights intervene from outside, from the neutral, 'uncontaminated' space of nature. It is therefore important for each episode to establish a threat or a problem that simultaneously affects both the Cartwrights and the townspeople, to establish a justification for intervention.

In 'The Saga of Annie O'Toole' (1959), Annie O'Toole and another man dispute the rights to a concession in a mining settlement. To avoid the conflict degenerating into violence, Ben Cartwright proposes that 'in the absence of official law, we must make our own law' and is appointed judge by unaminous acclaim. He justifies the Cartwright's intervention thus: 'it's not by ignoring the rest of the world that we will help our society become stable'. The genesis of the law is an individual of superior morality and intelligence whose arguments are accepted by other citizens as their own. Judging fairmindedly, Cartwright decides in favour of Annie, by far the more appealing personality of the two, on a legal technicality which happily brings legal form into line with 'human law'. The episode also relates the genesis of capitalism at a mining site where there is no official authority and therefore no social relations. The fiery Annie O'Toole sets up a restaurant in the camp in partnership with Adam Cartwright who supplies the food and fuel. Although she cannot read or write, Annie is an excellent cook and, the commentary informs us, 'has a certain gift for business' (increasing the price of her stew from $1.50 to $10 in the space of a few weeks, presumably in accordance with the laws of supply and demand, although one wonders how impoverished miners could afford to pay). Eventually, Annie makes a small fortune, sufficient to make a 'good' marriage and buy a country house. The conditions for acquiring wealth from practically nothing (a small parcel of land) are minimally reunited: natural skills, opportunism, a strong personality and an ethnic disposition (in this case, Annie's Irishness).

The episode 'Enter Mark Twain' (1959) relates the passing visit to Virginia City of journalist Sam Clemens, long enough to use his pen to destroy the ambitions of Judge Billington, a mayoral candidate in the pay of a ruthless railroad company that is out to seize part of the Ponderosa Ranch. Clemens destroys the reputation of Billington by dubbing him 'Professor Personal Pronoun' in view of the fact that he always begins his sentences with 'I'. A vain, conceited individualism does no more, in the episode's moral lesson, than hide an underlying submission and corruption. True individualism is manifested by Clemens, a 'character' who has travelled the length and breadth of the United States, exercising dozens of different trades before choosing to share his knowledge with his fellow citizens. Unlike some of the townspeople, who enthusiastically accept Billington's offers of free whiskies, Clemens has principles which he has acquired through experience: 'I pay for what I drink.' Clemens is the quintessential American populist hero, combining physical courage and intellectual shrewdness: it is while in the presence of the Cartwrights in a shootout with the railroad gang that he comes up with his famous pseudonym, derived from his boyhood memories of the Mississippi steamboats ('Mark the twain').

In 'The Stranger' (1960), a gambler, Sam Board, wants to buy some land without borrowing from the bank: 'I don't want any obligations to anyone'. Adam informs him that it is only by working that one can earn enough money to become a landowner and offers him a job on the Ponderosa ranch for $40 a month, and at the end of the year, ownership of ten heads of cattle. Ben Cartwright, we are informed, had to work for long years before he could buy the ranch which existed as a dream in his imagination long before becoming reality. The passage of a sect whose religion forbids them to use violence suggests an easier means of self-enrichment to Board, whose moral determination as a gambler and a drifter has led him to refuse Adam's generous offer. While stripping the sect of their belongings, Board kills the sect's leader. Feeling responsible for his death, Adam kills Board in a shootout: this natural justice on behalf of those who cannot defend themselves is at odds with the sect's pacifist creed and Adam loses the dead leader's daughter with whom he has fallen in love. The institution of the law, which exists to defend the weak against the strong, depends on a minimum of social binding, on the dual respect for the property and the opinions of others.

The ideological base of *Bonanza* was a very stable one and owed much of its success to the longstanding Sunday School tradition of dressing up moral homilies in secular adventures. Its only source of inner strain comes from the ambiguous nature of the townspeople in the series' moral universe. In order to dispense moral lessons, the Carwrights must be shown to be superior to others. Evil stems from the bad human nature of a small minority of individuals but for the threat to become a real one, of sufficient difficulty to warrant intervention and to generate narrative suspense, the evil must penetrate the townspeople who have less moral fibre than the Cartwrights. Here the series comes up against the real theological difficulty of accounting for the origin of evil, a problem that recurs in various forms in American television series. An all-powerful God created man perfect, in His own image. But the serpent, which tempts Adam and Eve to eat from the Tree of Knowledge, is also part of Creation. Explaining evil as an external force tends towards a dualism which undermines the monotheistic basis of Christian faith. Translated into secular form, this dilemma involves a constant oscillation between accounting for evil in terms of the imperfections of human nature and presenting it as an external force which disrupts the basic goodness of human nature. The Republic needs the moral guidance of superior individuals like the Cartwrights if populist values are to be upheld, but the consequent devaluation of the moral judgement of the townspeople is at odds with the populist belief in the capacity of plain people to distinguish between right and wrong. Although liable to be misled, the townspeople are quick to recognise the correctness of the Cartwrights' arguments when the crunch comes. This is because the Biblical homilies dispensed by the Cartwrights are already known and accepted by all in advance: the townspeople, like the television audience, needed constant reminding. As the 1960s wore on, this moral pedagogy lost favour with younger audiences as the ideological difficulties of using a Western setting mounted up. It was all very well to ground capitalist values in human nature and to explain away social disharmony by the bad nature of a small minority from 'outside' or the moral vacillation of the townspeople. But such a resolution depended on the perceived harmony of an embryonic capitalist society and its teleological extension into a New Deal America, whose 'traditional' values seemed ill-adapted to a new age of mass consumption. The Western was also left adrift when it came to addressing the social problems (racism, poverty, the Vietnam

War) thrown up in the 1960s, whose directly political terms demanded a more sophisticated and more relevant strategy.

Loyalty to the state

The Untouchables (1959–63), based on the true-life efforts of Eliot Ness and his small band of G-men to stamp out gangsterism during the Prohibition period, was an attempt to update the populist tradition. The Prohibition years represented a critical turning-point in the relative strengths of (wet) urban America and (dry) rural America: by the early 1930s, the population balance had definitely shifted in favour of urban areas. The moral evaluation of the city changes from a generalised condemnation to a more nuanced attack on specific targets. The character of Ness and his partners shows that the vices of the city can be resisted by those who are morally upright: similarly, the errors of well-meaning but naive out-of-towners or recent arrivals show that living in the city requires special skills in addition to a 'good' human nature. The major error is to take the American dream too literally, to equate the city with easy money and fulfilled ambition: a common trope is the naive young woman who wants to be a singer but becomes ensnared in that locus of sexual and financial vice, the (shady) nightclub.

The underlying strategy of The Untouchables was to displace the populist critique of big business on to big, illegitimate business. In purely business terms, little separates the gangster from the businessman. One of the last episodes, 'One Last Killing' (1963), describes the attempt of gangster Julius Flack to prepare what the voice-over commentary calls (ironically) an 'industrial reconversion' towards new business opportunities in the vice and narcotics rackets, in anticipation of the forthcoming legalisation of alcohol. This involves the dumping of hatchet men like Krupa whose crude, indiscriminate violence has become a liability ('When it is a question of killing someone, you're a master. But can you do serious business?'). Given one last chance to show his business acumen (raising $2 million in fresh capital without resorting to murder), Krupa comes up with a rearguard business opportunity, the theft and reconversion of 200,000 litres of industrial alcohol:

> Krupa: . . . because it's worth a million dollars.
> Flack: As if you could sell your junk to anyone else.
> Krupa: Julius, let's talk like two businessmen. I'm asking a fair price for guaranteed merchandise . . .
> Flack: You're talking like a rookie. If I'm the only buyer, you'll be forced to accept my price. It's worth only $100,000 to me.

The relations of force involved in this characteristic confrontation between small business and monopoly capital are identified with those between different hierarchies of gangsterism. The gangster is a businessman and reasons in business terms, but what fundamentally distinguishes him from the honest businessman is the flouting of the law and the use of violence to achieve illegal and illegitimate business aims, such as the construction of monopolies. On first sight, the choice of the Prohibition period seems an odd one for a moral theatre: Prohibition was finally voted down in a constitutional amendment in 1933 and the conventional wisdom had come to stigmatise the attempt to impose moral standards on Americans. But bootlegging was only one aspect of organised crime, a springboard for diversification into the more stable, long-term protection rackets which used violence to eliminate outside competition and could be extended upwards (to wholesalers) and downwards (to retailers) in the vertical integration strategies of big corporations. The inevitable result of protection rackets was an inflationary series of price rises as the costs were passed on to the consumer. In 1929, there were ninety-one different rackets in Chicago, whose direct cost to the city was a staggering $136 million a year and whose indirect cost could only be guessed at. This system – maintained by the use of force (in 1928 there were 116 bombings and 399 unsolved gang murders in Chicago) – amounted to an unofficial sales tax on ordinary citizens and an implicit threat to the authority of the state.[12]

Following in the footsteps of the New Deal, the series seeks to harness support for Keynesian state intervention from within populism (despite the latter's distrust of 'big government') by making common cause between the state and ordinary Americans against a condensed threat of monopoly capital and immorality. At a time when it was loudly proclaimed 'what's good for General Motors is good for America' and when fears over the symbiotic relationship between big government and big business were beginning to be voiced ('the military–industrial complex'), The Untouchables portrayed a small team of individuals representing the government (in alliance with honest citizens and honest business) fighting as relative underdogs against big illegitimate business. The business dimension of crime is continually insisted upon. The voice-over preamble to 'Junk Man' (1963) informs us that 'the secret of his success (is) brutality and murder'. The gangster in question, whose front for a narcotics racket is, symptomatically, as a junk dealer, complains that 'profits are getting lower and lower. . . . Ness has cut my turnover in half.' By situating itself in the pre-New Deal period – finally, a more important ideological reference than Prohibition – *The Untouchables* presents a negative world in which 'honest' free enterprise cannot survive and magnifies the moral distance beween the brutal, illegal methods of primitive capital accumulation and contemporary, 'civilised' big business which respects the role of the state. The attachment of the series to the coat-tails of the New Deal is made clear in the following voice-over commentary from 'One Last Killing': 'March 1st 1933, bank failures spread panic from one end of the country to the other. The American people put their trust in Franklin Roosevelt to restore calm.'

Only the state stands in the way of illegal business monopolies and the ordinary citizen. Gang 'empires' are presented as rival states, characterised by retrograde hierarchies: 'The word house was a very modest name for such a place. Castle was a better word. Waxey was the king. He had a court and the sinister-looking guests were his loyal subjects' ('The Waxey Gordon Story'). Gang leaders spoke of their 'territory', of 'taking over' new states. In the war between business and the state, gang leaders had little doubt who had made the right choices:

Waxey Gordon: Now if you had any sense you'd be looking into something with more money . . . do you know 'follow the leader'? You must have played it when you were a kid. All you gotta do is follow the guy who knows what he's doing and before you know it, you've made a bundle . . .

Eliot Ness: And what would you do with my job and everything it stands for?

Gordon (checks himself): . . . I know some other guys who work for the government and who . . . I got a pretty good idea of what you make, the dresses your wife wears, what she goes through to make ends meet. It's time to switch sides. You're wasting your life. You're a smart guy, you should at least take advantage of it . . . Lots of people go through my garbage cans. The smart ones find gold and the not-so-smart find only garbage.

Ness: For me, in a garbage can, there's only garbage.

Gordon: . . . I started from nothing, I did everything myself and now I've gotten to the top of the ladder, I wear the best suits with a different tie for every day of the year, I drive the fastest car and you know why? Because I've got a head on my shoulders, a brain that I use and I make money with it. And you? What are you? You're a piece of trash that you throw in the garbage can. You're a waste of time . . . Nothing's changed since I was a kid when the stuck-up brats would stick together and refuse to play with the others . . .

Ness: Perhaps they didn't like your rules.

Gordon: No, they were what you are today . . . cowards! (*slapped by Ness*) The last person to do that to me died in an 'accident'!

Ness: Get out!

Gordon: I'm going, good and faithful servant of the government!

In a system that encourages personal ambition (succeeding from nothing is the classic American dream) but refuses to allow state intervention on any vast scale to prevent this ambition from having negative social consequences, the only guarantee of social harmony is the moral vigilance of each and everyone. Personal ambition must be kept without reasonable grounds, those marked out by the law. In the 1950s, the boom in consumption, the extension of credit and the corresponding rise in juvenile delinquency and what was seen to be a slackening of moral standards aroused anxieties about a return to the law of the jungle that reigned in the 1920s, a ripping asunder of the social fabric. The gangsterism of the Prohibition years depended on armies of wayward, greedy young hoodlums, all seeking a short-cut to material success in a society whose moral values had been profoundly shaken by the war. One world war later, a renewed outbreak of juvenile delinquency could not be satisfactorily resolved in law and order terms (having attained 'social problem' status): the issue is displaced on to another, similar problem, that of the integration of ethnic groups, with different customs and rules, into the legal and moral framework of American capitalism. Tellingly, however, the gangster is portrayed as someone who has failed to reach adulthood, remaining in the egoistic petulance of childish gratification: the two references in the above passage to childhood games indicate that the real stake is youth as a key space of social reproduction, implying the possibility as much of decadence and degeneration as of renewal. Citizens who assert their individuality are those with a firm, personal set of upright moral values, refusing to 'play along with the others', in the case of the government agent, suffering personal hardship in the necessary fight to protect citizens from themselves, to help them keep to the straight and the narrow. The massive increase in the personal consumption of consumer durables which marked the 1950s engendered widespread fears relating to the 'manipulation' of citizens into 'satisfying false needs'.

The city is a more complex theatre than that of the Western. The traditional social fabric with its straightforward moral principles had broken down and all inhabitants of the city were vulnerable. Some were willing accomplices to wanton disorder: that familiar (and exciting) figure of the 1920s, the sexually incontinent blonde, resurfaced with a vengeance in 1950s crime fictions, usually as the motivating force behind the implacable descent from honesty into crime. Sexual immorality was integrally linked to illegality and crime. The slightest moral slackness visible on the body betrayed the direst corruption – the (blonde) secretary manicuring her polished fingernails on the job in 'The Waxey

Gordon Story' is also in the pay of the mob and an accomplice in the murder of her boss. Ness has few illusions about the capacity for honest resistance of his fellow citizens: 'There's a new denaturant in that alcohol that has to be separated to make it drinkable. . . . I don't want to have the poisoning of the population of San Francisco on my conscience' ('One Last Killing'); 'if we fail, they'll be enough narcotics in this city to intoxicate every inhabitant' (('The Junk Man'). Many episodes feature short interludes in which the voice-over commentary (the voice of pure authority) recounts how greed can lead to a sticky end. In the city, everyone is a potential accomplice of crime and disorder: social harmony required constant moral vigilance on the part of all. The voice-over introduction to 'Star Witness' (1960) declares: 'The (early) 1930s, a black stain on the history of the nation. Its citizens are only too happy to buy all the goods they want from gangsters. Organised crime is plunging its greedy hands into every sector of the country. . . . Gangsters pay no government taxes.' The episode relates the efforts of one courageous fishmonger to denounce the fish market racket (worth $40 million a year), overcoming his fear and the cynicism of his fellow workers as to the capacity of the law to do anything. A moral injunction is addressed to every citizen, for without co-operation the state is powerless: 'we've got to put millions of fists together to fight back'. Individual consumption is the weak link of the chain binding citizens to the authority of the state. Integrating New Deal values into traditional populism, the series suggests that the ultimate cause of crime lies in personal moral weakness, a reality of human nature to be compensated for by the rule of law. The intervention of the state in the economic sphere is displaced on to the maintenance of public order and justified in terms of this analogy, the figure of the gangster condensing a threat to the ordinary citizen which is at once criminal and economic.[13] In the burgeoning new era of mass consumption, with its unlimited new possibilities for greed, an alliance between private morality and the state seemed more necessary than ever if social decomposition was to be avoided. To this end, the experience of Ness and the G-men serves as an illustration of a general truth about human nature and the need for such an alliance. In 'A Taste for Pineapple' (1963), Ness concludes, following a period of temporary blindness after a grenade attack by a war hero turned psychopathic killer, 'a man who says he is never afraid is either a liar or a madman'.

At its prime, The Untouchables was followed by one American household in three. But for all its popularity, the series profoundly divided the public over its use of violence. The 'realistic', cold-blooded murders were assuredly an important part of its appeal, but each episode also provoked thousands of letters of complaint against its excessive violence. The series' strategy of using the Prohibition period as a *negative* example of an unregulated capitalism leading to a breakdown of social harmony in a war of all against all was (mis)interpreted by many as a *positive* example of the renewed possibilities of social violence in the form of juvenile delinquency. In other words, The Untouchables was accused of provoking the very moral decomposition it was trying to warn against. Refusing the way the series positioned them as potential accomplices of Evil, many turned this accusation back on to the series itself. Second, the strategy of transposing the fears relating to the successful integration of youth into a new consumer world on to the earlier integration of ethnic groups into 'respectable' capitalism ran aground on the hostility of these groups, shocked at what they saw as negative stereotyping. Later episodes toned down the violence and Anglo-Saxonised the names of gangsters. Clearly, however, the series' themes would have to be addressed more directly, in a contemporary setting.

Like The Untouchables, The FBI (1965–73) was based on fictionalisations of true cases. Here, even more so than in the earlier series, the obligations of citizenship are shown to be difficult and exacting. The enemies of the USA are ready to exploit the slightest moral weakness to obtain vital secrets. In 'Wind it Up and it Betrays You' (1968), the KGB agent takes out the photos of four American scientists working on a defence project: 'Here are four good Americans. . . . The chink in the armour of this one is ambition. He wants to be boss.' Without necessarily being evil, good Americans can unwittingly betray their country by having a false set of moral priorities; for example, putting friendship, family ties and sexual relationships before loyalty and patriotism. The frontier between being a good citizen and a traitor is exceedingly thin: unusual and unfortunate circumstances (the hand of 'destiny') can make anyone vulnerable. Looking for the American accomplice of pro-Castro terrorists among a ship's crew ('The Gray Passenger', 1968), the FBI agent asks what was to be a recurring question in the series: 'Has Colfax spoken to you recently about needing a lot of money?' Terrible consequences may follow ('the penalty for espionage is death') from an individual's moral weaknesses and the epilogue to every episode is specially designed to inform us of the eventual punishment suffered by the individuals caught up in the affair. Destiny hovers over the series, setting up trials of moral strength that some will pass and others will fail. The KGB agent has little doubt of its existence: 'Everywhere I go, new problems always catch up with me. It's my destiny.' Lisa, a Chicano ranch-owner, says to Billy Silker, a bank robber on the run: 'You can't escape your destiny' ('The Harvest', 1968).

The title 'The Gray Passenger' is a revealing one. Much of the drama in the series comes from an exploration of the 'grey' area of human nature which oscillates dangerously between good and bad, between voluntarism and destiny. For some, the issue has been settled. Asked by his mistress if he wouldn't prefer another, calmer job like bank manager or painter, the KGB agent in 'Wind it Up . . .' does not hesitate for a second – 'never'. For others, the scale may finally tip towards the good: the cynical Barbara Reyes, in 'The Gray passenger', saves her skin and her soul by co-operating with the FBI, to the surprise of her Latin-American, communist lover. But for yet others, the die is cast. In 'The Harvest', Billy Silker, who turned to crime after his father lost his land in Kansas, falls in love with Lisa and aspires to marriage and a 'stable life'. But he is unable to resist the pressures of his older partner to participate in another job. Broken-hearted, he declares:

Billy: Lisa, I thought people could change but I was wrong. I've nothing to offer you.
Lisa: (watching the crippled Martinez, once a famous bullfighter, engaging in a mock bullfight with a little boy): He's stayed the same Martinez, the best matador in Mexico, and not a crippled old man. He's strong, gracious and brave. You shouldn't try to change yourself. You can't do anything against your nature.

The 'job' goes wrong. In a pathetic death-bed scene, Billy promises to take Lisa back to his native Kansas and adds, before dying: 'It's not always easy . . . You can forget your mistakes but you were right, you can't wipe out your childhood.' In an attempt to portray Billy as fundamentally decent, the series is, once again in spite of itself, forced to invent reasons other than a bad human nature for his criminality. The obverse side of the American Dream, a predatory capitalism, is evoked in the form of the bankruptcy of Billy's father but left unexplored. We are led to think that had Billy been less ambitious and remained in his native Kansas, in spite of the difficulties, things may have turned out differently. Yet even this is partially undermined by the emphasis on destiny, fixed forever during Billy's childhood. The importance of childhood as the locus of social reproduction, a time in which the weaknesses of human nature are resolved one way or another for all time, is urgently underlined.

The obligations of citizenship pose special problems for those who have not benefited from the American Dream. That this problem needed to be addressed reflects anxiety as to the successful integration of poorer ethnic groups, most notably the blacks, whose most radical organisation (The Black Panthers) had adopted an explicitly revolutionary ideology. Blacks are notably absent from the series: the difficulties involved in the integration of an exploited underclass are displaced on to the quietist Chicanos. But even passive resistance was fraught with danger for the nation's security. Interrogating the Spanish-speaking mistress of an ex-South American President in 'The Gray Passenger', an FBI agent asks:

FBI agent: You're an American?
Barbara Reyes: Yes, I was born in San Fernando. My mother was so poor that she would get herself arrested every time she was due to give birth just so that she would have a roof over her head for the delivery. She did everything for me. She survived everything. That's what I'm doing too, surviving. See no Evil, hear no Evil, speak no Evil, that's my philosophy.
FBI agent: If you replace Evil by Truth, what does that give?
Barbara Reyes: The same thing.
FBI agent: You'd do anything to survive.

A serious problem has been raised which the FBI's house philosopher completely ignores, only too content to speak his lines, that the refusal to face Evil is a refusal to face the Truth (of the American Way). Why should Blacks or Chicanos, manifestly unfavoured by Destiny, feel any special attachment to American values? A propaganda vehicle for these self-same values, the series cannot resolve this question other than to hint that those who have been disadvantaged by fate must make a special effort. Destiny and human nature are erected into founding explanations of social injustice. But an emphasis on destiny tends to undermine the series' injunctions on behalf of a voluntarist moral effort. Crime and punishment are part of an implacable, predestined process: the series' strategy of fleshing out simple stories of crime with heart-rending moral dilemmas is often strained in the extreme. The pedagogical function of presenting moral dilemmas is based on the individual's freedom to choose the appropriate solution: once this choice is taken away, the dilemma disappears. The series attempts to negotiate this difficulty by presenting individuals torn between two possibilities which are worthy in themselves but inappropriately chosen, organised into an unsuitable hierarchy of priorities. In 'Anatomy of a Prison Break' (1966), Frank, an ex-convict, places his love for Cissie above the law:

Cissie: Frank, with all these cars, they're looking for mechanics everywhere in town. You could try to find work . . .
Frank: You don't understand, I love you. I'm through with little jobs here and

there, through with credit. You deserve better. The biggest car, the most expensive mink coat, and what do you say to a little trip to Rome?
    Cissie: Frank, it's you I want.
    Frank: Don't you understand? I'm doing it for you.
    Cissie: I don't want your mink coat or a trip to Rome. I don't want any of that.
    Frank: You don't know what you want. Open your eyes! Furniture falling to bits
. . . A roof that leaks every time it rains.
    Cissie: For a lot of people, that's already luxury.
    Frank: No, not for my wife.

Frank is not a bad person, but it is his inability to put his worthy desire
to please his wife into perspective that fatally leads to crime and tragedy.
More than ever, the blandishments offered by the consumer society
demand an unswerving allegiance to the law – the insatiable need to offer
one's wife or mistress a mink coat, an *objet maudit* which symbolises
women as sexual objects rather than wives and mothers, is also present
in *The Untouchables*, notably 'The Man in the Cooler'. As in 1950s crime
films, women often play the role of Eves for vacillating men, although
here it is clearly spelt out that there are other ways of satisfying one's
girlfriend or wife – by being upright and hard-working – than showering
her with gifts. Loyalty to the state is the fundamental principle of social
life. In 'The Kober List' (1968), the respectable Dr Matthew Kober is torn
between his respect for the law and loyalty to his (gangster) family. The
episode is organised to show that it is by retaining his respect for the law
above all else that he is ultimately more loyal, on a human level, to his
father than is his brother (a nasty piece of work) who has schemed to
eliminate his father and take over the family business. Once again, the
active co-operation of citizens is essential: it is precisely when citizens
lower their guard, sidetracked by purely material considerations, that
crime prospers. In 'Conspiracy of Silence' (1969), the FBI's investigation
of mafia real estate fraud in a housing development called 'Paradise
Regained' is frustrated by the unwillingness of witnesses to come
forward. Reese, an accountant, tells the FBI bureau chief, Durand:

    Reese: I think that the mafia is a myth but if it exists, it's the FBI's job to do
something, not mine . . . Listen, believe me, I'm ready to help you . . .
    Durand: Except I don't want to get directly involved? . . . A paradise where
everyone closes their eyes, a paradise of ostriches with their heads in the sand . . .
Mr Reese, the Cosa Nostra is a real cancer. To pretend it doesn't exist is pointless.
You've got to open your eyes and fight Evil. The FBI can win only if every citizen
lends a helping hand.

Confident of the rightness of their fight against crime, *The Untouchables* and The FBI are necessarily closed texts. Both series have the same formal structure, a spiralling closure of the circle of fate which reinforces the immutability of the social order. In both cases, a skeletal crime story is used to illustrate certain basic truths about human nature which are felt to be applicable to a new consumer society, generally, the negative consequences of placing individual loyalties (or worse, greed) ahead of social responsibilities. A formal distinction is made between the voice-over commentary which makes moral judgements on the characters and (private) scenes in which the viewer is placed on the same level of the characters, but is able to confirm the truth of the commentary for him or herself. Extending religious-based morality into the secular domain through the use of illustrative stories from real life, both series stitch together disparate scenes of public life (the law) and private life (crime) by passing constantly from a God's-eye-view of the world to a human one. Divine law demands more from ordinary citizens than merely respecting the letter of the law. There is crime, and there is moral complicity with crime by not fully co-operating with the authorities for a variety of understandable but illegitimate reasons.

By the late 1960s, the simple-minded conception of human nature in The FBI, paralleled in an equally simple-minded conception of law and order, had become offensive to many of the young (especially college students) for whom the repressive, illegal activities against the civil rights and the anti-Vietnam war movements rendered the FBI's occupation of the moral high ground derisory and hypocritical. The social origins of delinquency and violence, spectacularly impressed on the conscious-ness of Americans by the 1968 race riots, could no longer be ignored. The FBI could do no more than gesticulate in this direction, evoking and abandoning the dark side of American capitalism like an open wound which the series' ideological framework, with its voluntarist, moral explanation of crime, cannot bandage over. The confident equation of (Moral) Good with the 'Truth' of the 'American Way' exploited a powerful strand of the American populist tradition which was to remain influential until the early 1970s. But after 1968, the writing was on the wall: intense political contestation of the American 'system' and the deep division over the Vietnam War had transformed the American Dream into a lie for a sizeable minority. In 1970s police series, especially after the 'dirty tricks' revealed by the Watergate scandal, the FBI were to bear the brunt of the populist suspicion of federal bureaucracy.

Are the beings of your race worth it?

The Invaders (1967–68), takes the question of human nature to its ideological limits. One night, in the lonely countryside of rural America, an architect, David Vincent, witnesses a saucer landing: he alone knows that human-like invaders, fleeing their dying planet, have arrived to colonise the Earth. One should resist the temptation to see this series as a simple displacement of the Communist threat on to alien invaders who have taken human form, or to poke fun at its advanced paranoia. Completely sincere in the presentation of its own contradictions, The Invaders attests, despite itself, to a moment in which the Americans begin to doubt the universality of their system of values.

Much of the internal tension and unique atmosphere of this series comes from its unusual attempt to expose a utopian project (the unification of humanity; a common human nature) within the hate-filled, intensely patriotic framework of the Cold War. Fundamental American values are under threat, but given the increasingly violent internal divisions over the 'war against communism' in Vietnam, this threat cannot be politically located as in 1950s police and spy series. Following the strategy of the Western in collapsing capitalism and the law into a universal human nature, the threat is similarly grounded in biology rather than politics. The series' ideological project, that of post-war American imperialism itself, wavers between a narrowly political defence of American values and the generous extension of these values to all humankind.[14] In 'Summit Meeting', the alien 'Ellie' collaborates with David Vincent in foiling a plan to assassinate the world's leaders who have been reunited in a summit conference, organised by a pacifist Scandanavian prime minister (in reality a puppet of the invaders), to discuss measures to take against a worrying increase of radioactivity in the earth's atmosphere. The aliens have prepared a simultaneous coup d'état in every country so that their 'representatives' can take power in a strategy that oddly respects national political jurisdictions. 'Ellie', however, judges the plan to be strategically wrong, 'because it will reveal our presence to the human race which will then unite in a vast fighting organisation and quickly annihilate us'. The struggle is clearly a universalist one for the whole human race: in 'The Condemned' we are informed that the invaders have also set up bases in Great Britain, West Germany and the Soviet Union. In 'The Captive', the personnel of the Soviet embassy in New York are drawn into the struggle. Yet this pan-humanist aspect is constantly undermined by the series' Cold War reflexes in the form of verbal slippages: the arms manufacturer Cook is vouched for a 'real patriot' ('The Watchers') whereas the aliens are referred to as 'your compatriots' in 'Summit Meeting' and threaten 'our government' in 'The Condemned'. In 'Vikor', a protagonist building regeneration tubes for the aliens is said to be working for a 'foreign power'. In 'The Trial', Vincent asks an elderly alien couple: 'Who sent you here?' – 'A friend of the cause, Mr Vincent', they reply, using a term that refers directly to the Communist threat. The credits sequence shows the alien saucers approaching the Earth from space, homing in on the United States.

To assemble the elements necessary for the expression of its utopian, pan-humanist philosophy without confronting the political and economic obstacles to its realisation, The Invaders is forced on to a fantastic terrain, illustrative of the sheer difficulty of realising its project. In effect, the unity of the human race can only be realised by evoking a threat to the whole human race so that it can come together in a non-political, purely biological struggle for survival (another slippage is the application of the word 'race' to the aliens, a theme explicitly explored in 'The Vice' when a black police inspector is forced to choose between his loyalty to his own race (a 'black' alien due to be named as head of NASA) and his loyalty to the human race). Human nature must therefore be valorised as it stands, complete with its strengths (noble sentiments, 'love') and above all its weaknesses (hate, greed, racism, etc.). This relatively pessimistic vision of human nature, characterised as an eternal compound of good and evil, is often turned back onto the original project of the series, finally more concerned with the creeping immorality infecting the very American values it seeks to defend.

In 'Summit Meeting', Vincent discusses the relative merits of the two races with the (beautiful) alien, 'Ellie', in her hotel room (a repressed sexual setting):

Vincent: You must laugh at us on your planet, us poor emotional humans, so easy to fool.
Ellie: You're used to feeling emotions, so you find that normal. Do you want me to teach you our way of being?
Vincent: (with disgust): Not for anything in the world.
Ellie: Look at you! You feel love and also hate, pleasure and at the same time, immense pain. You love peace but make war. You despise each other. Believe me, your way of life is no better than ours!
Vincent: How could you know? You've never felt anything. You don't know what love is.
Ellie: No. But I don't know what hate is either. Isn't it better, to have known neither love nor hate?

The resolutely non-political terrain of the struggle makes it hard to argue for the moral superiority of the human race. What 'way of life' is being talked about here? Can there be such a thing as a 'human way of life'? The series' supranational framework prevents it from openly asserting the superiority or harmony of the American way of life as opposed to that of the socialist countries, whose system goes so much against the grain of human nature. But the slippage from 'our way of being' to 'our way of life', from biology to ideology, is a revealing one. In the setting in which the dialogue takes place, Ellie's offer to 'teach' Vincent hints darkly at 'unnatural' sexual practices without emotion, without love, a thought that provokes disgust in Vincent. A 'human way of life' is characterised by sexual reproduction within loving marital relationships, the experience of love being unfortunately offset in the human condition by the jealousy and hate that stem from extra-marital sex. The aliens are stand-ins for a creeping sexual immorality that threatens the American way of life, an anxiety the series cannot address directly for fear of being accused of promoting what it ostensibly seeks to denounce.

In one of the most moving episodes ('The Enemy'), also in a repressed sexual setting, Gale Fraser, a (young and attractive) nurse, has retreated to an secluded farmhouse in New Mexico, in a state of extreme mental fragility occasioned by the 'horrors' she has seen during her tour of duty in Vietnam. As a nurse, she sees it as her duty to care for everyone, regardless of political affiliation, including (the handsome) 'Blake', an alien who has been seriously injured in a saucer crash. Arriving on the trail in the midst of a dust storm which isolates the farmhouse from the outside world, Vincent establishes himself as Blake's 'rival': violently opposing the nurse's pacifist, supra-humanist creed, he attempts to convince her of the aliens' intention to exterminate humanity. But in wanting to kill Blake, Vincent is, in her eyes, equally ruthless. Although without emotions or pity, Blake asserts the legitimacy of his right to survive, arguing powerfully that human compassion is mere hypocrisy ('you humans always talk about love and brotherhood but in reality you're always killing one another'). No doubt intended as an 'understanding' critique of pacifism and anti-war sentiment at a time when consensus over the American intervention in Vietnam had broken down, the episode is on very shaky ground here. Being able to experience emotion is worse than useless in a simple biological fight for survival and insufficient in itself to establish the superiority of the human race. The cracks Blake's arguments open up can only be resolved rather crudely by having him revert to his original form, a physically loathsome Tyrannosaurus Rex-like creature.

In view of the discrepancy between discourse and action, humanist principles become inapplicable. How then can the moral superiority of the human race be upheld? In 'Panic', Vincent tracks down an alien responsible for the deaths of seven people in a remote part of Virginia. Infected with a killer virus transmitted by simple contact, 'Nick' pleads with Vincent:

> Nick: I didn't want them to die. But I can't control myself, I can't help it, I'm like that. But we're not all animals, believe me, Mr Vincent, we're not all sadistic brutes. Like human beings, some of us are good and some of us are bad. You too have your Neros, Al Capones and Hitlers: we're the same, most of us have to follow orders whether we like it or not. Believe me, Mr Vincent, a lot of us don't like what we have to do.
>
> Vincent: That's what the Nazis said once they'd conquered Europe.
>
> Nick: . . . Tell me, Mr Vincent, what are you trying to save? The beings of your race? Are they worth it? Look at the reality, Mr Vincent, they're savages.
>
> Vincent: And you, what are you?

In order to identify the aliens with Evil so as to give an ideological colouring to a biological struggle, the series is forced to explain Evil in human terms. The invaders are explicitly identified with the Nazis, but the latter were human and presumably expressed some aspect of human nature. So where is the superiority of the human race, with its Hitlers, Neros and Al Capones? Are not all humans sinners? For if in their actions, the invaders are clearly vicious psychopaths incapable of human emotion, they more than hold their own in the intellectual exchanges: in the above dialogue, Vincent is struggling to prove the alien's own point, that humans are morally no better than the aliens. Is Reason itself therefore a satanic trap? A fissure emerges as the transition between biology and ideology breaks down, evidenced by Nick's raising of the issue of volition ('following orders') for what is a purely medical condition. If the aliens are to be considered inferior, it is because *they are not creatures of God* but sentient beings without emotions, guilt, or sin, *beings without souls* whose dead bodies instantly vaporise. A very real theological difficulty arises. Was not the universe created by God? The existence of intelligent, fundamentally evil beings without souls tends towards the Manichaean heresy which accords creative powers to the Devil, a dualism that is very much present in American evangelical protestantism without ever being confronted theologically. Constantly drawing back from the implications of this contradiction, the series is shot through with a dramatic moralising of human dilemmas that strives to compensate for the very presence of the aliens, reduced to the role of catalysts. In some episodes, the aliens' invasion is given an indigenous political backdrop: in 'Life-seekers', Vincent collaborates with two alien agents representing the peace faction on their home planet and seemingly capable of moral judgement; in 'The Mutation', Vincent meets 'Vicki', a mutant alien who 'feels a stranger' on her own planet, believes that 'life has a meaning' and lost her father, also able to experience emotion, in a 'revolt'. Veering away from the brink of a species racism at odds with Christian teaching, the series implies that the battle between Good and Evil is truly universal, one that both races must fight out not only between one another but also, perhaps more importantly, within themselves.

In 'The Trial', Vincent arrives in Jackson City to come to the aid of Charlie Gilman, an old army buddy from Korean war days, accused of the murder of one Fred Wilk. (The friendship of Vincent, an architect, and Gilman, a foundry worker, in itself expresses the populist theme of organic links between 'good people' from all situations and callings). Gilman and Wilk were seen fighting in front of an open furnace, 'roaring like the gates of hell', as a witness later puts it: unfortunately for Gilman, the body of Wilk, an alien, volatised before witnesses could arrive on the scene. The defence argument turns on a legal technicality: the murder charge cannot be sustained simply because Fred Wilk was not a human being. But the moral validity of this argument is seriously undermined by the fact that Wilk's wife was Gilman's ex-fiancée: privately, Gilman confesses that jealousy was the real motive behind his fight with Wilk ('I didn't care whether he was a human being or not'). In a crucial scene, Mrs Janet Wilk is called to the stand:

Bernard (the defence attorney): Mrs Wilk, how long were you married to Fred Wilk?
Mrs Wilk: A little less than a year.
Bernard: And how long did you know him before marrying him?
Mrs Wilk: Just a few weeks.
Bernard: What do you know about his past, I mean, before you met him?
Mrs Wilk: Nothing at all. For all I knew, he might as well not even have existed before I met him.
Bernard: Your marriage – how would you describe it?
Mrs Wilk: My marriage was not a success.
Bernard: In what way?
Mrs Wilk: . . . He didn't touch me once.
Bernard: Why? Did he have no desire, no human drive?
Slater (the prosecuting attorney): Objection. The use of the word 'human' in this

context . . .

Judge: Overruled. A wife is a better judge of the behaviour of her husband than an attorney. I'm sorry to disappoint you on this subject, Mr Slater. Answer the question, Mrs Wilk.

Mrs Wilk: No human drive, no human desire.

Bernard: Why, in your opinion, couldn't Fred Wilk, who had all the appearances of being a man, a normal human being, have intimate relations with you?

Slater: Objection, your honour. It has not been established that he couldn't, only that he didn't.

Judge: Sustained.

Mrs Wilk: There was something cold about him, almost inhuman.

Slater: . . . I object to the sight of a wife destroying the reputation of her husband after her death.

Judge: Overruled and irrelevant.

Bernard: What did you say to Charles Gilman, the defendant? Didn't you tell him that your husband was not what you hoped for?

Mrs Wilk: Yes, I told him.

Bernard: Mrs Wilk, was your husband a human being, yes or no?

Mrs Wilk: I wish I knew . . .

. . . *Slater (cross-examining):* Mrs Wilk, you have stated that in some respects your husband was not a normal man . . .

Mrs Wilk: I don't think so, no.

Slater: You were married eleven months? (Yes) And you have a son who is four months old, I believe? (Yes) Can we conclude then that your husband, your ex-husband, was not the father of this child?

Mrs Wilk (after a long hesitation): Yes, sir (*exclamations in court*).

Slater: Will you tell the court who the father is?

Mrs Wilk (long hesitation): . . . Charles Gilman.

Slater: The defendant. Were you in love with him? (Yes) Are you still in love with him? (Yes) You never loved your husband. In fact, you were pregnant when you married him. You surely didn't encourage him. Could you really hold it against him for not having intimate relations with you?

Mrs Wilk: He couldn't . . .

Slater: You wanted him to be a normal husband but were you a normal wife?

Mrs Wilk: I don't think so, no.

Far from being a positive exposition of human as opposed to alien nature, this passage turns into a concern with 'normal' human behaviour. It is not enough to affirm the singularity of human nature as the possession of the quality of love and sexual desire. In themselves, these (biological) qualities are dangerous and must be disciplined into loving marital relationships. In the case of Charles and Janet, desire without marriage, and Janet's on-the-rebound marriage without desire have created a site in which the aliens have been able to intervene:

illegitimacy, the consequence of a moral lapse, threatens the very foundations of society and enables the aliens to falsely claim human parentage (an alien disguised as Fred Wilk Senior gives evidence that Fred Wilk was his illegitimate son). For it is in the socio-economic (deserted mines, abandoned factories, dying rural towns) and moral sites of human weakness (Gilman leaving town after getting his girlfriend pregnant) that the alien invaders are able to 'naturally' and effortlessly take their places and put the human race to the test. Outward appearances of conformity are thus insufficient without close, long established family and personal ties between citizens, of sufficient intimacy that the presence of moral judgement and the ability to experience real, sincere emotion in an individual can be testified to by others. Vincent observes that 'Fred Wilk lived here for one year, quite normally it seems, and was well integrated into the community' and prosecutor Slater argues '(Wilk) breathed, he ate, he cried, he laughed, he was a father and yet you affirm he was not a human being – what else could he be?' But neither Wilk nor Janet are natives of Jackson City. Against the threat of a creeping invasion, official documents (and by extension, the state) are worthless: in court, the alien Fred Wilk Senior blithely furnishes a birth certificate for his 'son'. Danger stems, therefore, from the lack of close social ties that integrate even unpleasant and difficult individuals into a community of trust. The arrogant Slater, suspected by Vincent of being an alien, is vouched for by the totally fair-minded judge (who resists Slater's oily reminder that political promotion to a higher court lies in the balance): 'You should have asked me before, Mr Vincent. He was one of my students at law college . . . but I never liked him.' Marriage and justice, the institutional expression of biology and morality condensed in the person of the judge, are the very foundations of society, both adequate compensations for the weaknesses of human nature. After Gilman has been acquitted, Janet asks, 'I like that judge: do you think he could marry us?' 'If the results of the blood test are all right', replies Vincent in what is as close as the series gets to making a joke.

The real theme of the series is the decomposition of small-town America and the breakdown of the family (divorce, extra-marital sex, illegitimacy and the 'generation gap'). In effect, the invaders have no families: in 'The Mutation', the mutant alien 'Vicki' tells Vincent that her special skills came from 'what you humans call a 'father', I think'. It is in the interstices of the breakdown of the family that the aliens are able to thrive and proliferate; in the wider sense, it is moral weakness, on a mass scale, that makes Americans vulnerable. In 'Vikor', a successful Santa

Barbara businessman, George Vikor, enters into a partnership with the aliens to produce the regeneration tubes so essential to their survival on the Earth. If the aliens have chosen Vikor for this task, it is precisely because of his overweening appetite for material gain over and above family obligations. A Korean War hero, badly wounded in the taking of Hill 317, Vikor explains his treason to his wife (who, neglected, has taken to drink):

Vikor: I want you to have everything. Can't you see, Jackie? Try to understand, they will be masters of the planet. You and I will rule the world, we will have everything we desire.
Vincent (interrupting): An excellent deal. He wants to sell nothing less than the human race.
Vikor (bitterly): Yes, our wonderful human race that I hate so much, cheats, liars and hypocrites. When I came back from Korea, I was tired of it all, the war hero bit, the medals . . . I was promised the earth until the day I had something to ask for. All I wanted was a small loan to start a business. That's when I saw what humanity was worth. They told me that a man who had undergone brain surgery was too much of a financial risk, that business was business . . .

Patriotic values are thus wronged by the banking and professional establishment who place their own interests above those of the pursuit of the Vietnam War, displaced on to Korea. The consequences of this selfishness, associated with a sincere but ill-informed pacifism, have harmful consequences on the internal cohesion of the United States. In 'Doomsday Minus One', General Beaumont, who has become sickened by war after losing his son in Korea, collaborates with the aliens' desire to test a radioactive anti-matter bomb and thus trigger a disaster that he hopes will end nuclear tests forever.

Only close family and social bonds, and an unswerving common sense and moral rectitude, can counter the aliens. An intimate detail ('Harvey was very superstitious. He refused to allow people to wish him good luck') enables Angela Smith finally to realise that her astronaut husband is an imposter in 'Moonshot'. But having taken a lover while her real husband was posted to the Far East, Mrs Smith is insufficiently interested in his return (seriously wounded after a terrorist bombing) to care that he has changed his tastes in everything and cannot remember the names of his friends. The (rebellious) daughter of scientist Nathan Tate collaborates with the alien kidnappers of her father out of hatred for his having abandoned his family ('The Condemned'): after his heroic death, she learns that her alcoholic mother had demanded he leave. In 'Labyrinth', Vincent is led to suspect the daughter of Dr Crowell who has been separated from his wife for fifteen years: after having spent this period in Europe with her mother, Laura Crowell has a distinctively 'non-American' way about her ('You should smile more often, Mr Vincent, you become almost attractive'), treating the threat of an alien invasion as a laughing matter. As in a detective novel, attention to domestic detail can provide important clues: in 'The Watchers' a young, blind woman realises that her uncle is an impostor when he mentions having notified the families of his assistants' death in an 'accident'. Only she knows that the two men in question had no family.

Resisting a creeping invasion which feeds on social and moral problems is a lonely, impossible task. As if to punish him for straying one night from the main road in search of a short-cut, Destiny has given Vincent a mission beyond a megalomaniac's wildest dreams: to save the planet all by himself, to convince those in authority (the police, the government, the army) who are only too happy to let sleeping aliens lie. Forced to fight a war on two fronts, against ruthless extra-terrestrials and also human moral weakness, Vincent runs headlong into the very populist values he seeks to uphold, for he too is a 'stranger' as he moves, rootless, from state to state. The isolated individual cannot pretend to know better than the 'silent' majority. Slater makes the same point in his sarcastic cross-examination of Gilman: 'You worked in the same factory as Wilk with 400 others and you were the only one to remark that he wasn't human. But of course you knew him better than the others. You knew him well because he married your ex-girlfriend.' The argument is a deadly one, for it suggests that moral reformers, those who think 'they know better', are acting for private, not public, motives. Any attempt to revive the populist moral code by enlightened, upright individuals is liable to criticism from the very populist strain it seeks to perpetuate. The morally truthful individual must be recognised as such by a wider community of trust: it is because Vincent's fellow citizens have succumbed to the internal threat of immorality, greed and materialism that his task is made all the more difficult.

But we know that Vincent is right. He has seen the invaders with his own eyes and we have seen them too. Yet this fundamental precept of common-sense empiricism – 'seeing is believing' – is undermined by the scientific insistence on external forms of 'proof' for 'theories' which have themselves arisen from observation. Criss-crossing the vast expanses of America, from Mississipi to New Mexico, from New York to San Francisco, David Vincent zeroes in on suspicious, bizarre incidents. In Virginia, seven hitch-hikers have been found frozen to death in midsummer

('Panic'); off the coast of Florida, two astronauts due to participate in a moon launch die in mysterious circumstances ('Moonshot'); in the Mid-West, a couple die of asphyxiation after breathing in the deoxygenised air given off by a crystal ('Wall of Crystal'). Condemned to the wrong side of the epistemological divide between theory and the facts, Vincent can never prove his allegations. To a disbelieving doctor in 'Panic', he can only reply: 'it's not a theory, it's the facts'.

As a theory of unexplained phenomena, this is simply unbelievable and some of the dramatic tension of the series comes from Vincent's own occasional self-doubts. Given their ability for instant dematerialisation, the existence of the invaders can never be proved in the exacting terms required by science. It is self-evidently shameful that military or government commissions should refuse to accredit the theory of extraterrestrial invasion, but there is no rational reason why this 'theory' should be given privilege over others as an explanation for strange phenomena, all the more so given the absence of material proof. But scientific rationalism alone is not an adequate basis for a moral code, or way of life: resistance requires a supplement of faith. In keeping with the series' populist precepts, little or nothing can be expected from the state or the military bureaucracy. All over America, however, from all walks of life, Vincent meets good, 'plain' people who are willing to keep an open mind, for which they are rewarded with an epiphany that can never be rationally argued. For all its talk of theory and facts, the series is clearly in religious territory here, imploring potential converts to accept a truth that flies in the face of the scientific rationalism that guides the establishment bureaucracy. As Vincent tells the scientist, Dr Crowell, a convert who has seen his research colleague dematerialise: 'You're a member of the loonies' club now' ('Labyrinth').

Each of the seventeen episodes of the series' first season (1967) followed an identical schema. The invaders prepare a terrifying plan to destroy the earth's inhabitants (carnivorous insects, provoking a nuclear war, modifying the climate, etc.). Vincent tries to alert the authorities who dismiss him as a lunatic: more often than not the only people to believe him turn out to be invaders themselves. Finally, Vincent manages to counter the machination but unable to prove anything, he is constantly brought back to square one. More than any other series, The Invaders poses the problem of seriality, the progression of events over time. In effect, the very form of the series implies a time-loop: the self-contained episodes can never really evolve without breaking out of the series format. The failure of Vincent to make any headway against the aliens left viewers frustrated. At Christmas 1967, a modification was made to the format in the form of 'The Believers', a group – one is tempted to say sect – which has faith in Vincent and offer him their time, money, knowledge and relations. This group of seven disciples, led by Edgar Scoville, the director of an electronics firm, continued until the death of the series in September 1968. But this modification was not sufficient to cover up the structural contradictions that the series contained from the outset. After forty-three episodes, it was abruptly cancelled without any closure of the conflict.

Seriality was not a problem for The Untouchables or The FBI, both of which present a fictionalised real within a 'realistic' time frame. In effect, the first episodes of The Untouchables are situated in 1929: four years and 118 episodes later, we are up to 1933. Similarly, The FBI draws on the narrative possibility of dividing police work into discrete 'cases', a factor which makes the police format an ideal form for action series. The Invaders, however, hovers between the series and the serial. It is as well to remember that it was modelled on an earlier Quinn Martin production, The Fugitive (1963–67), which featured Dr Richard Kimble, who roams from one small town to another in the search for a one-armed man who has killed his wife. In a very American nightmare, Kimble is on his way to the electric chair, unjustly convicted of his wife's murder, when destiny intervenes in the form of a train crash. Simultaneously fleeing the police and tracking down the mysterious one-armed man, the good and wise Dr Kimble nevertheless finds the time to solve the problems of numerous small town residents on the way. Later, after 120 espisodes, when the ratings begin to flag, Kimble is finally released from his ordeal. In other words, the outcome of the serial-series is already contained in its point of departure and it is only a question of time before Kimble's tribulations will end.

But this was not the case of The Invaders. How is the conflict to be resolved? Having established themselves in their earthly guises, the invaders would seem to be invulnerable to bacteria and viruses. In fact, they are so technologically and mentally more advanced (so we are told) that their surreptitious takeover would appear to be unstoppable. As 'Kathy Adams', an alien disguised as an attractive widow, tells Vincent in the first episode 'Beach Head': 'Don't try to resist us, you will be overcome. You cannot stop the inevitable.' And so it would seem: the aliens' ability to take human form, to penetrate the posts of command, and their disintegrating rays are in effect sufficient to assure the inevitable. The series form, however, logically demands an unstable stand-off between the invaders and the human race. Yet it is difficult to imagine how the invaders, with the advanced technology at their disposal (despite an unexplained reluctance to use it more than once), can be stopped: the lone efforts of Vincent, although highly effective, are derisory in terms of this goal. Maintaining the series form here involves denying its very possibility on another level: however advanced the aliens' technology seems to be, it has yet to reach the stage of serial production. The execution of a plan obeys very curious implicit rules: once materialised, the aliens' advanced science is effaced forever at the conceptual level, and the destruction of a single machine by Vincent amounts to a definitive loss for the invaders, now forced to find another ruse. The plots are often strained in the extreme: only incredibly lax security, slow physical reactions, and a perverse disinclination to use their superior intelligence prevents the aliens from drawing the benefits from a weapons gap heavily in their favour. Like the conflict between God and Satan in Manichaeanism, that which opposes Vincent and the aliens strives after a constant impasse. In this sense, the technology of the invaders is not so much advanced as evil, a sinister adaptation of electromagnetism: hence the 'regeneration trucks', the underground power stations, the cerebral haemorrhage machines. Although 'advanced', Evil in technological form is strangely inefficient: the disintegrating rays often miss their target, the heart-attack machines require the use of physical force on the victim, the brainwashing crystals are not always reliable against a revolver . . . But is not all (advanced) technology and the attempt to manipulate nature (including human nature) to human ends morally suspect, an affront to God? As the invaders are quick to point out, they are not the only ones to have invented the means of mass extermination, nor the only ones to use technology for dubious purposes. Explaining an electric shock chamber to a human who is about to suffer the consequences, an alien cannot resist drawing a parallel with the electric chair: 'You should know this technology given the widespread use you humans make of it. In your mental asylums, it's called shock treatment, if I'm not mistaken . . . If it's not efficient, one has only to increase the volume to human limits. A technique used in another of your human institutions' ('Summit Meeting').

The stand-off of technologies, therefore, is a stand-off of Good and Evil. The initial project of a pan-humanist morality is swamped by the alternative project of modernising the existence of Evil in technological guise. The theological roots of the series are never far from the surface. In 'The Storm', a tornado hits Miami 'suddenly, without reason, against all the laws of nature'. In a small fishing port on the Florida coast, Vincent befriends Father Corelli, a high-minded priest who unwittingly serves as a cover for an alien base in his previously abandoned church. After striking Vincent, who has been accused of rape by 'Lisa', an alien masquerading as a South-American member of his congregation, Corelli is seized with remorse: I'm not a just man, I'm a hypocrite. It's very easy to say I love all men because they're children of God. But I exchanged Good for Evil. For a few instants there, I really wanted to kill him. . . .'

Are the invaders also children of God? Is Evil therefore part of God's design? Corelli discovers the aliens' plan to artificially create a storm able to destroy Washington. More than ever, the aliens are dramatic stand-ins for a relationship with nature which is all too human. Ready to make the supreme sacrifice for his religion, taunted by 'Lisa' ('Every living being is a creature of God. Isn't that what your religion tells you?'), Corelli cannot bring himself to kill the aliens. Nor can he allow Vincent to use his weapon in the house of the Lord. From the summit of human moral integrity, he tells Vincent: 'I will pray for you. I will pray for us all.' Far from being a military problem (the use of military force is decisively rejected in 'The Peacemaker', where Vincent collaborates with the aliens to shoot down the plane of a mad General on a lone bombing mission which would compromise the possibility of peace negotiations), the invaders pose a purely moral problem which demands the help of God and the respect of the laws of nature. In an attempt to renew the religious basis of morality and extend it to the secular world of science, the episode formulates an alliance in which Vincent, an architect, with solid technical skills, is nevertheless in harmony with the foundations of religion in the quest for scientific proof. In what is perhaps a key discourse, the voice-over epilogue to 'The Storm' declares: 'Two men, two seekers of truth, one continuing his investigation in the skies and on earth, the others in the depths of human conscience. Both tirelessly continue their mission.' Both men have sacrificed sex and family life in the higher interests of humanity.

Having assembled the elements for the realisation of its ideological project, what is the series to do with them, if the situation is to stand still? The Manichaean struggle between human nature and pure Evil is necessarily – if the dramatic structure is to be fleshed out with 'human interest' – subsumed by ancillary problems bearing on the existence of human evil, or immorality. In no other series is the relation between the assemblage and the narratives so strained. Constantly, the series 'forgets' about the aliens and becomes caught up in its moralistic sub-plot. The aliens' physical disguises (an old couple, a black politician, a beautiful young woman, etc.) seem to have been chosen solely in terms of their capacity to set up and provoke human dilemmas. An alien's 'sensitive', Montgomery Clift-like appearance in 'Panic' sets up a romantic interlude with a young woman who has retreated to a remote farmhouse, jaded and cynical after a failed marriage in a big city. At times, the series breaks down completely under the strain. In the same episode, Vincent addresses the alien by his name ('get up, Nick'), thus bestowing on him human subjectivity.

According to the producer Alain Armer, 'the invaders are among us right now, in your town, perhaps even in your neighbourhood . . . the new neighbours on the other side of the street, the new teacher, that pretty secretary in your husband's office'.[15] At once anti-Communist and puritan, the mixed metaphor at the heart of the series' design could not be controlled. At a time when the Vietnam War was at its height and traditional morality was being called into question, the series' populist reflexes also harboured a destructive undermining of confidence in America's major institutions, in other words, a rejection of politics itself as the territory of 'pointy-headed' establishment elites suspected of betraying heartland values. The series is torn in two, unable to decide whether it is using the Cold War as a metaphor for creeping immorality or vice versa, each metaphor undermining the other. As in the McCarthyist paranoia, where the external signs of the communist ranged from the party card to any 'abnormal' behaviour, the means of identifying the aliens oscillate between firm biological signs (absence of a heart or a pulse; the difficulty, also experienced by gays and snobs, in bending the little finger) and the vaguest moral criteria (lack of enthusiasm for one's conjugal duties; inappropriate unfeelingness) which potentially applied to the whole human race. The portrayal of Communist spies in 1950s films as cold, calculating, emotionless beings whose powers of persuasion were practically limitless drew its force from a consensus wherein both liberal and conservative America were united in a relentless anti-communism which had become the very foundation stone of American values. In the face of the upheavals of the 1960s, this consensus was no longer viable: fundamental American values, everywhere called into question, were being betrayed from within. Unable to confront an external menace in the name of commonly held, universal values, The Invaders was the desperate swan-song of a conservative rural populism whose traditional morality no longer held sway in urban America (although a modernised version of a

C

religiously-based populism was to reappear in the 1980s: see the section on *Miami Vice*). The populist faith in the worth of simple, basic emotions and the distrust of science and reason was given its most extreme manifestation. Unusually intense, 'naively' sincere to the point of breaking down, *The Invaders* remains one of the most interesting American series.[16]

A superior vantage point

The project of a utopian, pan-humanist conception of human nature allied to a non-political exploration of present-day moral dilemmas was recast more convincingly in *Star Trek* (1966–69). Two hundred years in the future, peace and tranquillity reign on Earth; all divisive political and moral problems have been solved. The flaws in human nature (greed, sexual licence) have, through the process of social evolution, been ironed out into a dignified stoicism and moral control. By renewing the idealised values of Ancient Greece, civilisation has looped the loop: humankind, in alliance with other like-thinking races ('The Federation') which have accepted their leadership, is now in a position to go out and conquer space, to realise its manifest destiny. The device is an astute one: an optimistic version of a universal human nature (in its puritan American form) can be upheld while the problems of the twentieth century (in first place, the Vietnam War) can be displaced on to others. From their superior historical vantage point, the crew of the USS *Enterprise* confidently confront the problems of their own past. The structure of this ideological project is in many ways similar to that of Jules Verne (see Chapter 1), a point we shall come back to.

The displacement of what were current ideological tensions on to planets suitably designed for their resolution is evident in the episode 'A Private Little War' (1968). Captain Kirk and McCoy (the ship's doctor) arrive on a planet which has 'all the characteristics of Class M, a little like Earth' except, as Kirk explains, 'it's people have remained on its earthly paradise. They still hunt with bows and arrows. But they never make war. Absolutely peaceful.' Reporting on the planet for the Federation thirteen years previously, Kirk had written: 'inhabitants superior in some respects to humans. In evolving, it is certain that they will achieve a remarkable state of development in peace and fraternity.' On the basis of this report, a non-interference treaty has been signed with the Klingons, both galactic superpowers promising to let the planet follow its own 'natural' mode of development.

By breaking the treaty and arming one group of villagers with muskets, the Klingons change forever the history of the planet. Determined to avoid the planet being taken over by one superior armed tribe manipulated by the Federation's intergalactic superpower rival, Kirk arms the other tribe with identical weapons and gives instruction in their use. A long philosophical discussion takes place between Kirk and McCoy:

> McCoy: So that's the way you help them. You don't think one serpent's enough in this paradise? . . . You want them to completely destroy each other at any price?
> Kirk: Exactly. Each side receives the same advice and the same type of weapons.
> McCoy: Do you know what you're doing? Have you lost your mind?
> Kirk: The norm of development of this planet was a status quo between the villagers. The Klingons have changed all that with the muskets. If we want the planet to follow its normal course of development, we first have to balance both sides of the equation.
> McCoy: Jim, you're involving the planet in a war which will never finish. They'll fight year in, year out, massacre after massacre.
> Kirk: . . . So what's your sober and reasonable solution, Doctor?
> McCoy: I don't know what the solution is, but supplying weapons is not the answer.
> Kirk (with exclamation): Do you remember the twentieth century and the Cold War on the Asiatic continent? Two superpowers were involved, a bit like the Klingons and us. And none of them wanted to give way, none of them could give way . . .
> McCoy: Yes, yes, I remember. And for many years, it was real butchery.
> Kirk: The direction of the world was at stake. If we had allowed one of the powers to arm its friends without reacting, humanity would never have survived long enough to conquer space. No! The only solution is a strong opposition. A balance of power.
> McCoy: And if the Klingons give one side more powerful weapons?
> Kirk: Then we shall arm our side with weapons of the same force. A balance of power . . . Sometimes one has to make war to have peace.

Initially averse to the use of violence, the villagers learn to kill. Kirk is (as always) philosophical: 'It's not what I wanted, it's what had to happen. How long do we need to produce a hundred flint rifles? A hundred serpents for the Garden of Eden.' The biblical reference is thus explicitly made; the planet even has its Eve, the pacifist chief's sorceress wife who pushes her husband to acquire arms so as to take the houses and wealth of other villages.

Having reached a certain stage of technical and social development, humans are in a position to categorise and classify the rest of the universe. The norms of human evolution impose a standard for all intelligent development. Arriving on the planet, Kirk immediately remarks a deviation from the norm: 'thirteen years ago, these villagers had barely discovered how to forge iron. Scott received a discharge from a flint rifle. Normally, how many centuries are needed to make such a leap?' (Lt. Uhura: 'On Earth, it took about twelve.')

All life, all matter is understandable in terms of this norm. It is because humankind – having accepted the leadership of the United States – is well advanced on the scale of evolution that it is able to recognise problems which are similar to those of its own past. Kirk tells the villagers:

> We were in the same position as you in the past. Pickaxes and bows, and then the time came when wisdom was overtaken by arms to the point of destroying ourselves. This experience led us to adopt a code of behaviour for which we voyage to make sure that the same experience never happens to others. So that peoples can finally evolve without war and without weapons.

But the actions of Kirk on the planet and the justifications he gives for them are in total contradiction with this ringing declaration; if humans have been able to eliminate war from their own planet, they are totally unable to prevent it on others. Reflecting the limitations of the series' ideological project, all too constricted by the very real political impasses of American foreign policy on Spaceship Earth in the late 1960s, Kirk can do no better than to make a correlation between the planet's state of perfect tranquility and its failure to evolve beyond its earthly paradise. If the conquest of space is the teleology of evolution, war would seem to be a necessary stage, all the more that human evolution supplies the norm for the whole galaxy. This ambiguity between the series' utopian vision of human nature and the need to address contemporary moral and political realities is built into the very structure of the series, and is never really resolved. Any attempt to intervene positively in situations encountered by the Enterprise leads directly back to parallels with current problems that undermine the series' own arguments (superpower conflict, the Vietnam War, racial inequality).

So what is the point of the USS Enterprise's five-year mission to explore strange new worlds, to seek out new life and civilizations? Now that humans have achieved their destiny of intergalactic space travel and moral continence, the universe is fixed forever so that the historical and mythical past states of Earth can be represented by others. On one planet, we see the beginnings of Christianity re-enacted ('Bread and Circuses', 1968); on another, a salt-sucking monster disguised as a beautiful woman lures travellers to their deaths like Circe in the *Iliad*. These situations are observed, categorised and abandoned without any effective intervention being made. Like for the thin, emblematic characters of nineteenth-century adventure novels set in Darkest Africa (for example, H. Rider Haggard), strange and dangerous lands are hardly more than an occasion for observation and involuntary confrontation, a (brief) look at the mysterious Other. There is no thought of possession, conquest, absorption or assimilation: even though the existence of 'colonies' is part of the crew's mental horizon, prolonged exchange with alien forms can only endanger humankind's hard-won moral superiority. And like the voyagers of Verne, the crew of the *Enterprise* know that nature ultimately holds no surprises: nothing in the Universe can call into question science and the ultimate goodness of human nature, and every odd phenomenon can be explained in terms of previously discovered phenomena. The confrontation with alien life forms yields new facts but above all reveals the superiority, or at least the specificity of human nature. Each alien race encountered serves only as a philosophical sparring partner for the series' republican moralising. In many ways, *Star Trek* embodies to perfection a conservative form of positivism, a giant undertaking of classification without any *positive* project for improving society (a fundamental aspect of Comte's original design). The limitations of *Star Trek*'s conception of scientific reasoning are readily apparent in the following passage. In 'Wolf in the Fold' (1967), the ship's engineer, Scott, is suspected of three Jack the Ripper-style murders on Argilus 2, a rather decadent planet where space crews can partake of the pleasures of wine and women in an Ancient Roman/Arab decor. Although Scott is caught with a meat cleaver in his hands, the crew of the Enterprise know – because of Scott's intrinsic moral virtue – that he cannot be guilty. Logically, given the 'locked room' nature of the last crime, the killer can only be an immaterial being.

Spock (the 'logical', half-human, half-Vulcan, second-in-charge, unburdened with the experience of 'emotion'): Humans and humanoids are only a small part of known life forms. There are precedents for lifespans which are extremely long, practically immortal.

Kirk: We know that a man or a force has killed three women. If it's not a human being, it must therefore be a force, one capable of killing.

McCoy: But Sybo (a sorceress and latest victim while in a trance) said that it fed on death.

Spock: In the strict scientific sense, we all feed on death, even vegetarians.

McCoy: It also feeds on fear.

Spock: That backs up the hypothesis that it's not a human being. Life sustained by the emotions is not unknown in the galaxy. Fear is the most violent and powerful of emotions. . . . Computer, condense the ship's log for the past five minutes and compare the hypotheses with recorded life forms. Question: is such an entity within the possibilities of existing theories relating to this galaxy?

Computer: Drela feeds on the emotion of love. There are sufficient precedents for the existence of an unknown creature feeding on the emotion of fear.

Spock: Computer, extrapolate more precisely the composition of such an entity.

Computer: Answer; to meet its particular requirements, the entity must exist without form in the usual sense of the word. Probably, a highly cohesive mass of energy. An electro-magnetic field.

Kirk: Computer, could such an entity take on different forms?

Computer: Answer affirmative. Precedent: Militus, creature in the form of dense cloud on Alpha X 1.

Kirk: I've seen this Militus myself. In its natural state, it's gaseous and at rest, it's solid. Mr Spock, let's admit the hypothesis of the existence of such a creature.

Spock: . . . Jack the Ripper killed at will in the heart of the most populous city on Earth and was never identified. I suggest the possibility of a type of hypnotic screen which masks the presence of the killer from everyone except the victim.

Scott: Is it possible?

McCoy: Entirely possible. There are lots of examples of this type in nature.

Kirk: Very well. What do we have, Mr Spock? We have a creature without form which feeds on horror and fear and which can take on several forms to kill.

Spock: I suspect the victims are mainly women because women are more easily terrified and give off more fear than the male of the species.

There is something peculiarly Victorian about this dry, affectless exchange purporting to represent a scientific age of the future. Scientific method is simple deduction in the time-honoured Sherlock Holmes tradition, explaining new phenomena through the 'logical' manipulation of premises which, in this case, are founded on an intuitive knowledge of human nature. Science is merely the relation of the unknown to known common sense, an alliance of science and populist ideology whose future vantage point gives the lie to feminist attempts to redefine human nature. That Spock's observation of 'feminine nature', presented as a scientific fact, clinches the process of deductive reasoning confirms that the mission of the enterprise is not to extend the boundaries of knowledge but to prove the specificity and the perpetuity of human nature. The conquest of space is the teleology of evolution because it provides an ultimate theatre in which humans, confronting the same problems in space as their ancestors once did on Earth, can observe that their nature is truly immutable. The threat in space, often emanating (as here) from asexual life forms and always a test for human nature (the ability to experience emotion), is also an immutable threat: an immortal

Jack the Ripper alien being dogs human progress from nineteenth-century Whitechapel to the colonisation of the galaxy, eternally punishing women for falling out of step with codes of sexual morality (the Ripper victims, the decadent planet Argilus 2) and scientific rationalism (the sorceress Sybo).

The confident mock-scientific reasoning which informs *Star Trek* is based on an ultra-empiricist conception of science as a giant accumulation of facts. With all existing knowledge stored in the computer, scientific method is child's play, the tautological movement from facts to deductions back to facts again. It is little wonder that human nature is the ultimate scientific object, continually 'proving' itself in its confrontation with reality and serving as a 'theory' for explaining it. Everything that can be known not only will be known but, in its broad outlines, is already known: human nature can only be proved over and over again, setting absolute limits to scientific progress. *Star Trek* represents an optimal world in which progress is perfectly adequate to human nature: logically, any further advance must be refused. In its own terms, it is a static, deeply conservative world, which draws on the romance of science, only to reject it.

This contradiction emerges clearly in the episode 'The Ultimate Computer' (1968). A computer genius, Dr Richard Destrom, the inventor of the standard computer equipment for all the Federation's spaceships, has designed a new supercomputer, the M5, which can replace virtually the whole *Enterprise* crew, including the captain. Predictably, Kirk is not overjoyed at being replaced although he has no immediate answer to Spock's logical argument: 'We must use (the M5) in the interests of science. It would not be reasonable to try to ignore the importance of such an invention.' Surely, one cannot refuse progress: as Destrom explains: '[the duotronic computers on your ship] are as archaic as the dinosaurs if you compare them to M5'.

But Destrom's technological advance destroys the teleology of human evolution, the conquest of space, the logical extension of a forever expanding free enterprise system. As he argues:

Now, it will be useless to travel in space, to voyage to hostile worlds where so many men have died. Man was made to live and not to sacrifice his existence in the discovery of unknown worlds. What's the point of dying in order to conquer space if the computer can do it without us? Try to understand. I don't want to destroy the human race, I want to save it.

In terms of the series' ideology, this abandonment of territorial expansion in favour of a life of earthly pleasure is wild and dangerous talk: paradoxically, beyond a certain point, scientific progress itself becomes hopelessly regressive. The attempt to link scientific reasoning to a static conception of human nature, a necessary bridge between the series' utopian future and its relevance to present-day problems (displaced on to other worlds) comes apart here: in the inevitable conflict between scientific change and a human nature which cannot change, it is the latter which is affirmed, forcing the series to renounce the very basis on which its utopian future is constructed. Yet Destrom's question – what is the point of conquering space? – a question that challenges the very ontology of the series, cannot be satisfactorily answered on its own terms. The series weakly avoids the problem by presenting Destrom as a crazed genius who, having won the Nobel Prize at the age of twenty-four, is now suffering from mid-life depression. The inability of the genius to produce revolutionary theories on demand leads to frustration and misanthropy.

Fortunately, the M5 has a fatal flaw. Modelled on Destrom's brain, the machine has an overly-developed survival instinct and sense of its self-importance and cannot distinguish between friendly and hostile space vessels. But Destrom has also inculcated it with his own remorse ('to kill is to go against the civic and moral laws on which our society has been based for over a thousand years'). The enduring laws of an enduring social system are neutrally based on formal logic.

Computer: A computer cannot commit murder. It is against the laws of man.
Kirk: You've already killed the crew of the Excalibur . . . It's you and you alone, the murderer. What's the penalty for that?
Computer: The death penalty.
Kirk: So who is going to pay for this act? For all those innocent victims?
Computer: The computer . . . must . . . pay (*self-destructs*).

Humans are the measure of all things, whose ultimate achievement is common sense and the ability to experience emotion, both brought into harmony. A fellow starship captain, Bob Wesley, is faced with the agonising decision of destroying the Enterprise before it destroys his own ship. By dismantling the M5, Kirk leaves his ship's defences exposed, gambling on the compassion of his colleague and his own insight into human nature.

Kirk: I know Bob Wesley. I counted on his common sense.
Spock: His most logical choice had to be compassion.
McCoy: Compassion, surely that's something that a machine can never feel. It's

perhaps that which accounts for the superiority of human beings. Does that shock you, Spock?

Spock: No, I maintain that machines are more efficient than human beings, but not better.

So machines must be kept in their proper place, under the control of humans. In a far-off future where international political divisions have been overcome, where the project of an 'Alliance for Progress' under American leadership and values has been realised, the crew of the USS (Free) Enterprise is a happy human family in miniature, directed by the youthful, Kennedy-like Captain Kirk: the Russian, Ensign Chekov, was expressly added in the second season towards this end. However, all arguments based on a fixed conception of human nature are also implicit arguments for an existing social order which expresses this nature: human society is therefore part of the natural order of things. What is therefore 'better' about human control is the social system in miniature on the Enterprise, an order that technical advance can only disturb.

Kirk: The machine in the place of man. Impressive, perhaps even practical.

Spock: Practical, but nevertheless not very desirable. (The M5) is undoubtedly a very efficient servant but I would not like to serve under its orders. Captain, a vessel like ours is also run by loyalty towards a man, and nothing can take the place of that loyalty.

The efficient running of the vessel, like the efficient management of society, is dependent on submission to a hierarchy. Hundreds of years in the future, we are back to the very beginnings of the capitalist order: all of the unranked personnel are given the title 'yeoman', a reference to that historical class of small freeholders of common birth who were given the virtues of staunchness, loyalty and courage. Like the intrepid colonists of The Mysterious Island, the crew of the Enterprise are forced to return to the sources of capitalism in order to realise the republican ideal, the highest stage of human political development. The 'neutral' terrain of space is used as a theatre for the affirmation of this ideal but where are the sources of conflict – the essential basis of all narratives – to be found? All the obstacles to the realisation of a perfect human order have been conjured away: in fact the social order of the Enterprise is so much characterised by mutual respect and acceptance of one's place in the hierarchy that there is little basis for inter-personal conflict. In this respect, Star Trek continues the nineteenth-century tradition of organicism in which society is portrayed as a 'family', a 'partnership' (Burke), a living organism whose collective values are assured by a strong state.[17] In the Conradian translation of this project, the ship becomes the perfect micro-community, where ideals of duty, loyalty and hierarchy (every man has his station) can be convincingly affirmed against a common enemy – the sea. Yet this is undermined by a submerged anxiety relating to the reality of the voyages of conquest: imperialist domination of primitive peoples strips away the coloniser's thin veneer of civilisation, potentially confronting him with the core of evil at the heart of human nature. Space, too, reunites the perfect community against a shared natural danger to the foundations of human nature, one which demands that voyagers come heavily armed with moral resolve. The worst fate that can befall the crew members of the Enterprise is to be stranded on a strange planet, cut off from their community and losing their moral bearings.

One possible answer to the problem of finding trans-class, trans-historic threats to all humankind in deep space is to portray the galaxy in systematically pre-capitalist terms, a device common to science-fiction romances ranging from Asimov's Foundation series to Herbert's Dune. The future is a reworking in space of colonialism, capitalist accumulation and superpower rivalry against the Klingon Empire (Chinese) and the Romulan Empire (Russians), both marked by an extreme aggressivity and rigid, feudal-like military hierarchies which set them apart from the republican 'Federation' (Free World). As if conscious of the fact that feudal spaceships implicitly call the question the natural superiority of capitalism as a springboard for the conquest of space, the series tends to resort to magical elements. Without any visible technological advance, and invariably without the means of social and sexual reproduction, other beings nevertheless possess highly developed biological powers (telepathy, materialisations of illusory images) which can put human nature to the test. Associated with 'primitive' beliefs and customs, magic – sometimes the property of a planet itself – is an alternative to scientific development, independent of any social and historical agency. Unlike humans, such beings are trapped in biology: the singularity of human nature is the balanced blend of scientific logic and emotion, ideology and biology.

Although the primary concern of the Enterprise's mission is to provide occasions for the ratification of the moral superiority of the human race, sometimes this superiority is only relative. In 'Arena', the Enterprise engages in hot pursuit a Gorm vessel which has wiped out a Federation colony on Cessius 5 'illegally' installed in Gorm territory. A superior race, the Metrons, intervenes to prevent a war: the conflict is reduced to a hand-to-hand combat between Kirk and the Gorm captain who are transported to a distant planet. The fate of two crews depends on a fight to the death between two individuals. The Metrons explain to the crew of the Enterprise: 'We have observed you and taken note that your violent instincts are natural and inherent . . . You are not civilised. Your actions and your instincts prove it'. Against his reptile-like opponent, Kirk displays superior intelligence by producing a primitive form of gunpowder. Magnanimous in victory, he refuses to kill his wounded opponent. A Metron appears to Kirk: 'You are more evolved that we thought. Perhaps there is hope for your race . . Perhaps in several thousand years, your race and mine can find a durable basis of understanding. You are only half-civilised but there is hope.' Kirk concludes: 'Our species has a lot of promise, despite its present state of barbarity. Perhaps in a thousand years we will be able to prove it.' The disincarnated Metrons, who represent a higher stage of evolution, have gone beyond material reality to live a purely spiritual existence, beyond the production of the means of existence and, therefore, of class relations. Republican democracy, for all its faults, is only a stage in the *spiritual* development of humankind. The series here betrays the limits of its project of presenting space conquest as a panacea for existing problems.

The theological premises of *Star Trek* also emerge here. The goal of all races is the moral perfection of the universe before the Fall, a mission made all the more difficult for humans by the liberal sprinkling of planets whose state of paradise hides a satanic trap (the surrender of free will in exchange for bliss). Technical progress, although impressive, is spread rather thinly: faster-than-light spaceships, talking computers (giant encyclopaedias) and teleportation (this last feature added to save money on spaceship landings) take their place in an otherwise largely unchanged world. In 'Tomorrow is Yesterday' (1967), a 1960s security guard is accidentally beamed on to the Enterprise where he is dumbfounded at a display of one piece of twenty-second-century technology: a primitive prototype of the microwave oven. The romance of technology, characteristic of the early, Wellsian period of science fiction, is less in play here than a romance of a moral leap forward for the human race, for it is through the conquest of space that moral evolution becomes possible, beyond the greed of the consumer society. On the Enterprise, the baser emotions of sexual jealousy, lust, greed, delusions of grandeur and unwarranted ambition have been brought under control. Reason and moral continence reign supreme. This gives the series its oddly stiff, stilted character: bodies exist in space because ideology requires them to be there, to propagate the twinned values of free enterprise and human love throughout the galaxy. Humans travel in space as monuments in a moral enclosure that prevents consequential exchanges or reactions with other beings for the simple reason that they have come in advance bearing the highest values: in the contact with alien beings, they can only lose their tribal purity. The perfect society (of which the Enterprise is a microcosm) is a rationalised hierarchy in which sexual desire, source of disorder and chaos, is overcome by what amounts to military discipline: in this sense, the spaceship is the perfect site for the 'natural' existence of a human nature without desire, either for sex or for material goods.

Without base emotion, the half-Vulcan, half-human Spock (who holds forth the utopian promise of well-bred manners outside present social relations) is present to confirm the concordance of pure logic and positive human emotions like love and compassion, an added bonus which makes the human race unique and even superior. In 'Requiem for Methuselah' (1968), an alien force field takes human form, exchanging immortality for the experience of physical love, the highest form of knowledge in the universe. Metaphorically linked to sexual procreation, the (free) expansion of capital becomes a noble value, in concordance with the biblical injunction to 'go forth and multiply': in the same episode, Kirk ringingly declares that 'it is in the nature of our species to be free . . . Our species can survive only if it has obstacles to overcome . . . We live on thousands of planets and are still expanding.' The real mission of the Enterprise is to 'fertilise' the galaxy with human values, only occasionally stopping to question its anthropocentrism.

The optimism of Star Trek drew much of its force from the political context of the mid-1960s, from the twinning of two great projects: the Apollo space programme (which aimed at a moon landing by the end of the decade) and Lyndon Johnson's 'Great Society' programme (which aimed to eliminate poverty in America within a generation). Social progress and technological progress were inextricably linked, an optimistic vision of the future that rapidly sank in the quagmire of the Vietnam War. Ideologically stranded in the far reaches of space, the crew of the Enterprise were in a less than ideal position to address burning contemporary issues. This is even physically visible: the crew are often left standing stiffly to attention, while one of their number pronounces a sermon for the inhabitants of the planet earth in the late 1960s, straining to communicate over the time divide. This was a characteristic it shared with the Western: it comes as no surprise that the producer Gene Roddenberry originally modelled the series (working title Wagon Train to the Stars) on the 1950s series Wagon Train which recounted the interminable trek of 1840s pioneers across virgin territories.

Despite its cult following, *Star Trek* was not particularly popular with a wider audience who considered it overly 'intellectual', a consequence of the fact that, set in space, its ideological project was difficult to collapse into 'natural' activity: at the height of its popularity in 1967, it was ranked only fifty-two in the top hundred programmes. Furthermore, advertisers were dissuaded by its disproportionately adolescent audience. After seventy-nine episodes, the series was cancelled in June 1969. However, for a cult minority, it had an undeniable ideological force: not only did a mountain of fan letters helped reverse plans to cancel the series after one season, but to this day there are some 350 fan clubs in the United States (and some fifty in other countries) which continue to 'spread the word' through conventions and newsletters.

The series we have discussed in this chapter were not a transparent window on the burgeoning consumer society spearheaded by the very medium of television. Rather, their insistent moralising within the framework of a pure, pre-consumption epoch of capitalism (the Western) or a post-consumption stage (*Star Trek*) betrayed widespread anxiety over the breakdown of social discipline. The strategy adopted initially was the rearguard one of establishing moral guidelines which the practice of personal enrichment had to respect, a strategy somewhat at odds with that of the advertisements that framed these series, also striving to appeal to a universal human nature but this time one of desire and need.[18] By the mid-1960s, the obsessive concern with moral weakness and greed was becoming increasingly irrelevant to a society that was qualitatively different from an earlier stage of capitalism. The specificity of the new consumer society demanded a different approach, one that privileged an accelerated rhythm of consumption over the certitudes of an unchanging human nature.

The pop series

Designed bodies

If we are to understand the way in which ideological determinations replaced psychological archetypes in the design of characters, we must first outline the integration of television series into the world of design and the key economic role of the latter.

After the Second World War, design came under the influence of information theory which saw the object as an element in a whole, as part of a code. This vision of design replaced the earlier idea of the individual styling of objects.[1] The mass production of designed products and the fragmentation of a previously standardised market demanded a context, a homology between a series of different products and the consumer into what came to be known as a 'lifestyle'. The possibility of transferring a master motif to a whole range of products had already become evident in the 1930s with the use of the 'streamlining' style, initially designed to lower air resistance in planes, in the design of cars, trains, refrigerators, ovens, biscuits and other products. Streamlining broke the dominant idea of design that 'form follows function'.[2] The acceleration of the cycle of obsolescence brought with it a corresponding acceleration of the production of design codes, the periodic reshuffling of styles.

In an epoch of abundance, it was gradually recognised that demand did not necessarily follow the possibilities of production.[3] Consumption had to be constantly stimulated through a symbolic enhancement of the use value of objects, impregnated with social connotations drawn from 'pop culture' (music, subcultures) which became increasingly synchronised with the production cycle in the 1960s. Just as in the 1930s, when the sponsoring of products by film and music stars was a way of reducing the risks of mass production by associating the object with an existing value already ratified by the public, the cultural industries were called on to play a special role in the creation of social use value: it was, in effect, inconceivable that advertisers alone could invent and impose new fashion cycles.

Most of the initial creative impetus came from subcultures based around pop music, a relatively 'open' medium which, without the heavy production costs and responsibilities of film and television, was more adapted to the rapid shifts of style required by the fashion cycle. Subcultures in the 1950s had prepared the way by implicitly attacking the conformity of existing modes of consumption. The beatniks, for example, adopting the model of black jazz musicians, reacted against what they saw as, in the words of Norman Mailer, 'a slow death by conformity with every rebellious and creative instinct stifled',[4] exploring the possibilities of *experience*, beyond comfort and security, and yet to be integrated into mass commodity consumption.

Something of the difficulty in coming to terms with this new mentality can be seen in the violence of the moralist denunciations of rock and roll, and the 'moral panics' associated with youth subcultures which continued through the 1960s. A new ideological project, integral to the functioning of an advanced capitalist society, stressing individual pleasure and a freer choice of lifestyle, ran headlong into existing ideological configurations based on moral continence and social discipline. This clash of values became a major social fault line: in the 1960s, liking The Rolling Stones or not implied a whole set of attitudes, almost a choice of lifestyle. The important role played by the magazine *Playboy* in mediating between the marginalised 'beat generation' and more respectable society, proposing a pleasure-oriented existence which included a relaxed approach to sex, can be seen in its relentlessly didactic tone in the second half of the 1950s. The 'Playboy Adviser' section offered to answer 'all reasonable questions – from fashion, food and drink, hi-fi and sports cars, to dating dilemmas, taste and etiquette', foreshadowing the later, more developed notion of a lifestyle ethic based on styles of commodity consumption. But the transition towards this was not always an easy one: 'what's IN today is OUT tomorrow . . . [if] you are now unsure, you are more SQUARE than HIP', *Playboy* readers were warned (March 1958). 'A British chap I know wears buckskin shoes in the higher shades with sports clothes. Is this proper?' asked a worried reader in the March 1964 issue. Inevitably, the following letter appeared in the *TV Times* concerning the television series *The Avengers*: 'Patrick MacNee (John Steed) always has marvellous clothes, including shirts and ties . . . Are they his own?'[5]

In this new world of total design, stars played a strategic role in integrating the human body into the design code, transforming it into a master design surface. The process of designing pop stars had begun in the 1950s when, just as designers turned their back on the idea that 'form followed function', pop impresarios refused the idea that the 'look' of singers necessarily stemmed from their natural 'personality'. The synchronisation of the half-life of singers with the fashion cycle led to a constant, frenzied search for new talent. Early rock stars were modelled on James Dean and Marlon Brando and in Britain, Cliff Richard was modelled on Elvis, but this method of launching physical lookalikes of existing stars was increasingly inappropriate, all the more so given the difficulty of coinciding the right appearance with real singing ability. Fabian Forte, discovered by a Philadelphia entrepreneur at the age of fourteen for his 'Elvis with the boy-next-door' look, had two years later tried the patience of three singing instructors, but with his voice electronically treated, his records nevertheless became hits. The jazz critic John S. Wilson wrote:

Recording techniques have become so ingenious that almost anyone can seem to be a singer. A small, flat voice can be souped up by emphasising the low frequencies and piping the voice through an echo chamber. A slight speeding up of the tape can bring a brighter, happier sound to a naturally drab singer . . . Wrong notes can be snipped out . . . and replaced by notes taken from other parts of the tape.[6]

The manipulation of the voice in the recording studio opened the door to a greater manipulation of the *image* of the singer whose original personality was no longer inviolable. An entirely different 'gaze' is at work in the following:

As the airplane door opened, down the steps came a quiet, polite Southerner . . . (British producer) Jack Good remembers thinking: Oh dear, this won't do . . . Mr Vincent is going to have to change his image. Fortunately, says Good, Gene Vincent suffered from a bad leg – having fallen off a motorbike – and wore leg irons. This gave me the clue. As he limped, I saw that he must become a Richard III figure, dressed entirely in black, including black gloves. He must hunch his shoulders and lurch in sinister fashion toward the cinema before singing. I arranged on his first television appearance for him to walk down several flights of stairs so that his limp would be emphasised. I also gave him a medallion to wear around his neck to make him look more Shakespearian. When I say him gingerly trying to negotiate the steps, I had to run around the back of the set and shout, 'Limp, you bugger, limp!'[7]

Less provocative than rock because of the need to appeal to a mass, family audience, television also had its part to play in the dissemination of new styles. Characters in series were no longer social archetypes representing various facets of 'human nature' but designed to double as fashion models. The credits to the popular 1964 spy series *Danger Man* inform us that lead actor Patrick McGoohan's clothes are designed by 'The Fashion House Group of London'. The conflation of the two roles in a new 'modernist' discourse which collapsed ideology into design is strikingly evident in the following excerpts from a *TV Times* article in 1963 on *The Avengers*:

> (*Said fashion expert Michael Whittaker*): 'You might say I designed this wardrobe for the new, modern, 'let's go' woman . . . Cathy is glamorous. But she is practical too and her wardrobe has to reflect this . . . Culottes – those divided skirts – are just right for a woman who one minute has to look poised and serene and the next could be jumping into a shooting fray with a band of thugs.' 'These clothes are new and certainly diffferent,' *said Patrick Macnee*, 'and I think they capture perfectly the image of the new woman . . . I think the clothes also capture perfectly the enigmatic, indefinable personality of Cathy.' (*Said Honor Blackman*), 'These clothes couldn't be more perfect for Cathy. I don't think I've ever had a professional wardrobe which has helped me capture the essence of a character so sompletely.'[8]

The gaze of pop

Through its glamorisation of the new and the rapid turnover of fashion, the 'gaze of pop' made the constant stylistic obsolescence of products, the acceleration of the consumption cycle, not only legitimate but positively exciting. In a widely quoted 1960 letter, the British artist Richard Hamilton defined 'pop' thus: 'popular, transient, expendable, low cost, mass produced, young (aimed at youth), witty, sexy, gimmicky, glamorous, big business'.[9] The mass production and 'artificiality' of the world of commerce were valorised in relation to the 'elitism' of high culture: in Britain particularly, pop seemingly combined the energy and talent of art students and youth subcultures, the intellectual skills of a new middle-class of designers, technicians, artists, media people and teachers, and the institutional might of progressive business and the government. This informal, unstated alliance was loosely organised around a self-conscious modernism which waged war against a clearly identified figure of contempt, the old-fashioned person of all classes, the brown-ale drinking workingman, the stodgy bourgeois and the pompous aristocrat. Much of the energy of pop in Great Britain came from the Mods, a subculture that carried the self-consciousness of fashion to a wilful fetishism that involved conferring their own value on (consumer) objects (scooters, amphetamines, desert boots, suits, the Union Jack, rhythm and blues, soul music) by the simple act of selection: the Mod was the prototype of a new, 'active' consumer, free to invest objects with a symbolic dimension that was totally arbitrary to their function.[10] The emergence of a pop culture around which trans-class battle lines were drawn seemed to confirm the utopian possibility of a transcendence of social class in a new society in which relations of consumption were replacing relations of production as the centre of existence.[11]

Pop music and youth subcultures represented the cutting edge of the new pop culture, always on the front line and more often than not spilling over into moral panic territory. But behind the front lines, other media also had their part to play in the less spectacular but more influential extension of the pop ethic into the mainstream of society. One of the strengths of pop was its ability to take form in several different media: films, television series, novels and, last but not least, comics. Some pop texts like James Bond, The Ipcress file, and Modesty Blaise existed in two or three media forms. An important cultural movement, pop was a highly coherent ideological strategy whose success was to some extent reflected in the 1964 Labour victory and the government's subsequent belief in a 'white-hot' technological revolution as a spur to social evolution, an idea which participated in the pop romance of mass gadgetry. The combination of social-democratic politics with more sophisticated 'continental' lifestyles is apparent in the following passage from Len Deighton's 1962 spy novel The Ipcress file: '. . . I bought two packets of Gauloises, sank a quick grappa with Mario and Franco at the Terraza, bought a Statesman, some Normandy butter and garlic sausage . . .'[12] Pop in its television guise had the particularity of engaging with, and proposing a resolution of, the contradiction between individual (consumer) pleasure and more traditional values of patriotism and duty. One of the advantages of pop in television form over pop in novel form was that the look of pop could be understood at a glance, with a richness that needed pages of description in a book: the perfect pop text Modesty Blaise sometimes contains two or three pages on end of descriptions of decor.

Danger Man: . . . the tough life we lead

Why did the spy genre become the dominant fictional form of the pop ethic? In Cover stories, an analysis of the ideological foundations of the popular spy novel, Michael Denning[13] demonstrates the importance of patriotism and imperialism to the form's appeal. From the beginning, from Le Queux to Oppenheim, the stake involved was the defence of the Realm. The singularity of the spy was a gift for impersonation, a deadly cultural mobility that could cut across national boundaries. As

Denning argues, the ideological strategy of early spy thrillers is to privilege a national consciousness over a class one, the threat coming from those who placed class over nation. In Buchan's *Thirty-nine steps*, the hero Hannay is able to trump his adversaries by using tactics of disguise he has learnt from his mentor, the Afrikaans scout Peter Pienaar, to move up and down the class structure while staying within the nationalities of the British Empire, unifying them in a common patriotic loyalty against 'aristocratic supra-national dynasties, international financiers' or 'tub thumpers of world revolution' (Denning). The threat to the nation comes at once from the top and the bottom of the class structure and there is little doubt that it is the middle classes (incarnated here by the character of Hannay, a mining engineer) which form the backbone of society, in alliance with good and reasonable people from the other classes. In Buchan's *Mr Standfast*, Hannay explains that 'you can wash out the old idea of a regiment of scallawags commanded by dukes . . . The hero of this war is the plain man out of the middle classes.'[14] By the 1950s, the amateur spy had given way to the professional technician, but what is striking about the James Bond character is the confusion over his class status. Whereas Bond appears to be something of an 'aristocratic clubman' in the Fleming novels, a continuation of the tradition of 'snobbery with violence', he takes on a more 'man of the people' aspect in the Sean Connery film versions, a 'classless' moderniser. Patriotism and duty are preserved within a new game which allows for pleasure and individual autonomy: the confrontation with foreigners, in a foreign theatre of operations, is a source of pleasure as well as danger. Inextricably linked to patriotism and the overcoming of class divisions, the spy genre becomes additionally coded with discourses pertaining to tourism, conspicuous consumption and sexual pleasure, an ideal terrain on which to confront and explore the tension between duty to a higher authority (the state) and the individualism produced by the new consumer culture. The very figure of the spy functions as a resolution of this opposition, combining pleasurable interludes in exotic locations with service to the state. As Sean Connery put it, 'Bond is quite right in having all his senses satisfied – be it sex, wine, food and clothes – because the job, and he with it, may terminate at any minute'.[15]

As well as being an agent of national or imperialist interests, the spy brings into play a new gaze on the world of objects: he is, to use the expression of Denning, 'licensed to look' and is also, in turn, the object of the gaze of others, a perfect, 'cool' surface unruffled by uncontrolled emotion or ambition. In its pop version, the spy genre was very much a

British ideological strategy where, in the absence of a tradition of republican populism as in the United States, a trans-class discourse nevertheless had to be situated in class terms.

Danger Man (*Secret Agent* in the United States) has rarely been absent from the world's television screens since 1965. Although it is now seen as a classic pop series, this is largely despite its premises, based on very traditional ideas of superior British fair play. Announcing the new series in September 1960 (in its initial twenty-five-minute version), the *TV Times* introduced secret agent John Drake in these terms:

> As [he] wends his knightly way across the world, seeking out villainy, his fists will be as virtuous as his cause. Those who fall before him will have been clobbered with a fairness which will make the Queensberry rules look almost criminal . . . [The] relentless demand for reality [in the fight scenes] extends to the tender moments of the series . . . though he carefully avoids romantic entanglements . . . He is fair. He is considerate. He is a gentleman . . .[16]

Distinguishing himself from the 'Bond type of agent', Patrick McGoohan (Drake) comments: 'Some of (Bond's) encounters with the opposite sex are not really fit for a family audience . . . Drake is a more serious character. Much closer to what a real agent should be. And he never gets emotionally involved with a woman.'[17] There can be no better illustration of how the effect of 'realism' is obtained from the minutest thread of opposition to a postulated fantasy: making a virtue out of the necessity of catering for a more sensitive television audience, Drake's 'no sex on the job' attitude is sufficient to render him as a *real* secret agent. Recognising the foundedness of this, a viewer wrote to the *TV Times*: 'Patrick McGoohan is one of the few actors who actually looks and sounds like a spy.'[18]

Interestingly enough, the early twenty-five-minute episodes contain a first-person narrative, a clue to the secret agent's origins in the private-eye figure with its attendant updating of the tradition of romantic individualism, but this time working – more or less autonomously – for the state. The only early episode I have seen, 'The Relaxed Informer', features a young woman who is tricked into giving away defence secrets under hypnosis, and a naive scientist duped into working for the Soviets, both classic Cold-War tropes. But although the Cold War still features as a backcloth to Drake's adventures, the reference is misleading in another way. The relaxed tone and the evident pleasure of Drake in his 'job' are light years removed from the paranoiac insistence in the 1950s on duty as opposed to pleasure. For the secret agent, there is no clear demarcation line between work and leisure.

One of the reasons for the high quality of the second series (1964–66) is the variety of its scripts, each episode tailoring quite different dramatic themes to the series format. For this reason, Drake's political persona varies from episode to episode, some concerned with anti-fascist themes, others with anti-Communist ones, others with private threats to state security.

A good place to start is with an atypical episode ('The Ubiquitous Mr Lovegrove', 1965) which relates a dream sequence after Drake has lost consciousness in a car accident. The dream framework is useful in that contradictions can be presented in their strong form without the need for 'realistic' resolution. Using his cover of 'travel agent', Drake goes to a gambling club where he is surprised to find that a 'John Drake' has signed an IOU for £500. Drake denies all knowledge of, and all responsibility for, his gambling debts to the club owner, Alexander. The two John Drakes are one and the same, the secret agent and his double, his disguise, and Drake cannot renounce the debts of his other self. In a scene set in the luxurious apartment of Alexander, in which Drake and Alexander appear only as mirror-images, the latter proposes they do 'business':

Drake: The day I do business with you, Mr Alexander, is a long way off. I don't think our professions have much in common.
Alexander: You have chosen a very interesting profession.
Drake: Travel agent is one way among others of earning a living.
Alexander: How's that, Mr Drake? Living in luxurious surroundings, taking frequent overseas trips? I've been following your career for some time. What were you doing in Cannes, Mr Sybot? In Cairo, Mr Maxwell Ryder? Somewhere in Africa, Major Sullivan?
Drake: What are you getting at?
Alexander: That you're in the service of the government, Mr Drake. Of course, you're not a simple Post Office employee. Spy is a little too theatrical. Agent is more discreet.
Drake: Travel agent.
Alexander: No, Mr Drake, I prefer travelling agent . . . Despite all this luxury, I'm a very poor man. I'm only the manager of Almarks, not the owner. For a long time I've been looking for a way of breaking free and standing on my own feet. I want to spend the rest of my life in an atmosphere of independence.
Drake: Get yourself sent to an old people's home.
Alexander: My dear Drake, I fear that the wine served in that type of establishment would be of very unsatisfactory quality. I propose that you pay me the sum of £10,000 within twenty-four hours, otherwise every embassy in London will be informed of your identity. You will be definitively exposed.
Drake: Are you sure you've got the right John Drake?
Alexander: Which John Drake do you think you are?

There is a problem of identity here. Drake has two roles to play, as travel agent and secret agent: as such, he is torn between two moralities, one of pleasure which threatens his downfall and one of service to the government, unable to reconcile his 'cover' in a world of leisure with his real role (or is it?) of duty to his country. His blackmailer Alexander represents one of the new dangerous classes, a *nouveau riche* (and Balkan immigrant to boot) who is too ambitious to accept the rank of member of the lower management class, and has given himself airs of culture (classical music, good wine) surpassing those of a mere club manager. Contact with a high bourgeois, even aristocratic lifestyle has corrupted the vulgar, self-seeking Alexander to the point of blackmail, betraying the government of his adopted country. Yet Drake too has betrayed his duty for failing to discipline himself from succumbing to vice (a failing he refuses to recognise . . . or is it all a terrible machination?), so putting himself in a position of weakness. He has failed his government but also his superiors and ultimately, himself. His chief is furious:

Boss: I no longer have confidence in you. You lied to me. You are an incorrigible gambler and I refuse to pay your debts. Do you think the Treasury would settle £10,000 just like that? You've got a strange conception of public funds. You should have thought a bit more before gambling. I know it's often necessary for you to go out to casinos and offer yourself the company of women of dubious reputation.
Drake: That's just to compensate for the tough life we lead.
Boss: I work as hard as you do and I think that a two-week bicycling holiday is more than enough.
Drake: Buy a tandem, and next time I'll come with you.

If Drake has been impersonated, he has no means of proving his innocence and cannot count on the government to help him out. Ultimately, he is very much alone, an individual (whose independence is evident in his insolence) forced to fend for himself when things go wrong. The most dangerous aspect of his job is not the physical danger but the loss of his identity and self-control. The ultimate enemy is the enemy within himself, a point laboured by scenes of Drake wrestling with the 'Other' in the mirror.

Summoned to respect his 'debt of honour' like a 'gentleman', Drake attempts to bargain with Alexander. Thanks to his polite treatment of Alice Fairbrother, a middle-aged 'merry widow', Drake uncovers the secret of the casino: Alice has noticed that a certain gentleman always wins on the roulette. He is, Drake learns, Lovegrove, managing director of a turbo-jet engine factory from which there have been leaks. The rigged roulette table serves as a means of 'legally' paying him off for microfilms in the gambling chips which are left as a tip for the croupier. Drake's boss is incredulous: 'If he were only a vulgar subordinate . . . but he's a Captain. Unfortunately, he must have friends in high places.' In the denouement, it transpires that the real chief of operations is the humble doorman of Almack's who feels 'betrayed' by Alexander: 'It took me years to build up our network and you have ruined everything through greed.'

Within Drake's dream, the identity of his boss becomes confused. At times, he assumes the guise of Drake himself, the doorman, the croupier, a salesman for the insurance company of the Eternal Father. The traitor is now Alexander, now Drake's superior, now Drake's own double. In this jumbled world of social mobility and class role-reversal, all guidelines to an individual identity have broken down. The threat to society comes at once from the lack of moral commitment from the ruling classes, the ambitions of the lower classes (who are not to be underestimated) and the greed of the *nouveaux riches* who place wealth ahead of patriotism. This social confusion coalesces in the casino, a place of leisure and vice in which Drake must, paradoxically, fulfil his duty. The *doppelgänger* theme reinforces the links with the Romantic tradition, obsessed with the question of a dual identity. No-one can be trusted, not even Drake himself: the upturning of the social system also destroys the ideological certitudes that unify the individual personality into a morally responsible 'subject'.

However, the tension between discipline and individualism is more easily resolved by presenting Drake as the medium between two extremes. In 'Fair Exchange' (1964) Lisa, a former British agent prematurely released from a psychiatric hospital, slips away to East Germany with the intention of killing Pohlman, a spy chief who had tortured her on a previous mission. Drake is instructed to stop her for fear of provoking a dangerous diplomatic incident. His attempts to co-operate frankly with his East German opposites run into difficulties because of the Byzantine machinations of police chief Colonel Berg, who wants to use Lisa to eliminate his rival, Pohlman. Two forms of unacceptable individualism are expressed here: the sympathetically portrayed Lisa is nonetheless emotionally unstable and her 'unofficial' mission, although understandable, is clearly at odds with the national interest which cannot allow itself to be inflected by personal considerations. On the other hand, the naked, personal jockeying for power which characterises the secret services of the German Democratic

Republic undermines its efficiency and compares unfavourably with its more 'civilised' British counterpart. The series often uses comparison as a safety valve, displacing the tension between the individual and authority on to a foregrounded (but secondary) opposition between the British and other races. We shall return to this point.

Clearly, *Danger Man* is obsessed with the question of what it is to be an agent in the generic sense of the word, to act on behalf of others. In 'It's Up to the Lady' (1964), Drake tails the wife of Sir Charles Glover, a prominent civil servant, who has mysteriously disappeared. Tracking her down to a remote Greek frontier village, Drake persuades her to reason with her husband not to defect into Albania: she cannot adapt to foreign habits and cuisine and is continually haunted by the country she has left behind. Finally, Sir Charles, a well-meaning, supremely unpractical idealist, agrees to accompany Drake back to Britain on the understanding, given by Drake's superiors, that he will not be charged. To Drake's dismay, Sir Charles is immediately arrested on his return. Drake too has been betrayed: the national interest does not always correspond with private morality. In 'Double Game', Archer, a former British agent who has set up his own private spy ring in Beirut, selling secrets to the highest bidder, is eliminated by a British secret service killer after being unmasked by Drake. Drake can only make known his disgust at such methods, 'worthy of our enemies'. His emotional response marks the 'free' agent off from the blind obedience in totalitarian systems, but the issue of individual freedom, even within the framework of liberal democracy, is sharply focused. His freedom to consume in exotic places, to frequent the sites of pleasure, is no more than a 'compensation' for his enslavement to a government bureaucracy, a philosophy that McGoohan was to recast in *The Prisoner*.

Private enterprise also poses a danger to national security. In 'The Battle of the Cameras' (1964) Drake is on the trail of A. J. A. Kent, head of a private international company that specialises in selling stolen information. In a Côte d'Azur casino, Drake poses as a gambler and engages in conversation with Martine, Kent's assistant:

Drake: . . . I earn my living by playing what are commonly called games of chance.
Martine: You must live dangerously.
Drake: Let's just say that I take calculated risks. What about you?
Martine: Oh, I like taking risks too. I've nothing to complain about. Fate has been kind to me up until now.
Drake: I'm sure you manage to get what you want.

Martine: Of course, when I pay for it. Everything has to be paid for in one way or another, doesn't it?

The rhetoric of capitalism, associated with risk-taking, has been reduced to a game of chance, a common trope in spy series. There is no free money: whoever wins does so at the expense of others who lose in what is a zero-sum game. Everything has to be paid for: the price of absolute freedom, an unregulated capitalism of private brokers of state secrets, is the undermining of society itself. After Drake gallantly offers Martine one of the chips he has won from her on the roulette wheel, she remarks:

Martine: I thought you British used to say 'Loser pays'.
Drake: Perhaps in the last few years, Britain has come up to date.

Up to date means accepting a greater social mobility, allowing the lower classes to try their luck on the condition that the lucky winners be made to redistribute a small part of their 'new money' to the losers. In the new social consensus guaranteed by the welfare state, whoever wins pays back a little in taxes, a necessary sacrifice to assure the adherence of the losers to the game. (At Almack's, the game is rigged in favour of the *nouveaux riches*, a decidedly greedy class). For the very system of private enterprise is essentially two-faced, torn between social obligations and personal ambition: symbolically, half of Kent's face is covered by a black leather mask, the result of an acid attack. Far from being a respectable businessman, he 'presents only one side of his face, like the Ace of Spades'. Private enterprise, like the casino, must be kept under close surveillance and control by the state, necessarily limiting the possibilities of individual freedom.

The threat to society also comes from above. The other dangerous classses are the old aristocracy and the high bourgeoisie, reactionary classes which refuse to accept the welfare state. In 'Such Men are Dangerous' (1965) Drake disguises himself as a released prisoner to penetrate 'The Order', an assassination bureau which executes personalities who have been condemned by its directors. The leader of The Order, identified only as the 'General', explains its philosophy to a group of ex-prisoner volunteers who have been assembled to undergo a training course in killing techniques at Lyndon Manor, his vast country estate:

Our Order is international and is based on discipline and the authority and morals that ensue from that discipline. Men are for the most part honest but by nature incapable of managing their own destiny. They need a guide, which automatically leads to the adoption of the methods of our Order – discipline and blind obedience to those who hold the authority. All this time, the so-called democrats who govern us have been fooling the people by passing themselves off as idealists, but in fact they are nothing but decadent and corrupt demagogues. These men are dangerous and must be eliminated. Eliminating them will create a force . . . And it is through their elimination that the world will rediscover the discipline and morality that the hope for a better future rests on.

Resistance to the new order of consumer capitalism has been pushed to the extremes of discourse. Words like 'discipline' and 'morality' are here unambiguously identified with fascism, a dangerous rearguard action from the last remnants of the old ruling class from an earlier stage of capitalism. This negative example also implicitly presents the new manager class as enlightened and progressive, 'modern' in outlook. More than ever, this class, along with the new, 'liberal' middle class and the upwardly mobile skilled working class, a powerful trans-class alliance in favour of modernism, are the common-sense middle ground between old and new money, between two political extremes. Drake learns that one of the Order has been arrested after the attempted assassination of a black diplomat:

Jackie (a woman colleague): (he was) active for a while in an extreme left group, then fell out with them and got in touch with the British Nazi Party a year or two ago. And then, one day he went to a meeting of the 'Crusade'. He'd gone to heckle, but like St Paul, he saw the light. He became a convert and by the time of his arrest was an ardent supporter.
Drake: That group of pious bigots.
Jackie: Bigots, certainly but I can't see them inciting people to kill. I was at their last meeting at the Albert Hall; they were all respectable, well-off people.
Drake: Perhaps so, but they have dangerous ideas and a lot of money behind them.

Drake makes a semantic deduction: 'crusade, order, the two go together'. The religious intolerance associated with the word 'crusade' hides a politically dangerous obsession with order. An upper-class moral crusade serves unwittingly as a cover for a fascist hit squad, providing it with essential logistic support. Two dangerous classes are reunited in one threat: the reactionary upper class and the lumpen proletariat (the ex-prisoners). To complete the puzzle, the General's wife tells Drake she 'was born in the Gorbals and often went hungry as a child. . . . On one side are the winners and on the other the losers. I want to be on the right side.' This involves being as vicious as her husband, and Drake cannot give her the benefit of the doubt.

The old guard can also be ruthless capitalists. In 'Whatever Happened to George Foster?' (1965), Drake discovers that rioters in the young republic of Santo Marco are being paid in sterling for their activities against what is, we later learn, a 'progressive' government with policies of self-reliance. Back in London, posing as a travel agent, he investigates the 'Society for Cultural Relations with South America' which has spent a large sum of money – a sum it cannot account for – on 'cultural activities' in Santo Marco but practically nothing in the rest of South America. Drake pays a visit to the head of the society, the powerful, well-connected Lord Ammanford, whose extensive financial interests in Santo Marco are threatened with nationalisation. Ammanford is uninterested in Drake's suspicions:

> Drake: Must I conclude then from your tone that what is happening in Santo Marco is of less interest to you than your profits?
> Ammanford: Oh, Mr Drake, your idea of capitalism is outdated.
> Drake: But not my idea of democracy.
> Ammanford: Listen, through the investment of capital in that country, we are helping the people gradually to escape from the mire of ignorance and stagnation in which they wallow. If they're not helped, they'll starve to death.
> Drake: Who could blame them for wanting to be self-reliant?
> Ammanford: You seem to be hostile to progress, Mr Drake.
> Drake: Freedom is more important for me.

Drake's social–democratic principles are derisory compared to the sheer institutional might, both political and economic, of Ammanford whose philanthropic cover for economic imperialism has now become unacceptably paternalist. Drake's superior tells him: 'You know very well, Drake, that in the modern world, politics and industry are inseparable.' But Ammanford has a chink in his armour, a false identity assumed as a young man. After diligent private detective work, Drake discovers that Ammanford's real name is Foster, and that he worked before the war as a garage mechanic. Leaving behind a wife and family, Foster had changed his name to Jones and married a rich heiress to whom he had been giving driving lessons. Drake is able to make a deal: either Ammanford closes down the Society or else he will be exposed as a bigamist. In a final gesture of selflessness, Drake dedicates his victory to the 'ordinary people' of Santo Marco.

Ammanford is that dangerous animal, the ambitious working-class man who has tricked and bluffed his way into the higher reaches of the bourgeoisie and does not hesitate to use his power: as he tells Drake, 'I can break you, physically, professionally and morally, and you can do nothing against me.' Only a private weakness can destroy those who, in new-found positions of power, have retained traditional instincts of class hostility, a private weakness that Drake ruthlessly exploits for higher ends. In this sense, he is acting out of character, obliged to be moralistic in a way that his usually liberal outlook finds difficult to accept. For Ammanford's bigamy is not a moral issue in itself. His second marriage is a loving one, justifying his class mobility: he describes his first wife, who has refused him a divorce, as a 'horrible woman' and this is borne out when Drake visits her. Wealthy from the handsome rent she has received from Ammanford all these years, she represents the prudish, hypocritical morality of the lower middle class, obsessed with keeping up appearances. Were there not a greater cause at stake, Drake's implacable pursuit of Ammanford would be clearly unfair and unreasonable.

For mobility, however problematic, is the order of the day. The very epitome of unacceptably outdated social relations is the master–servant relationship, a theme that arises several times in the series. Although Drake is in the 'service' of the state, he maintains a high degree of autonomy from his employer, as befitting 'modern' social relations. One of the most efficient means of penetrating the lair of the reactionary old guard, however, is to disguise himself as a servant: it is an undeniable source of pleasure for the viewer to see Drake forced to act out an unsupportable servitude to a dying class, vainglorious and petulant, blind to its inevitable comeuppance. In 'The Hunting Party', (1966) Drake enters into the service of the obnoxious Basil Jordan, an ex-Oxford ne'er-do-well, and his wife, heiress to the Wormsley chemical group and one of the richest women in the world. Basil's hobby is model car racing, evidence of a class unable to grow up, to adapt to the times: humiliated by his wife's taunts that he is incapable of earning a penny on his own, tired of depending on her pocket money, he has organised a way of making his own fortune. Luring prominent diplomats and civil servants to his wife's Swiss castle estate for a weekend's game-shooting, Basil uses the hypnotism skills acquired at Oxford (instead of studying) to extract secrets from his guests during their sleep, secrets that he subsequently sells to a Greek spymaster.

Class contradictions organised around the poles of 'tradition' and 'modernity' are often displaced on to an opposition between the British and other nationals, to suggest that class struggle in modern Britain has been rendered archaic by progress, singularly lacking once the Channel has been crossed. In 'No Marks for Servility' (1964), Drake is once again required to disguise himself as a servant, this time to the (presumably Greek) property shark, Gregory Benaros, who has enriched himself, in the context of positively feudal social relations, by cheating poor peasants out of their land. The British secret service will have none of this and arrange for Lady Fielding, a friend of Drake's boss, to rent her villa in Rome to Bernaros who, like all *parvenus*, jumps at the chance of worming his way into the graces of the British upper crust. On Lady Fielding's recommendation, Drake is hired as a butler by Benaros who proceeds to treat him like a dog, much to the embarrassment of Benaros's terrified English wife. Seething at Benaros's crude insults and unable to stomach his wife-beating, Drake crushes a glass in his hand in order to maintain his self-control. The incident functions as a vignette of a nightmare world in which free-born Englishmen and women are at the mercy of 'inferior' cultures, trapped in 'backward' social relations. Given the task of organising an important business dinner, Drake proposes an impeccably tasteful menu which is rudely overruled by Benaros who, in a supreme gesture of vulgarity, orders out-of-season pheasant to be flown in from. . .Johannesburg. The dinner guest, an American banker, is unimpressed by Benaros's obsequious flattery and turns down his request for a loan, supposedly designed to 'help my people overcome their misery'. Unable to do normal business, Benaros responds by kidnapping the banker's daughter.

The threat to the nation's security from the Oxbridge old guard and the *nouveaux riches* is often combined with the threat posed by alien cultures and ideologies. Briefed for a mission in Singapore ('A Very Dangerous Game' (1965)), Drake is warned by his chief that 'these people (the Chinese) have had 3,000 years experience in this game'. Taking the place of an alcoholic British Council lecturer who has been unmasked as a communist spy, Drake establishes contact with the local communist chief, Chi Ling, a dapper, bow-tied Eurasian with an impeccable Oxbridge manner, who demands 'total obedience'. Using his modern equipment (bugs and tape recorders), Drake unmasks the real head of the Communist spy ring – the Oxbridge head of the British Council himself. The treason from Britain's traditional elite threatens its world supremacy from within: aristocratic, old school-tie values are not only inappropriate to the age of new technology but a liability. The credibility and force of such characterisations draw, of course, on the historical upper-class traitor Kim Philby, but middle-class suspicion of the elite can also be found in G. K. Chesterton's *The man who was Thursday* where a character declares 'the rich have always objected to being governed at all. Aristocrats were always anarchists . . .'[19]

Anxiety over Britain's place in world affairs is evoked and addressed. If Britain's decline is to be checked, a new class must come to terms with the reality of decolonisation: many of Drake's interventions in Third

World countries involve nipping in the bud plots from an old guard, whether colonial or indigenous. The colonies are now a threat to the British national interest. In 'Colony Three' (1967) a communist spy plans to infiltrate Britain with the false passport of someone 'returning from the colonies'. In 'The Mercenaries' (1965) a colonial rearguard poses a Rhodesia-like threat to the independence of African countries; in India, a Colonel Blimp figure, unable to come to terms with decolonisation, has become a spy for the Chinese ('The colonel's daughter'). In 'Yesterday's Enemies' (1964) the friendly head of the Lebanese secret service tells Drake that 'your country is ten centuries behind', a discreet reference to the 1956 Suez fiasco whose watershed importance was becoming clear. What is more, the threat is specifically located. In the same episode, Archer, a former British agent, cynically tells Drake: 'One day the oil here will run out. The country that controls the world's oil will dominate the world, and it won't be England.' But adherence to British criteria of modernity is the yardstick by which Third World politicians are to be judged. In 'Fish on the Hook' (1964) the urbane manners of the Egyptian authorities are shown to be no more than a thin veneer on a cruel traditionalism which encompasses torture and murder. The only Egyptians portrayed positively are those with British sympathies and attitudes. To complete the affiliation with the Suez fiasco, the mysterious agent that Drake must rescue is an Israeli woman spy who has married an Egyptian cabinet minister in the line of duty.

Most of these themes come together in one of the best episodes of the series, 'Colony Three'. Some 400 Britons have disappeared in recent years: in defiance of all rhyme and reason, they come from all social classes and none were engaged in sensitive areas of work. Taking the place of an obscure civil servant who is to due to 'defect', Drake finds himself behind the Iron Curtain in the company of two compatriots – a young woman, Janet, who is in search of her librarian boyfriend, and a middle-aged electrician, Rendall, who has been promised higher social status ('I'm an electrician, er, I mean an engineer'). They are conducted to Hambden New Town, a giant school whose object is to train Communist spies to acquire English reflexes down to the last, everyday detail. The town – a veritable human zoo – has therefore been peopled by real Britons from all trades and callings, representative of the real class mix of a typical English town. The spies are working on the theory that to be 'English', one does not have to live in the physical reality of England. The school's deputy director, Richardson (who, like the other Slavs, has taken an English name) is 'English' in everything but patriotic loyalty:

'Most of the time, geography is just an illusion, features on a map, words on a stamp. That's all it takes to give a country its real identity. After all, you're in the country that you believe yourself to be in. Mr Donavan (the director) says that countries are subjective things.' No-one will ever be allowed to leave New Hambden. Janet learns that her boyfriend died while trying to escape and that she is to take his place: although decent and without political motives, she is punished for being old-fashioned and insufficiently independent by following in the steps of her boyfriend. Rendall is furious at being asked to resume his work as a mere electrician. In an allegorical, schematic representation of England and its sharply divided class system, Rendall and Drake are made to share the same room: Rendall's class jealousy towards Drake is compounded by the latter's apparent collaboration with his jailers, his respectable social status in the village at a desk job. Drake is forced to bear not only Rendall's 'uncivilised' habits (leaving his socks to soak in the washbasin, borrowing Drake's electric shaver) but also a belligerence that compromises the mission. Disillusioned by his lack of promotion prospects, Rendall has redeemed himself, discarding his communist ideas and reverting to type as a patriotic, English working-class bulldog whose unwillingness to co-operate troubles the directors: 'Like a lot of English party members, he's a bit confused having to follow our norms. That pushes him to be even more English than usual, more independent.' But others are willing to co-operate. At a stuffy, 'typically English' cocktail party, Drake meets 'Sir' Anthony and 'Lady' Denby, the former merely Mr Denby of Foreign Affairs at the time of his disappearance. Revolted by this upper-class treason, Rendall disrupts the evening, taking aback one of the students whose conscientiously acquired English politeness cannot deal with Rendall's threats of physical violence.

The village is an experimental project, contested by the Communist Party authorities who are jealous of its relative independence, the inevitable consequence of its true-to-life Englishness. The latter is a truly difficult quality to acquire: 'We must assimilate your curious little customs. Driving on the left, politics on the right; animals kept in the home, children sent to boarding school, hating privilege and defending the privileged, loving gold and despising wealth. When we leave Hambden, we shall be more English than the English.' But the spies are learning a rather stiff, old-fashioned deference which is rapidly disappearing in the new Britain and are completely unused to the working-class independence shown by Rendall. His mission terminated, Drake is forced to leave behind Janet, and his superiors in London can do nothing for her. Chillingly, in a very 1960s nightmare, she has 'ceased to exist'.

The episode should not be reduced to its Cold War framework. The context of the series as a whole (not to speak of its later extension into *The Prisoner*) suggests that the town is also intended to evoke the new towns in England itself, also an unacceptable form of social engineering, a directed, enforced modernisation that suppresses individual freedom. 'Modern' is not simply the 'new', but implies certain conditions of individual consumption, something totally absent from Hambden which can cater only for standardised, compartmentalised needs: 'The plan of our village is simple. . . . The residential quarters are further to the west. That's where you'll live. The commercial centre is over there, and here is the library. Behind it is the school. . . .' The residents are obliged to resume the trade or profession they have left behind. Theirs is very much an 'anti-world', an alternative present in which existence itself – conceived of as the satisfaction of individual desires – is laminated, reduced to serving the state.

Two conceptions of technology are opposed, one 'old-fashioned' and the other 'modern'. Seeking nothing less than to transform the inner life of the spies, the town is a heavy, cumbersome machine, whose construction has mobilised considerable resources but which is destroyed from within by a single individual using portable, micro-technologies (a signal emitter in his pen, a camera in his typewriter). The use of the gadget, omnipresent in the series, marks a radical break with previous conceptions of modern technology, characterised by exponential increases in the power of electromagnetic machines and most notably represented by the gigantic power plants of the 1936 film *Things to Come*. With benefit of hindsight, we now know that the line of the future passes through increasingly miniaturised and individualised information-processing technologies: the gadget foreshadowed a future in which advanced technologies were to be consumer products on a mass market. Freeing state of the art technology from its military–industrial connotations, pop got the future right, not only in the type of technology but in the way it was to be used. This was not necessarily a dominant representation in the 1960s: in conservative versions of the future like *Star Trek*, which continued in the style of 1950s science fiction, one still saw lights flashing, electrical circuits exploding, levers pulled, switches and knobs furiously flicked and turned. . . In contrast, the gadget was deployed without brute force, coolly and dispassionately, closer to the programming values of today.

Designed (in both senses of the word) for a precise, functional use, the gadget plays an important role in the accomplishment of the mission. Through the use of miniaturised, concealed cameras, listening devices, tape recorders and closed-circuit video, Drake gathers information that would otherwise be beyond the resources of a lone agent. The deployment of gadgets also allows the secret agent to overcome the passivity of his fellow lone operator, the private eye. In *Danger Man*, the information-giving role is transferred to the gadget, freeing encounters with others for ideological rather than purely narrative ends and enabling the planting and monitoring of electronic bugs to become an 'active' process which slows down the narrative to the strains of cool bass lines and jagged harpsichord notes.

The character of Drake – the very name suggests virility and noble, patriotic antecedents (the reference to Sir Francis Drake is explicitly made in 'Parallel Lines Sometimes Meet' (1965) – is a condensation of the pop alliance between the worlds of fashion and advanced technology. Drake is always impeccably dressed, his clothes barely ruffled even after fights and chases: most episodes could also be read at least in part as a prolonged demonstration by a male model. At the same time, he is also a skilled manipulator of gadgets and instruments. As well as technical skills, his missions also demanded acting ability and a vast general culture (for the credibility of his impersonations). Drake thus assembles, in the design of his character, the roles of technician, artist and intellectual, different facets of the new middle classes. Like Richard Hannay, Drake moves up (disguised as a major, or a diplomat) and down (servant, criminal) the social scale, drawing the best from other classes, the charm and consumption skills of the well-off and the disrespect for authority in the new working class. But above all, Drake moves *across* the social scale, adopting the disguises of travel agent, teacher, journalist, writer, photographer, engineer, businessman, disc jockey and civil servant, representing the range of skills possessed by the new middle classes and the range of attitudes and behaviour. The foundation of pop in a delicate blend of art (including the erotic arts) and technology is also manifest in the novel *Modesty Blaise*. Having bugged the cell of Modesty and her Cockney partner Willy, the villain's fussbudget, Scottish accountant reports on their conversation thus:

it's all on tape. For what it's worth. Ooh, just desultory stuff . . . a girl in Santiago; poems of C. S. Lewis; fixing a quartz-iodine headlamp on her car; Bourdon Street, New Orleans, and Al Hirt's jazz combo; . . . Harold Pinter . . . some electronic rubbish about a square wave generator ... Otto Klemperer conducting Beethoven's Ninth; a girl in Singapore.[20]

The art/technology mix is also a blend of the old and the new, Beethoven and electronic generators: Drake himself is a carefully crafted design of the new, modern person, running a continuity line between the moral uprightness and politeness of tradition and the light, ironic touch of the new, integrating both into a more liberal-minded, relaxed personality that is receptive to change. As the ideal representative of the modern person, the spy added cultural, political, technical and social skills to his professional baggage, knowing that his cover depended on avoiding errors like ordering red wine with fish (like Red Grant in *From Russia with Love*).

Danger Man is also interesting formally. In its pop strategy of refusing to reduce discourse to the expression of a human nature, the voice is often disembodied, processed by tape recorders, television screens and assorted listening devices. The unusual ideological density comes from the complexity of its project, its forceful integration of the pop elements described above within the terms of the dominant ideology of service and patriotism. Pop irony and moral seriousness are constantly in tension, the signs of consumption and technology straining against more traditional values. The positioning shots of London and other capitals like Cairo, Rome or Singapore which begin most episodes, perhaps intended to reinforce the difference between dangerous foreign cities and London, where diverse world wrongs could begin to be put right, could also be read as a nod to pop's cosmopolitanism in which the foreign is a condition of excitement. For style and consumption values are foreign or continental. The ultimate pop heroine, Modesty Blaise (also an ideologically charged name, marrying coy femininity to confidence and passion) was brought up in Iraq and Tangiers and operated world-wide before settling in England: all of her culture, apart from that learnt on the street, has come from a polyglot Hungarian Jewish philosophy professor. Rather than reinforcing his Britishness, Drake's presence in foreign cities is a chance for him to show off his cosmopolitan skills, his degree of ease in another culture. The design of the 1960s spy, with its resolution of the opposition between duty and pleasure, was a highly unstable one: pushed too far either way, the spy tends toward a self-seeking mercenary or a colourless bureaucratic operative, a mere *agent*. As the decade wore on, the spy genre fissured into two distinct forms; on the one hand, the 'ultra-realist' genre made popular by John

Le Carré in which unglamorous, shadowy characters went about their business in a morally ambiguous world; on the other, playboys who carried out vague missions in tourist playgrounds against secret international organisations. Drake is somewhere between both genres, but his reliance on bugging and camera devices points towards the realist spy genre which tends to a moral equivalence of all secret services. Drake's gadgets, however, are used 'cleanly', for the most part in less advanced countries which rely on cruder techniques like torture to obtain information. The confident assertion of British modernity was nevertheless dependent on a strategic absence at the heart of the series: for a series so obsessed with comparisons between Britain and other countries, the lack of references to the United States was symptomatic of an inability to confront its social democratic politics with a more advanced version of modernity. Greater sensitivity to questions of imperialism and state interference in private life eventually told against the British spy as a modern culture hero, except in obviously spoofed forms: the sordid, reactionary bungling described in Peter Wright's *Spycatcher* – whether true or not – has surely closed the chapter definitively on the romantic image of the spy. In the 1960s, however, the spy was uniquely positioned as someone who hid his game behind a 'cool' exterior, refusing to allow emotion to disrupt the clearsightedness of his gaze on the modern world.

I am not a number

In 1966, Patrick McGoohan recast some of these themes in *The Prisoner*, undoubtedly the most enigmatic series of all time and one which still maintains a cult following in many countries. After resigning for mysterious reasons, a secret agent (played by McGoohan) is kidnapped and taken to a seaside village resort, which contains every leisure facility but from which no one can escape. In effect, the residents – nameless and reduced to numbers – are prisoners and worse, have no way of distinguishing between fellow prisoners and jailers. Originally, a miniseries of seven episodes was planned, but the producer demanded another nineteen for the American market. Finally, on the basis of a forty-page synopsis by McGoohan, seventeen episodes were made. Each episode was but a variation on the same story: the nominal administrator, an ever-changing Number Two, sets in motion a sophisticated ruse designed to uncover the reasons for Number Six's resignation. Number Six (McGoohan) counters the ruse and escapes, only to be defeated by another counter-ruse which brings the situation back to square one. The assemblage was so tightly constructed that only one basic narrative was possible.

It is plausible to see *The Prisoner* as a parable of the modern world, an updated, Kafkaesque micro-society in which leisure on a mass scale has brought with it a sheep-like conformity, a 'soft' repression in which 'clean' techniques of mind manipulation are used to discipline troublemakers who assert their individuality. In 'Checkmate', convinced he has discovered a psychological ploy to distinguish prisoners from jailers, that only prisoners, used to subservience, will unflinchingly accept orders from another prisoner, Number Six teams up with a fellow rebel, an electronics expert who has refused to play the role of human chess piece. But his masterly escape plan is betrayed by his partner. As the episode's Number Two tells him: 'I was sure that you would recognise the jailers by their subsconscious arrogance, but you forgot one thing. The way you directed the escape operation with such authority per-suaded the others you were one of ours.' Number Six is trapped in a double bind: his individualism leads him to resist authority but also to impose his own authority on others. Fellow individualists can logically only resist him in turn.

In 'Free for All', Number six wins an election on a 'freedom' platform to be the new Number Two only to find that he is a figurehead and that the real Number Two all along has been his maid, playing the part of a childish, rather ignorant supporter. In the village, one can never be certain who is playing what class role nor, in a superficially egalitarian leisure society, where power really lies. Questioning the village council ('Who do you represent? Who elected you? What country do you owe your allegiance to?), Number Six is told: 'you are not allowed to ask questions relating to their private life'. The consecration of private life in bourgeois ideology is transformed into a sinister veil for the public sphere, reserved for those in the hidden reaches of power. The alle-giance of the villagers has been secured by the provision of a comfortable leisure existence for which they have surrendered their freedom and their individuality.

In the final episode ('Fall Out'), Number Six earns the right to choose between governing the village and leaving it. He finally comes face to face with the mysterious Number One, whose real identity is hidden behind a mask. Beneath this mask is another mask, that of an ape, beneath which, in turn, is . . . Number Six himself. After programming the destruction of the village, he returns to London, where the last images are identical to those of the opening minutes of the first episode. The denouement is a loop-the-loop whose *doppelgänger* theme captures the limbo between bound agent and free agent, each individual being his own jailer.

In the long sequence that opens every episode, the McGoohan character resigns in a fit of anger from his official position. His Lotus sports car is followed by a hearse. He prepares his luggage: passport, plane ticket, tourist brochures. A pallbearer in top hat and tails descends from the hearse and inserts a gas canister through the keyhole. When McGoohan awakes, he finds himself in the 'village', peopled by pleasant, nameless conformists in identical late-Victorian uniforms living a comfortable life in a baroque toytown. Number Six, as he is designated, is in 'Hell' and, in the words of Sartre, 'Hell is other people.' In the 1960s translation of existentialism, Hell is a bureaucratic consumer society, the ultimate source of alienation ('I am not a number, I am a free man'). The village is trapped in a curious timewarp between Trad and Mod, a bizarre assemblage of Victoriana (the penny-farthing bicycles, the uniforms) and 1960s modernism (the mod cons, the surveillance and brainwashing machines). Hell is an oxymoron, an old-fashioned modernity in which advanced technology is used to increase the possibilities of state control and repression rather than those of individual freedom. Like its contemporary pop series, The Avengers, The Prisoner visually translates the figurative into concrete forms: the residents become literal living chess pieces ('pawns'), playing chess reduced to physically moving from square to square according to the dictates of the jailers. A resident who makes his own move is a 'defective piece' who is promptly taken to hospital. The co-operation of the 'pieces' in the game is secured by the possibility of promotion to 'king' or 'bishop' or demotion to 'pawn' ('Checkmate').

The Prisoner both invites and resists interpretation of the kind I have attempted here. Manifestly, viewers were invited to draw their own conclusions, a prospect that excited a cult minority but undoubtedly bewildered most. This was a logical consequence of the series' existentialist strategy of interpolating viewers to recognise their own unfreedom, to confront the jailer within themselves. But individualism here is defined in terms of the rejection of society itself: the only way to 'exist' (in the existentialist sense) in the village is to escape . . . but where? As the final episode reveals, there is no escape, no 'outside' in which individuality can be 'freely' realised outside social constraints. For individuality is a double-edged sword. Content to satisfy their personal desires in a leisure paradise, the villagers are finally too 'individualist' to join forces with Number Six: they are 'non-people' to the extent that their existence is a purely private one.

For all of its originality, its forceful representation of a nightmare world of 'soft' repression, The Prisoner suffers, in retrospect, from an ideological thinness, an obsessive concern with individual freedom in a setting which is too facile to allow the issue to be treated with the necessary complexity. The problem is thus insufficiently focused: in a political confusion peculiar to the 1960s, a 'radical'-minded anxiety over state interference in private life and the use of the media to manipulate citizens into a dull conformity spills over into a conservative attack on the welfare state itself, seen as effacing the individual personality into a mere number. Like Leavisite literary criticism, to which the series is distantly related, this was a gratifying world view for an educated middle class, enabling at once resistance to a commodified, mass-mediatised society and a rejection of the mindless consumption habits of the 'masses'. The right to have a 'name' and the cultured sensitivity that went with it, to exist as more than a cog in the machine, was finally founded on the value of rejection. It is only by resigning and positioning himself against the backdrop of the village – which, without work, is also without social classes – that Number Six can impress upon us the true singularity of his existence.

The threat from above, the threat from below

The Avengers was a more rigorously 'pop' series than Danger Man, whose 'pop' elements were still enclosed within a framework of existential anxiety and political dilemmas. Foregrounding the pop obsession with designed surfaces, The Avengers eliminates all trace of a human nature from its content. These features were an integral part of another style of series that made its appearance in the United States at the beginning of the 1960s in opposition to the Western, eschewing the 'realistic' illustration of human 'truths' in favour of 'glamour', the imagery of conspicuous consumption. The producer of Burke's Law (1962–63), which featured a handsome, womanising, millionaire amateur detective, the very epitome of the leisure classes stigmatised by populist tradition, declared: 'everyone was preparing psychiatry and psychology shows, series with deep problems. We felt that TV needed something glamorous'[21] (my emphasis). This consumer orientation began to find favour with a younger, more urbanised audience, one that was more interesting to advertisers.

There is an important 'pop' idea in the above quotation. Once 'expressive design' had come into its own, once the look of an object was not intrinsically related to its function, 'it is the surfaces that matter, the surface is matter' (Dick Hebdige).[22] Pop rejects 'depth', the idea that the true meaning is hidden behind the surface appearance, a fundamental axiom of the television play constructed around the 'in-depth' exploration of character. For pop, 'psychological depth' (or 'deep problems') can only detract from the display of designed surfaces which are themselves rich in meaning. In the words of Paul Barker, '(pop art's) secret depth is that there is no secret depth'.[23]

A second feature of pop art that was to find expression in series was the arbitrary juxtaposition of contexts, the 'illogical' combination of fetishised objects (as in collages). Pop refuses to get 'to the heart of the matter'; its movement is sideways rather than downwards, 'in depth'. This was also a controlled ideological strategy for poking fun at selected targets of the establishment old guard: a mafia meeting disguised as a bishops' conference ('The Little Wonders') was just light-hearted fun which required neither justification nor apology. The strategy was a highly successful one in that it forbade anyone to take it 'seriously': even though the joke was on them, vicars and bishops could only applaud with the rest for fear of passing for old-fashioned bores. There was always something jokily sadistic in pop, whether in its provocatively emotionless approach to death (a pretext for witty remarks after Steed and Peel have timed their arrival seconds too late), or in the wicked, metaphorical regression of opponents of the new consumer order to an infantile stage of development, fanatically tending to their model train sets and plans for world domination like so many beastly schoolboys. In Losey's film version of Modesty Blaise, the accountant McWhirter (and the viewer) are frustrated by not being allowed to look at the spectacle of an agent having his neck broken by the sadistic Mrs Fothergill: McWhirter is forced to do the accounts with his back turned and the viewer can participate in the pleasure only by following the expression on master criminal Gabriel's face. The passage from 'perverse' sex to fashion is epitomised by the slippage of the word 'kinky' from the 'illogical' combination of pain and (sexual) pleasure to the appearance of suitably unusual juxtaposition in dress and design. The 'hidden depth' of a sexual metaphor is given a 'banal' concrete appearance. Deliberately seeking references out of context, juxtaposing opposites, pop engaged in what Dick Hebdige calls 'facetious quotation'.

The third crucial feature of pop, a consequence of its rejection of 'psychology' and 'depth', was its flattening out of social life, its transformation of the figurative into concrete representation. Nothing, not even the life of the mind, escapes the world of design: even metaphors are given appearance. To some extent, this is inherent in the very notion of design, which translates an abstract concept into concrete form: as we have seen, the emergence of a universal streamlining style translated the metaphors of 'speed' and 'modernity' into a variety of forms (certain clothes were 'as fast and slick as a jet plane'). Similarly, the combination of opposites in 'kinky SM sex' became a metaphor for similar juxtapositions in fashion. The reduction, or 'flattening out' of ideas, maxims, metaphors and clichés into real objects was integral to pop style: in *Modesty Blaise*, Mrs Fothergill *literally* dies by 'kicking the bucket'. In *The Avengers* episode 'The Interrogators', an undercover informant is shot dead while alive and kicking . . . a football.

Having abandoned the situation of characters and situations in terms of psychological motive and human nature in favour of design codes, the new type of series nevertheless had to be understood, its designed surfaces correctly 'recognised' and 'read'. 'Pop' series required a new gaze from viewers, one that was ready not only to accept patent artificality but derive pleasure from it. The flat, superficial world of the comic hero had previously been dismissed as 'childish' by the middle classes, some of whom (notably schoolteachers) considered its very existence a threat to the nation's cultural and moral health. The new heros were nothing if not comic-book characters: to resist them was to fall foul of pop's newly acquired right to draw the demarcation line between the Old and the New. To be 'modern' or be laughed out of existence. Concerning the quintessential pop series, *The Avengers*, some critics were initially confused. On BBC radio in 1963, Harry Craig confessed: 'It's impossible to watch this stupidity, this excellent stupidity, this silly excellence without being struck by black thoughts about design and vision, about content and about form. You see, it is made brilliantly . . . *The Avengers* is excited surface. What is it about? Search me!' While George Melly opined: 'if this had been a send-up of everything bad and modish on television, it would have been brilliant, but it wasn't a send-up . . . It made the commercial break seem terribly honest.'[24] Kingsley Amis, however, provided a legitimation of the new gaze that is worth quoting in full:

Whenever anyone sets about poisoning off most of the human race or blowing up London, Steed and Cathy (Gale) are sure to turn up, often it seems by the merest chance. This on-the-spotness is often a snag in thriller series; *The Avengers* cleverly turns it into a virtue, something to enjoy. At least two highbrow critics have shown themselves too dim to see this. 'Who actually employs Mrs Gale?', they ask triumphantly, as if they'd spotted some fatal flaw. But the whole point is that the question of employment doesn't arise. These are a pair of heroic free-lancers, inspired amateurs who knock off a couple of world-wide conspiracies in the intervals of choosing their spring wardrobe. All this is, so to speak, a wink at the audience, a joke shared with them . . . This kind of game is impossible unless the producers have confidence in their audience, who must have the mental agility to appreciate the odd satirical nudge while still believing in the story as a thriller. I don't think it's fantastic to call such mental agility 'sophistication'. At the opposite end of the scale . . . comes the viewer who can't distinguish between fiction and reality. I'm thinking of the Coronation Street fans who wrote to Len Fairclough threatening to come and fill him in if he didn't mend his ways. Non-sophistication could hardly go further.[25]

An enormous shift has taken place. Psychological identification with characters on the basis of commonly established moral criteria is here dismissed as 'unsophisticated'. Previously, 'unrealistic' protagonists like Bulldog Drummond, Fu Man Chu and the Saint had a less than cerebral reputation, to put it mildly. The pop gaze establishes a new regime of truth for the television series, no longer based – however inadequately – on the 'outside world' but on the higher reality of design. Once dismissed as 'escapist', this new reality was now valorised as 'sophisticated', which explained its attraction – its necessity even – for those seeking to operate successfully in the modern world. Externalised on the body, style becomes publicly visible, one's personal lifestyle choices open for all to read: failure to consume correctly, at the proper rhythm, was to expose oneself to rebuke for being a 'square'.

The terms used by Amis ('mental agility', 'sophistication') are apt in another way. They suggest the degree of mental effort and achievement in attaining a new gaze on the world of things. Just as the rejection of aristocratic classicism involved the studious cultivation of a more sensuous imagination (romanticism), the development of a modern consumer mentality necessitated a new attention to detail. This meant learning to concentrate one's gaze on surfaces in a world in which fetishism had been extended to almost all objects (and to people themselves), henceforth massively invested with systems of signification. The inability to read surfaces correctly amounted to a lack of 'sophistication', a failing that could ultimately compromise one's performance on the socio-sexual market.

The Avengers, a title later so much at odds with its content, began as an entirely different series, still conceived of in terms of psychological realism. A Doctor Brent sets out to 'avenge' the death of his fiancée, cold-bloodedly murdered by a drug gang after she has opened a package of heroin mistakenly delivered to Brent's surgery. The police can do nothing and in despair, Brent teams up with Steed, a mysterious under-cover agent who is fighting a general crusade against organised crime. The actor Ian Henry described Keel as 'a most attractive character (who) combines toughness with compassion and serves as the conscience of the team'[26] while Steed, whose affiliation remained unclear in the early episodes, was designed to be 'sardonic, suave and cynical, with a flair for elegant clothes, an eye for the women and a not too fastidious ruthless-ness in getting his own way'.[27] Steed, then, was a new type of off-beat hero, 'a wolf with the women' and 'not too popular with the police',[28] a freebooting counterpart to the more orthodox moral qualities of Dr Brent: together, they formed a complementary team in the fight against crime, a combination of conscience and cynicism, work and pleasure. The first episode went out live in January 1961.

The doctor and undercover agent formula was dropped after only three episodes of the second 1962 season. The Keel role was changed into that of a woman, Cathy Gale, a cool blonde with a PhD in anthropo-logy, an expert mechanic and photographer skilled in firearms and judo. Cathy Gale's part was written as if she were a man: the actress Honor Blackman described her role as 'the first feminist to come into a televi-sion serial; the first women to fight back'.[29] When recording began in May 1962, the fashion expert Michael Whittaker was brought in to design Cathy Gale's clothes to keep ahead of current fashions throughout the coming winter season and her leather trousers and high boots eventually came into vogue. The part of Steed was revamped as a 'modern-day Beau Brummell', with dandified Edwardian-style clothes and the impeccable manners of an English gentleman. A formula gradually evolved: a crime hunt with 'kinky', eccentric characters and a cool pop humour which involved dialogue that was 'inappropriate' to the situation.

What is important here is that ideological themes have been built directly into the characters' design, reducing them to ideological machines rather than 'real' people. No attempt is made to relate the ideological themes of the series to 'human nature'. In 'The Warlock' (1962), a Soviet spy, Markel, has teamed up with a warlock, Cosmo Gallion, to extract information from scientists working on top secret research projects but are also interested in the occult. The threat comes from the illegitimate combination of modern science with 'the promise that Evil, intelligently controlled, is more powerful than Good', a point of view that Steed thought 'went out with the middle ages'. In the episode 'Mandrake' (1964), a doctor and his associate run a sideline business based on poisoning their clients' rich benefactors and arranging their burial in the arsenic-laden soil of a Cornish cemetery. The doctor's descent into crime is explained as being due to the fact that he 'just couldn't keep up with all the new techniques'. This is a pop explanation – psychology has been reduced to ideology, motives are no longer necessary. Protected by the ever present, none-of-this-is-serious irony, characters are reduced to their ideological determinations.

Avoidance of the 'yardstick of social reality' became an increasingly pronounced part of the series' ground rules after 1965. Fantastic plots are juxtaposed with banal, ordinary locations; simple gadgets lie behind supernatural appearances. Nothing is what it seems. A luxury hotel contains a concentration camp . . . a marriage bureau hides an assassination agency . . . beneath a graveyard is an underground city and secret army . . . the moat of a Scottish castle contains a fleet of submarines . . . As Steven Chibnall[30] points out, the threat to society generally comes from one of two directions: on the one hand, a rearguard refusal of modern technology by diehard reactionaries (retired colonels, fin de race aristocrats); on the other hand, from lunatic scientists who want to extend machine principles to human beings. The nodal point around which the series' oppositions are organised is the very ideal of modernity: its acceptable dose – not too little, not too much – lies in the median ground between the two extremes, personified in the pure friendship between Steed and Emma Peel (M(an) appeal), the proof that traditional and modern values can coexist in a pure complicity, the question of sex being heavy-handed, messy and irrelevant – in a word, psychological. In 'Death at Bargain Prices' (1965), a retired department store owner reminisces about the past: 'a glorious age, gracious, leisurely and ordered . . . A machine was a thing of joy then, built to last a man's lifetime. Now it's out of date before it's left the assembly line. Out of date! They say this is where I belong, a discontinued line.' His desire for revenge, stemming from a pre-pop conception of consumer durables, consists in forcing an atomic scientist to transform the store into a giant atomic bomb.

In the famous 'House that Jack Built' (1966), Emma is lured to a remote country house where she finds an 'exhibition dedicated to the late Emma Peel' complete with old television news interviews of Emma Knight, as she was known at the time. Having succeeded her father as head of Knight Industries, Emma sacks the firm's automation expert Professor

Keller: 'I couldn't agree with his methods. Automation to the utmost degree. Replace man with machine. Subjugate him to it. Equate man with machine? I don't think it's entirely possible'. Keller has spent his retirement building an 'intelligent house' to prove her wrong and avenge his dismissal. His taped voice explains:

You laughed at my theories. You were wrong. The machine is not only man's equal but his superior. I am dead. Only the house survives. This house is a machine, an indestructable machine. It will last 1,000 years, perhaps forever. The mind of a machine cannot reason, therefore it cannot lose its reason. That is its superiority. It has no breaking point. But you will be mad.

In 'The Cybernauts' (1965), another deranged scientist, Dr Armstrong, a cripple confined to an elaborately automated wheelchair, is persuaded that government by automation will be the 'ultimate in human achievement'. His plan is to take over the planet with a killer army of remote-controlled robots: 'This is the age of the push button ... We human beings are fallible, temperamental and so often unreliable. The machine, however, is obedient and invariably more competent.'

One form of the threat from below is posed by the vulgar *nouveau riche* class who ruthlessly pursue ambitions of power and wealth – Thatcherites before their time – without the civilising restraint of the old elite. In 'The Fear Merchants' (1967), the 'Business Efficiency Bureau', a group of humourless psychologists, offer the service of 'eliminating the competition': applying market principles to the letter, they provoke mental breakdowns among their clients' competition with the aid of modern methods (questionnaires, computers and a lie detector) for exploiting psychological weakness. Their latest client is Jeremy Raven, a grown-up adolescent whose line is mass-producing fake classical ceramics in execrable taste. After three leading managers in the porcelain industry have suffered mental traumas and regressed to childhood, Steed pays a visit to Raven, a rather 'anal' character, who explains:

I cannot tolerate the slightest defect. I am aiming for absolute perfection . . . Youth to the fore and all that. I don't deny having inherited a great tradition and quite a few archaic methods, unfortunately but I'm going to change all that. Do you know my motto? 'Creation through automation'. Put a classical piece in every household.

Unfortunately for Raven, his rivals refuse his offer of a merger: 'Real fossils. They think that modernisation cannot regulate human life.'

The head of the Bureau, Pemberton (whose slicked-back hair and dark glasses give him a lean and hungry, 'competitive' look), explains to Steed:

'With the modern methods of psychiatry, we shall study your competitors, explore their entire life, specify their defects, their weaknesses: we shall pierce their armour.' The conception of a psychological trauma used here is an extremely 'flat' one: the mere appearance of the object of repressive fixation (a bird, spider, mouse, car travelling at speed) is sufficient to trigger off a mental breakdown. Similarly, in classic pop style, the psychologists cannot resist giving concepts a concrete form by writing key words (motivation . . . potential demand analysis) on the walls of their office. Pemberton and his associates have found a means of extending the market: 'The mind is our territory, fear is our merchandise.' The reduction of people to objects, the manipulation of the mind as an object, was an archetypal pop theme which had to be addressed to the extent that pop itself was engaged in the same reduction of people to designed objects. Boundary lines had to be drawn between what was legitimate and illegitimate in this process, a line that passes through the satisfaction of (sexual) desire. The threat to society comes from those who put ambition and greed ahead of pleasure: the figure of the (impotent) scientist who is too involved in his projects to have cultivated the simplest social graces was a common trope in the 1960s, as was that of the unattractive, physically ambiguous and ambitious woman professional (here represented by the mannish Dr Voss: the character of Rosa Klebb in From Russia with Love also comes to mind.) Deriving pleasure from object-commodities (which potentially includes people) is highly legitimate; manipulating objects for purposes of social climbing or doctrine highly illegitimate. Doctrine in the 'neutral', modern world – sociologists like Daniel Bell[31] proclaimed the 'end of ideology' as a consequence of the consumer society – is reduced to harebrained schemes to take over the planet. Ambition is acceptable only in that it does not detract from the pleasure of others and stays within the rules of the new managerial capitalism. Steed himself declares: 'If we wish to be present on the world market, we must eliminate waste and increase productivity.' But there were right and wrong ways of going about this.

Danger also comes from a fascist rearguard who envisage the future in non-consumer terms, an alliance of advanced technology and military discipline which directly contests the power of the welfare state and its liberal consensus. In 'The Invasion of the Earthmen' (1969), Commander Brett runs the Alpha Academy, a boarding school for young men and women, along military lines. His real goal is to send deep-frozen killers into space:

The Earth, overpopulated, underfed, its sources of wealth dried up ... Like schoolchildren fighting to be top of the class, East and West seek the ideal means of interplanetary travel; when this has been perfected, my army will travel to distant planets and we shall colonise them. An army of soldier-astronauts to exterminate the other astronauts.

In 'The Interrogators' (1969), a fake Captain Mannering takes advantage of the blind obedience to military discipline and secret service bureaucracy to persuade agents to undergo a mock interrogation after which they give away vital secrets in the bar – 'the one place where we were allowed to relax, to lower our defences': too much discipline and a lack of discipline are combined into a single point of weakness. Another form of danger stems from channelling the libido into illegitimate causes. 'My Wildest Dreams' (1969) features a futurist 'Aggresso-Therapist' who teaches patients to 'triumph over their inhibitions' and the 'restrictive laws of society', to become primitive killers, once again in the cause of ruthless business competition.

This was going too far. The need for an alliance between advanced technology and fashion becomes evident: for want of adopting the light-hearted, relaxed modal personality which is part and parcel of being modern, the anally-retentive, obsessive rising class run the risk of compromising modern society by taking the possibilities for social promotion through technological advance too seriously, exploiting them beyond their means and confusing the social hierarchy. The consumption skills of the upper class, their ability to derive pleasure from fine things like champagne, become a model for the whole of society. No longer in the thick of class struggle, the liberal-minded aristocratic gentleman was henceforth a socially neutral figure, one who was au-dessus de la mêlée: another example of this 1960s prototype was Simon Templar ('The Saint' in the series of the same name) who deftly and elegantly intervened in the contentions of lesser mortals, putting distasteful petty-bourgeois greed back in its rightful place. True modernity was a duality of technology and art, science and fashion, discipline and pleasure, private enterprise and the state. A narrowly defined technological modernity, symbolised in the person of the lunatic scientist, represented a dangerous drift towards a socially rearguard authoritarianism.

This theme recurs over and over again in The Avengers. In 'The Hidden Tiger' (1967), another humourless fanatic, Dr Manx, has devised a plan for taking over the country by fitting cats with miniature receivers which can transmit brain waves capable of transforming them into ferocious killers. He tells Steed: 'Few humans will survive, but for the happy few, there will be unlimited wealth.' In 'The Living Dead' (1967), the plebeian Masgard, decked out in tasteless medallion and boxer's helmet, has constructed an underground city with slave labour and is preparing to emerge from his shelter with a 20,000-strong army to take over the country after an atomic bomb has been dropped on the hapless inhabitants of Britain. A class reversal has taken place: above ground, Masgard is a mere estate manager for the 16th Duke of Benedict who serves as a cover for the project. By temporarily escaping to the surface, the 15th Duke, thought to have been killed in a mining disaster five years previously, has triggered off rumours of ghosts on the Benedict estate. It is the way Masgard gives orders to the Duke that first arouses Steed's suspicions; meanwhile, underground, the 15th Duke has been reduced to a slave worker. As the pun in the final set piece makes clear, the 15th Duke is the 'ghost in the machine', a pop translation from the figurative to the concrete. Similarly, the underground city, whose grey square buildings and absence of cars resemble a 'socialist' city, an anti-consumer society, is a literal representation of the threat to the social consensus 'from below'.

The theme of class reversal is also to the fore in 'Who's Who' in which an enemy agent has invented a machine able to transfer the mind, body and psyche from one person to another. Two lower-class assassins, Basil and Lola, swap bodies with Steed and Emma, enabling them to infiltrate the British spy network and wipe out half of its agents. (In a pop joke, the 'flowers' of the secret service have code names – Tulip, Daffodil, Poppy, Bluebell – to match their buttonholes). Physically identical to Steed and Emma but betraying their class origins in their gum-chewing and neck-nuzzling, Basil and Lola are enraptured with their newly luxurious lifestyle: '(They) were on to a good number. A posh appartment, a good life.' The real Steed is furious at the vulgar manners of the two assassins: 'My last bottle from 1947, not even put on ice. My cigars! He has cut off the end with his fingers! What unspeakable individual are we dealing with?'

In 'The Winged Avenger', a comic-strip artist brings to life his own creation, dressing up as The Winged Avenger, a Batman-like figure who viciously claws to death deserving victims like the nasty publishing tycoons Roberts and Son and the industrialist Damayn who has automated his factories and made thousands redundant. In the words of Steed, the victims are all 'ruthless businessmen (who) treat their personnel badly and mercilessly wipe out their competitors'. A condensation of the 'threat from above' and the 'threat from below', higher judge of men and killer beast, The Winged Avenger represents an individualism taken to its lunatic extreme: 'I have come to purge the world of evil. I bring justice and vengeance to those beyond the reach of man and law ... Creator and beast fused into one individual, indivisible, omnipotent.'

The presence of anachronisms, a juxtaposition of the past and the new, was also a pop device used in *The Avengers*, designating the 'perverted' modernity of the villains, a backward-looking confusion of the past and the present. In 'Epic', a bald Germanic film director, Z. Z. Von Schnerk, makes dreadful, unintentionally camp movies featuring, for example, a centurion standing in front of a 'Police Department of San Francisco' sign. Acting involuntarily in the mad Von Schnerk's greatest work, 'The Destruction of Emma Peel', Emma is attacked successively by a medieval queen, a cowboy, first-World-War soldiers, Cossacks and Red Indians. In 'Escape in Time', Steed and Emma are confronted with a mysterious anachronism: a fellow secret agent is found in the Thames, shot dead by a sixteenth-century bullet. Thyssen, the owner of an opulent country estate, has apparently invented the perfect escape route – a time machine which allows criminals to escape into a past peopled by Thyssen's own ancestors. After paying a fortune, clients have a choice between what amount to the Edwardian, Victorian, Georgian and Elisabethan eras, all, incidentally, golden moments of the traditional elite. At separate intervals, Steed and Emma, posing as criminals on the run, both choose the Georgian era, Steed because 'Samuel Thyssen the libertine is more my type' than the Edwardian, racehorse-owning Thyssen, and Emma, after dismissing the Victorian and Elizabethan eras for their puritanism and lack of independence for women, because it was a 'refined era' with 'intelligent women'. Although dressed in Georgian costume, Emma is sent by Thyssen's 'time-corridor' to the Elizabethan era where she is seized by Matthew Thyssen, the notoriously sadistic witch-hunter:

'*Matthew Thyssen*': This strange costume is an invention of the devil. Its purpose is to seduce and bewitch men, to stimulate their desires ... You are a heretic, a witch.
Emma: I'd like to see you in the twentieth century.

Surprising Thyssen on the point of applying a white-hot poker to Emma's flesh, Steed is aghast: 'Good heavens, what happened to the gracious manners of 1790?' Fortunately, history is a linear progression: to escape, one has only to move from one room to another: 'We have come from 1560 to 1968, next stop Venus!' The episode proposes that the Georgian era is to the Elizabethan one as the Modern era is to the

Victorian one. It also resolves the contradictions inherent in Steed's character design by establishing 'traditional', Georgian precedents for the new era of refined consumption and pleasure, and suggests at the same time that the puritan Victorian era is superior to the Elizabethan one only in that sexual repression has replaced physical torture. For the worst possible motive of greed, Thyssen has reverted to the most sadistically reactionary part of his aristocratic make-up. In true pop style, the concepts of time and history are reduced to designed 'things': the time machine is really a series of perfectly furnished rooms where clients are cruelly and campily put to death by Thyssen in period costume.

The second Diana Rigg series (1967–68) and the Linda Thorson series (1969) were made with American backing and were successful in the United States, though it is certain that most of the class references discussed above were lost on an American audience for whom the series had a quaint British charm in its juxtaposition of the traditional (country house, fox-shooting) and the modern (robots, atomic power plants). A sudden decline in the American ratings following a scheduling change led to the series' cancellation, and a derivative, Franco-British financed revival in 1976, The New Avengers, was only moderately successful. In its time, however, The Avengers had an undeniable quality and force.

Professional modernists

The Man from UNCLE, an American translation of pop, was inflected by the distinctly American tradition of camp, which was ideologically motivated to deride those incapable of adapting correctly to the modern world. Camp is not so much a genre or sub-genre but a strategy for reading, for refusing and reappropriating an original message whose 'cover has been blown'.[32] As such, it represents, along with canonisation into a 'great' (or 'alternative') tradition, one of two possibilities for reviving a text outside its original context. The force of a camp response is that it confers an instant superiority on the audience over the text, the former's ability to 'see through' and derive (sadistic) pleasure from the text's very badness (Cecil B. De Mille films, for example) being the proof of its 'sophistication'. It is, in short, an assertion of difference through the celebration of the ideological uselessness of a text. In the UNCLE series, however, camp elements were strategically integrated into a confident affirmation of the values of a modern consumer society.

The idea of UNCLE began to take form in October 1962 when the advertising agency J. Walter Thompson took up the idea of converting some of Ian Fleming's books into a television series, taking its cue no doubt from President Kennedy, who declared himself a James Bond fan in a *Life* interview. (Watch your spy series more.) In the basic assemblage, two agents, the exhuberant, easy-going Napoleon Solo (the name suggesting a well-bred individualism) and the quiet, moody Ilya Kuryakin work for a multinational security organisation called UNCLE, constantly saving the word from the evil designs of an apolitical international crime organisation called THRUSH (almost certainly a jokey, winking reference to the common name for a vaginal infection).[33] The assemblage enables the series to affirm a pan-humanist, internationalist creed in a world in which competing political philosophies have been consigned to the dustbin of history by the emergence of a modern consumer society.

Much of the visual humour comes from the incongruous hamminess of the villain parts. In one of pop's most brilliant formal devices, a discourse of great moral earnestness ('speaking with forked tongue') is mouthed by manifestly insincere villains, duping 'non-professional' protagonists (often from backward cultures like Arabia, Greece or Japan) who commit the error of taking discourse and emotion, rather than design, at face value. But for the audience, hypocrisy is immediately recognisable in certain tell-tale signs: the unfashionable clothes and mannerisms, the over-seriousness, the lack of humour, the repressed sexuality. The UNCLE agents, on the other hand, combine a crisp, no-nonsense technical discourse with 'charm' – quips, smart put-downs and seductive smooth talk, an alliance of the technical and social skills so essential to pop's brand of high modernism. Secondly, unlike the sexless THRUSH agents, Solo has a voracious appetite for the naive and attractive women thrown up in the course of the mission. The popularity of the series and the positive attributes given to the UNCLE team consecrated the victory of consumption and pleasure values over those of the moralistic 'stuffed-shirts' that were the target of *Playboy* ire in the 1950s. The dangerous fanatic is no longer he who gives free rein to his sexuality but he who does not.

UNCLE (originally a sound-evocation of Uncle Sam and the UNO but converted on audience demand into an acronym, United Network Command for Law and Enforcement) is an international secret organisation whose American headquarters is hidden behind the fitting room of Del Floria's Tailor shop. In itself, this is a pop gag: a men's fashion boutique serves – literally – as a 'front' for a secret service, just as the agents' fancy-dress outfits serve as a 'cover' for their work. The device also suggests that a liberal-minded establishment is operating – once again literally – 'behind the scenes' to ensure the welfare of citizens. In keeping with the series' end-of-ideology options, Solo's partner, the jazz-loving Illya Kuryakin, is an officer in the Soviet navy. Their adversary, THRUSH, impressively endowed with an international network and the latest technology, is an enormous bureaucracy with its own career structure, pension plan and absurdly rigid regulations.

In 'The Indian Affairs Affair' (a.k.a. 'The Oklahoma Bomb Affair', 1966) Carson, a THRUSH agent, has taken over an Indian reserve by holding hostage its chief, High Cloud. In a grotesque reversal of historical truth, Carson, a fanatical Indian-hater, tells High Cloud: 'The Oklahoma Massacre. A whole company was wiped out by a handful of bloodthirsty rebels. It was people of your race that committed this atrocity, almost a century ago. The date changes nothing for me. Indians have no sense of Good and Evil. That's why they're still savages.'

The West of the 1870s, pictured as an idyllic primal state of American capitalism in series like *Bonanza*, fulfils the same role as the Victorian epoch for British pop series. Carson's *passéisme* is of the salacious variety, cross-fertilised by fears of racial decline. Laying his paws on the chief's daughter, he cries: 'I hate Indians, just like my father and my grandfather before him, but you have to know your enemy. You savages have a few secrets I'd really like to know. Our times have seen the degeneration of the white man, his vitality is fading, whereas you Indians still have all of your basic instincts intact. . . .' A psychological anxiety has been 'flattened out' into a racist puritanism, devalorised in relation to those who, marginalised by the traditional bourgeois mode of existence, have retained their basic (sexual) instincts. The alliance between the 'primitive' libido and consumer modernism is similar to that found in the discourses surrounding rock music of the same period.

In the episode's sub-plot, Carson profits from a difference of outlook between Chief High Cloud and his daughter Charisma to destroy the former's morale and obtain his cooperation. Evil no longer inserts itself in the interstices of moral weakness but in those of puritanism, the inability to accept the pleasures of the modern world. Charisma works in nightclubs, cabarets and gambling saloons doing tribal war dances in her spare time to finance her university studies, something her traditionalist father cannot accept, while the reservation Indians are decked out in headbands, warpaint and . . . suits and ties. As in *The Avengers*, anachronism (the battle of Little Big Horn is re-enacted with jeeps and scooters; the first time as tragedy, the second time as farce) is a device for making directly visible the illegitimate ideological sedimentation of survivals from the past.

In 'The Sort of Do-it-Yourself Dreadful Affair' (1966), written by science-fiction writer Harlan Ellison, Solo adopts – reluctantly – the disguise of a boring Swiss banker for a mission in the Bahamas. A THRUSH scientist, Dr Pertwee, has produced a series of beautiful super-women, kidnapping living New Yorkers and replacing their brains with electronic circuits, 'a compound like that made by Burke and Hare in the cemeteries of Edinburgh in the eighteenth century'. The THRUSH direc-tor, the sexually repressed, aptly named Lash, who has invited a number of bankers to finance his project, declares the highest of high-minded ideals:

we wish to liberate man from exhausting, assembly-line work . . . We have perfected an alternative concept of automation by using – how shall I put it? artificial humans . . . Cheap, easy to maintain and indestructible. Slaves that can be programmed according to your wishes. Think of it, you will be able to realise all of your desires.

Unfortunately, Lash has other plans for his 'living dolls'. In an unguarded moment, his voice takes on a Hitlerian pitch:

Hundreds and thousands of well-armed, indestructible slaves that will march, march, march and sweep away everything that lies before them, achieving victory in a few invincible days. Neither bullets nor bombs, nor tanks can harm them. Soldiers without a soul, without a conscience. A huge army covering the planet, marching, marching . . .

In this modern version of the Frankenstein myth in which objects of (male) desire are transformed into mass-produced robot-soldiers, the renunciation of the libido becomes monstrous, fascistic, misogynous, the dangerous inability to transcend a primitive, puritan stage of capi-talism. The advancement of technology and liberation from the drudgery of work cannot be separated from the experience of new forms of pleasure, the *sine qua non* of true modernity: in this respect, Lash's artificial human slaves represent a perversion of modernity, an attempt to create an alternative future with categories from the eighteenth century, to return to the very beginnings of capitalist work relations in which human beings are reduced to the role of raw materials in the production process. Automation, inextricably linked in the 1960s to a new age of leisure, is rejected in favour of mechanising the human body itself, or more precisely, the female body. In Lash's world, sex becomes a

mechanised, programmed work activity in which female desire is
annihilated.

In the episode's sub-plot, Solo comes into contact with a THRUSH
woman scientist, that familiar pop figure, the frigid workaholic whose
obvious sexual potential is spoilt by unsightly horn-rimmed glasses and
who is incapable of communicating in anything but the most abstruse
technical jargon. The strategic importance of this type of character, a
female counterpart of the 'anal' scientist, was to serve as a demonstration
of the liberating effects of the 'Playboy philosophy', especially when
practised by expert (male) 'professionals'. 'Sophisticated' viewers had no
doubt about 'what she needed', a service that Solo – with the series'
discreet benediction – was only too happy to provide. In a recurring pop
theme, the villain of the piece is petty-bourgeois ambition, here
associated with anxiety over the growing role of women professionals:
'Do you think I want to spend all my life as a quiet office worker for a
bank without any future? I'm worth more than that.' But the master
seducer Solo has a strong card to play against the desexualised THRUSH
social relations. 'Mr Solo, I'm terribly lonely in this job. There is no place
for love. My relations with men are purely professional.' A trade-off is
being offered: a loosening of the moral screws in return for keeping
personal ambition in check, a permission to indulge in the pleasures
offered by the new consumer society without upsetting the order of
things. Professionalism conceived of in the narrow terms of work relations was dangerously ambitious, obsessive, irredeemably old-
fashioned. Self-realisation was to be displaced into the domain of consumption and pleasure.

The same trope re-emerges in 'The Nowhere Affair' (1966). In a ghost
town called 'Nowhere' in the hidden recesses of the Nevada Desert, Solo
stumbles upon a THRUSH headquarters situated in an abandoned mine,
furnished with banks of computers as far as the eye can see and guarded
by cowboys dressed entirely in black. To escape interrogation, Solo takes
an amnesia pill which temporarily effaces his memory. Furious that Solo
is able to 'retain' important information in his 'subconscious', the
THRUSH chief, Longolius, is forced to call on Tertunian, a cybernetics
expert hired by THRUSH 'to study the influence of various emotional
factors on the loyalism of THRUSH members' (forbidden any love
life except with express permission). Tertunian's reasoning takes Longolius, who has never heard of the word libido, by surprise:

We must call on the most animal instincts, which man cannot defend himself
against. Fear is the most ancient but Mr Solo knows no fear . . . Another basic

instinct is the libido and there, my dear Longolius, lies our last chance . . . (The libido) is the interest that one has for the opposite sex and our subject has had immense experience in this area. His Achilles' heel seems to be women and if we can find his ideal partner, we'll have succeeded.

Confident that '(his) machines never make a mistake', Tertunian programmes 2,000 files of suitable THRUSH 'female personnel', limiting his sample to the Pacific Coast to save time. To everyone's surprise, the machine chooses agent Z 897, none other than Mara, his studious, bespectacled assistant, who confesses her lack of expertise in this domain:

> Tertunian: I thought that THRUSH women received lessons on what men and women do together in private.
> Mara: I didn't do that course. I could have, but I preferred integral calculus . . .

At the sight of a revolver, Solo's memory comes flooding back: the notion of psychology used by pop comes straight from behaviourism. The themes of conditioning and deconditioning were common ones in pop as is shown by the frequent use of the brainwashing motif which explored the line between what was legitimate and illegitimate in this process: adaptation to the modern world demanded a deconditioning from puritan constraints, an argument hammered by advertising ideologues as early as the 1920s who sought subjects open to advertising's attempt to 're-condition' consumers. Mara's THRUSH training is no match for Solo's lovemaking skills; the seductress is seduced. The computer has not made a mistake but the new age of modern technology 'naturally' goes hand in hand with more relaxed attitudes to (sexual) pleasure: the use of computers to enforce a repressive moral regime can only backfire. But for Mara, the damage has been done. As she explains:

> I have never known any other way of life. THRUSH has always been everything for me, father and mother, church and country. The organisation took me in when I was four . . . They clothed me, fed me and trained me to follow a goal that until today I thought was my own . . . The problem is that none of this can be wiped out. THRUSH does things so thoroughly that I am programmed for life.

A conservative upbringing is not a problem for pop ideology: the answer for Mara is simply to take a strong dose of amnesia pills which wipe out all memories except for those of pure pleasure, in other words, her lovemaking with Solo. From one instant to another, Mara becomes a born-again member of the consumer society, able to freely choose her own goals, a jar of pills (contraceptive pills?) instantly destroying twenty years of sexually repressive THRUSH programming.

THRUSH, then, is a buffoonish outgrowth of the crime syndicate with its own forms of social organisation that contrast unfavourably with those of the modern state and concentrate all the vices of an earlier stage of capitalism: the heavy-handed, imperialist attempts at world domination, the sexual repression, the racism, the treating of its personnel as disposable objects, the rigid, bureaucratic rules and regulations, the moral hypocrisy, the tasteless clothes. The liberalism of the 1960s, directed against traditional morality, was necessarily forced on to the terrain of sexual repression: what appears in retrospect as a rather puerile male fantasy was an integral part of a coherent 'Playboy Philosophy' which constructed sexual pleasure and 'free' consumption as pivotal issues for broader political concerns.

For all of its insolence and its constant visual and spoken sexual innuendoes, UNCLE, like the British pop series we have discussed, was nonetheless grounded in the promotion of an interventionist state, presented as a more appropriate guarantor of the new consumer society than the injunctions to moral discipline in rural populist ideology. In this respect, the series is a distant cousin of the earlier The Untouchables in its confident condensation of the values of individualism and state intervention in the same assemblage. The opposition between the sympathetic, modernising state represented by 'professional' free-lance individuals and an undisciplined, gangsterish free enterprise system, a central one in The Untouchables, is explicitly to the fore in the UNCLE episode, 'The Round Table Affair' (1966). Due to the absence of extradition treaties, the miniscule European principality of Ingolstein has become a haven for gangsters the world over, who thrive in its feudal social relations. A small-time crook and huckster, Arthur King, has seized control of the state treasury by cheating on the naive Prince Regent at poker and running up a vast national debt which international gangsters are only too happy to pay off in return for immunity and a strategic base for their operations. King is not happy about the reigning princess's return from a convent school near Paris to clean out the stables with the help of the UNCLE agents:

Do you think Artie King is going to let himself be dispossessed? Taxes, the treasury, everything belongs to me, everything is mortgaged to me, it's to me that fishing rights, hunting rights are paid. I've got rights on space all the way from here to the stratosphere, and if I want to, I will also use my seigneurial rights. They belong to me too.

It is only when the greedy, ambitious King switches sides after falling in love with, and marrying, the strong-willed Head of State, Princess Victoria, that the gangsters are hoist on their own feudal petard.

Eschewing the dire threats of punishment for moral transgression advanced in the 'human nature' series, UNCLE nevertheless contained light-hearted, but didactic invitations to 'wise up', to get more sophisticated, to learn new skills for living in a modern society which offered new possibilities for social mobility. A common trope, found in almost every episode, is that of the naive and stupid ingénue who has pushed her charms too far. In the sub-plot to 'The Master's Touch Affair' (1967), an American model is lured to the Lisbon villa of THRUSH chief Pharos Mandor where she becomes a virtual prisoner:

I came here two weeks ago and every day I ask (Mandor) to let me go and every day he tells me 'tomorrow'. Every day he promises. What is going on? Do you know who he is? I pose for newspapers; if you glance at magazines from time to time you must have seen my photo. One day I was invited to a very fancy party, a famous shipowner . . . organises them almost all year round. A servant came to show me the guest list, you've never seen anything like it, kings, queens and all that and a helicopter just for me . . . Anyway, when I landed here there was no-one except Mandor and besides, the champagne wasn't even on ice . . .

After the mission has been concluded, Kuryakin offers her a book which contains 'pearls of wisdom' – a list of all the authentic millionaires in America and Europe: 'in future, don't get into a helicopter with just anyone', advises Solo. Intended as a device to provide a vicarious identification for the viewer, the integration of innocent ordinary people into the adventures also underlines the difference in social and technical skills between them and the UNCLE agents who, as 'professionals', set the standards for the new age. The structure of many episodes was based on a doubling-up of the fight between the old and the new on two distinct levels: one, epic, between UNCLE and THRUSH in which the future of the world is at stake; the other, down to earth, in which repressive customs and family obligations are grappled with by 'amateurs'. Adapting to the new skills required by a consumer society on an everyday, individual level is structurally linked to a grand opposition against a perverted modernism combining advanced technology with a simultaneous desire for personal power and repression of the libido. In 'The Adriatic Express Affair' (1965), a THRUSH ancienne belle who directs a beauty salon and is bitter about her own ageing plans to let loose a chemical that will eliminate the male desire to reproduce. Other THRUSH projected misuses of technology include high-frequency sound machines ('The Birds and the Bees Affair'), an ion-projection machine ('The Dippy Blonde Affair'), a heavy magnetic metal to disrupt world communications ('The Yukon Affair'), a brain-altering machine ('The Brain Killer Affair'), a sense-increasing drug ('The Minus X Affair'). Unlike in *The Invaders*, where the transformation of nature is morally suspect in itself, the question here is into whose hands these scientific inventions will fall.

UNCLE went out for the last time, after 104 episodes, in February 1968. During its third season (1967), a clone series *The Girl from UNCLE* featured agent April Dancer who added 'female' masquerade and seduction skills to the spy's professional baggage but was overcome by slipping ratings after twenty-nine episodes. The radical refusal of realism, a consequence of the equally radical elimination of all hint of psychological depth, led to increasingly weird plots that began to pall, the conscious use of camp walking a fine line between sophistication and mere bad taste. In retrospect, UNCLE was a curious series in which fast movement and fight scenes (made possible by extensive use of the hand-held Arriflex camera) were combined with an old-fashioned theatricality in which the protagonists circled and paced around obviously artificial studio decors: this, and the rather rank sexism, place its modernism firmly in the 1960s, although it does preserve a certain period charm. By the end of the 1960s, the impact of the Vietnam war and a tense domestic political context meant that the utopian, Kennedyan myth of a progressive, modernising establishment on which the series ultimately depended had lost most of its credibility. Incredibly, a smear campaign by conservative parents' groups, who lumped it in with *The Untouchables* as being too violent, killed the possibility of syndication re-runs during the 1970s. Given the harmless spoofing that characterised the series, such attacks almost certainly reflected a deeper ideological unease over the spread of 'permissive' values.

The first series to adopt some of the formal solutions of pop (programmed action from an assemblage of characters who are ideologically rather than psychologically determined) but without pop's irreverence was the highly successful *Mission: Impossible*. For 171 episodes, during the period 1966–73, the regular members of a para-state organisation, the Impossible Mission Force, coolly carried out their meticulously programmed simulations with the most ideologically minimalist strategy ever devised. A self-destroying tape and an envelope of photos riskily left in banal, everyday locations such as a fishing hut, a circus roundabout, a library or a gas station reminded viewers that the secret mission has, in some ultimate sense, the lives of ordinary Americans at stake. Dialogue between team members was limited to the technical and the expository: a grave threat to American security had to be excised in forty-eight minutes, and there was no time for civilities. To keep up the appearances of freelance individualism, the IMF chief (Dan Briggs and later, Jim Phelps) is given the choice of accepting the mission but no provision is made for refusing the request of the Department of State: 'Should you accept this mission. ... Good luck, Jim.' In a matter of seconds, questions of individual choice and loyalty to the state are evoked and passed over. In this sense, the ideological determinations are gratuitous in relation to the narrative: rather than being explored as such and integrated into the plot, they are simply used as background 'colouring'. In a further example of ideological minimalism, music rather than dialogue is used to maintain narrative continuity in long sequences in which the team sets up its equipment. This formal device was to be used even more radically in the later series *Miami Vice*.

The ideological project of pop is reinvested into a serious, modernised political framework that affirms American world domination in a neutral, dispassionate, 'technical' manner. The threat to American and world security comes from backward political systems, an even-handed mixture of communist and fascist dictators. For diplomatic reasons, these threats cannot be dealt with openly by the state: the maintenance of the *Pax Americana* required a surgical intervention that left no (messy) traces, an appealing fantasy for a nation bogged down in a losing war. The IMF team regroups the trans-class alliance of pop: Jim Phelps, the managerial 'brain'; Cinnamon Carter, the actress/seductress; Rollin Hand, the master of disguise whose ability to manufacture faces on demand impressively combines acting and technical skills; Willy Armitrage, the 'muscles', and Barney Collier, the black electronics wizard whose very presence is proof of technical modernity's liberal-mindedness. The ability to solve the world's problems by clinical means thus depends on an alliance of art and science, the co-operation of managers, actors, intellectuals, technicians and manual workers, all specialised 'professionals' in their given field and occasionally comple-mented by a guest expert (dentist, cybernetician, etc.) for a particular mission. At the beginning of every episode, the IMF 'director' casts the roles in the mission by perusing a file of publicity stills of potential team members on standby. The possibility of using 'artificial' design and acting techniques to remodel reality is proposed as a serious strategy for treating threats to the modern international and national consensus cleanly and efficiently. As in UNCLE, a liberal establishment of professional specialists stands guard over the welfare of ordinary citizens.

The minimal assemblage from which each narrative is entirely programmed also meant that the series could adapt to changing circumstances. After 1969, following the reduction of its budget after the takeover of the producer Desilu by Paramount, and greater doubts over, and sensitivity to, American interference in foreign countries, *Mission: Impossible* moved operations back to the United States to engage in the fight against domestic crime. The elaborate simulations previously used against the secret services of the Eastern People's Republic or dictators in the flyblown wastes of Camagua or Lombuada were now employed where they were more needed, against American crime syndicates. The foreign interventions, although important in the earlier episodes, could be detached from the assemblage without destroying the whole, a factor which explains the series' unusually long life span traversing both spy and police genres. As a police series, *Mission: Impossible* was less successful and never achieved the high ratings of its first three seasons: the ideological determinations of the team were too rigid for the fight against urban crime which demanded 'humanised' individuals whose relation to authority was more ambiguous.

The moment of pop

The moment of pop has come and gone. It is impossible to recreate the excitement provoked by the emergence of a modern consumer society, the seduction exercised by pleasingly designed objects, the overwhelming presence of a greater aesthetic sensibility. But pop has passed into our common-sense expectations of the worlds of advertising, fashion, music and television and foreshadowed many of the characteristics of the present 'postmodern' vision of the world.

From the beginning, the series had to confront specific problems relating to its form, problems based on continuity and coherence, and the generation of a large number of narratives from the same static assemblage. The credibility of earlier, 'human nature' series was largely dominated by notions of psychological realism, the relative presence or absence of a variety of universal moral virtues determining an individual's actions and the general narrative possibilities. The continual creation of the violent conflict demanded by the 'adventure' series from the problematic of a fixed human nature gradually ran into difficulty: as we have seen, long-running Western series like *Bonanza* and *Gunsmoke* eventually became episodic soap operas in a Western setting in which the pretext for violence always comes from 'outside'. Series in the 1960s were strongly influenced by the formula established by drama anthologies: the same leading actor(s), the same basic situation but with different stories and guest stars every week. But by the end of the 1960s, this formula of adapting widely different stories to the same assemblage began to break down as social tensions needed more direct, ideological resolutions. The care of time between episodes (what does David Vincent do to earn a living?) and the contradiction between the ideological and the psychological determinations of characters posed problems for series that still ultimately made claims to realism.

By abandoning all pretence to psychological realism, pop was able to resolve the problem of seriality in a new way. Like commodity designs and advertising symbols, the prefabricated characters were throwaway, ideological determinations. Time was collapsed into the assemblage: characters and decors were always *immanently* present, their meaning forever fixed in advance. In the resulting, (stereotyped) narrative, the action is simply *programmed* from the original design. The *tour de force* of pop was to have resolved the contradiction between a reified world of commodity values in which personality is transferred to things, and the possibility of individual action. For to the extent that the hero is ideally designed in ideological terms, any serious impact on society would undermine or at least change the terms of the initial assemblage. In the absence of psychological conflict, the heroes' experiences are reduced to a form of *positioning* in relation to objects and other people, carefully posed scenes which do little more than show off the ideological determinations of the heroes to their advantage. As we shall see, this formal solution for 'wasting time' was adopted by police series as cops paid visits to eccentric or 'interesting' characters at best marginally related to the simplified main plot. This became caricatural in the 1980s series *Miami Vice*: long sequences of dog races, basketball matches, disco dancing or pop concerts are justified only by the fact that they serve as a background for one of the protagonists who happens – advantageously or otherwise – *to be there*.

Bypassing the unwieldy, strained combination of changing ideological strategies with immutable expressions of human nature – which gives drama its 'heaviness' – pop boldly assumed the essential artificiality of all ideology, now invested in fashion and design values, and wore it on its heroes' sleeves. It is this which gives pop its quality of 'lightness': designed representations could be mainlined directly without tortuous explorations of an individual's psychological make-up. Strongly didactic, pop's ideological 'rush' gave instantaneous pleasure to those with the sophistication to read the signs correctly. The pop series represented the high point of a specifically television style of fiction in which form and ideology were inextricably merged.

The integration of the programmed action of pop into the American police series was also a necessary condition for the domination of world television markets, over and above purely economic factors. The rejection of psychological determinations for characters allowed American series to cross national boundaries without effort. In effect, the in-depth exploration of an individual's psychological make-up is always profoundly rooted in a national culture: as film club audiences know, this is not always readily accessible to those outside this culture and may need to be 'processed' (in the case of American Westerns and *série noire* films, through French existentialism). The ideological minimalism of *Mission: Impossible* enabled it to be screened in eighty-seven countries: its political colouring was not integral to the narrative and, with a little effort, could be ignored. In spite of its British origins, the ultimate victory of the moment of pop was perhaps the real popularity of strange American assemblages like Kojak in a hundred countries all over the planet.

The police series

In the wider genre of action series, the police genre has become increasingly dominant since the end of the 1960s and has been present since the very beginnings of television. To some extent, this was a predictable consequence of the need to justify the portrayal of 'entertaining' physical violence by casting it in 'realistic' social terms so that a pedagogical alibi could be established. Early police series in the 1950s like Dragnet immediately took on strong documentary overtones with dispassionate professional dialogue ('All I want is the facts, ma'am'). This marked a shift from the efforts of amateur detectives to collective, state activity in the fight against crime, no longer an arbitrary disruption of an organic harmony but a constant, pervasive part of the urban experience. Stephen Knight argues that the effects of the war in both Britain and the USA contributed to this new perception of crime: 'total war involved both general experience and widespread acceptance of bureaucratic organisation and communicated a notion that security could come from organised, technically skilled collective effort'.[1] The pedagogical nature of a documentary approach to crime is aptly shown in this presentation of Dragnet in a 1955 issue of the TV Times: 'in this episode . . . we are shown the methods used by the American police to track (an escaped robbery suspect) down'.[2] The moral lesson, that crime did not pay, was spliced into the implacable nature of standard police procedure: the conventions of realism tended to preclude the moralistic speechifying contained in the Western. But for many American viewers, the moral overdub was lost in the mix. After the outcry provoked by The Untouchables, the police series went into abeyance in the United States throughout most of the 1960s. By the end of the 1960s, however, political conditions made its revival a matter of some urgency.

In Great Britain, on the other hand, the police series proudly waved the banner of realism throughout the 1960s, integrating some of the formal properties of the soap opera (construction of an in-depth personality by focusing on the continuing dramas of everyday life) within what was presented as an accurately rendered description of routine police work. One of the practical difficulties of this format was that realism required a large number of regular characters and therefore complex plotting and writing as in a theatrical piece: the British police series was something of a cross between soap opera and drama. This formal solution was not taken up on American television until the 1980s, when Hill Street Blues episodes were farmed out to different writers in fifteen-minute segments. Realism demanded that stories be sometimes left with threads dangling, sometimes even with police failure: this was not yet acceptable for many American viewers, for whom the presence of violent crime was justifiable only by its eventual punishment.

The combination of police work and private life in the pioneering British series Z Cars was initially controversial. After its opening night (2 January 1962), the Chief Constable of Lancashire, in whose territory the story was laid, protested that a policeman's wife had been made to seem like a 'slut' in an episode dealing with the theme of marital difficulties. Built into the series' brief was the idea that police officers had 'feelings like the rest of us, and wives and girlfriends, and squabbles back home and headaches about easy payments and tomorrow's racing form'.[3] The importance of realistic characterisation over story was underlined by the series' producer Richard Beynan:

Our scripwriters start with the assumption that a police constable is a human being who happens to have chosen the profession of law and they take it from there. Otherwise we'd be left with nothing but plots. Who wants bare plots when they can watch a policeman reacting as a human being to crucial situations? As time goes by, you can see his character undergoing an organic growth.[4]

Police series like Z Cars and the later Softly, Softly aligned themselves with the technocratic, managerial reformism of the 1960s Labour government. Whereas The Avengers explored the ideological consequences of the new liberal consensus, police series established its 'human' dimension. A new ideology of security was presented, showing policemen who understood, and related to, the human qualities of the adversaries, judging them on their individual merits: this demanded at least some awareness of the social origins of crime. Modern police work, a judicious compound of technology and human experience, was a pragmatic solution to particular problems without the authoritarian illusion of totally stamping out crime through moral injunctions and repression.

The 'realistic' portrayal of professionals at work ran aground on the sheer complexity of modern social relations. Critics praised the authenticity of *Mogul* and *The Troubleshooters*, which related the affairs of a multinational oil company, but real-life executives had reservations about their treatment of management: 'as far as I can see, Mogul is run by Stead, Izard and Thornton single-handed. I've got 6,000 people working for me in this building alone.'⁵ Similarly, real police work demands the co-operation of dozens of personnel and long hours of routine administrative work. The integration of 'realistic' details from private life provided a way out of this difficulty. The close association between this selective realism and liberal humanism, and the underlying strategy of legitimising modern police techniques in the fight against crime is evident in this appraisal of *Softly, Softly* by the actor Stratford Johns (who played Superintendent Barlow): 'It is the most realistic of television police programmes. It is also, I think, the most human . . . Living of the backs of serving police officers, we strive never to cheapen their attitudes, betray their confidences or underrate the magnitude of the tasks they face on our behalf.'⁶

Police series began to re-emerge in the United States towards the end of the 1960s after the camp absurdity of spies had begun to seem like a flight from the searing political divisions provoked by the intervention in Vietnam and by racial inequality. What was worse, opposition to a political error and to previously segmented domains of injustice was being extended into a global contestation of the very foundations of the American economic system. The broader cultural consequences of this political and ideological crisis presented itself as a generation gap, and it was in this space that new ideological strategies urgently needed to establish themselves. For television executives, this was also economically important: some of the more radical elements of the new 'youth culture', whose influence was spreading among the college-educated, rejected commercial television programming wholesale as 'mass intoxication' of conservative values. A new type of hero was needed to breach the divide between young and old, between civil society and the 'Establishment'. This was to be a new breed of policeman, an individualist who worked within the system in his own, unorthodox manner, upholding the social order but fighting injustice from above as well as below and protecting the citizens from a psychopathic criminal class by virtue of his superior personality. The private detective of the Chandler type, a romantic individualist who is 'anti-establishment' because of his special sensibility and cynical knowingness (rather than any political conviction), was collapsed and remodelled into an offbeat representative of authority and the existing order. An early, somewhat conservative prototype was *Ironside*, which took pre-evasive action against accusations of violence by casting its middle-aged protagonist in a wheelchair, victim of a would-be assassin's bullet in the spine. Two idealist, young police officers, Ed Brown and Eve Whitfield, and a young black bodyguard, Mark Sanger, are his arms and legs, and his antennae for youth and racial questions. It is Ironside's human qualities, his superior knowledge of human nature and his tolerance that enable him to solve crimes in an individualist, professional way despite (or because of?) his physical infirmity. Even so, the series' resolutions of social conflict were sometimes strained when 'youth' questions were addressed. In one episode, Eve discovers that one of her girlfriends has a serious 'marijuana problem'. From the lofty pedestal on which the series places him, Ironside finds a compromise solution that enforces the law without being too repressive: condemned to one year's imprisonment, the 'criminal' acknowledges his wisdom and thanks him for the fairness of his judgement. This is unconvincing to say the least: the policeman as a neutral mediator of social problems was still envisaged in unacceptably paternalist terms for younger viewers, a weakness rectified in later series like *Starsky and Hutch*.

Similar comment could be made of *Mod Squad* wherein three idealistic ex-hippies, a representative group of male, female and black (with an Afro hairstyle), work undercover for the Los Angeles police, using their street credibility to solve cases (usually involving social injustice) beyond the reach of orthodox police methods. A ground-bass is sounded here by two underlying themes that were to prove crucial in 1970s police series: the police as social workers in a society in which crime is endemic; the need for 'street skills' in an alliance between the police and marginal social elements in the fight against injustice and big crime.

A neutral space

The longest-running police series of all time, *Hawaii Five-O* ran continuously from September 1968 to April 1980. In seeking to address the burning problems of racial integration and youth revolt, the series transposes the issues to the 'neutral' territory of Hawaii, a multi-racial state without black ghettoes and major racial violence. The island's natural beauty not only gave the series a stylish look but provided a backdrop against which crime seemed more obviously unnatural. As in *The Untouchables*, the police team is an ethnic mix: Steve McGarrett, a poker-faced inspector with quiff and sideboards, and his three assistants, the young Danny Williams, the Chinese Chen Ho Kelly and the Polyne-sian Kono.

The same formal structure as *The Untouchables* is adopted but this time without the moralising voice-over commentaries, whose efficacy had clearly waned. The police have no private lives; only very occasionally do private emotions intrude (an ex-girlfriend of McGarrett, a murdered fiancée of Williams) to show that they too are 'human' and personally threatened by crime. Theirs is a neutral, professional space from which they can intervene into the private lives of others. By virtue of being situated in an island paradise, detached from the political strife of the mainland, the series was able to continue the 1950s argument that crime was a moral, rather than a political, question: it is the weaknesses in an individual's make-up, evident in private life, that lead to crime. A space is carved out in the centre of society from which sympathetic authority figures can clean up the problems provoked by the discrepancy between personal ambition and social possibilities, from placing personal greed ahead of the law. In 'Beautiful Screamer' (1970), two young women are strangled, a verse of Byron written in lipstick on their bodies. The killer is Walter Gregson, who has financed a construction company with his wife's money: the two victims, selfless teachers at the Hawaii Junior Blind School, have been murdered in order to make the intended murder of his wife look like the work of a psychopath with a penchant for Byron. Gregson's wife wants a divorce: 'I know how hard you've worked, but at what price? Never any time to be with me, no question of starting a family, no time for anything that really counts.' On the point of strangling his wife, Gregson gives a rational explanation of his actions (and allows McGarrett to arrive in time): 'Going into business requires capital. I got hold of yours, your pretty little bundle of stocks and shares. So when you spoke of separation and divorce, that's when I saw the danger. Do you think I would let the law go through our accounts when there is a simpler solution? I've got to do it, Sally.' The descent into murder as the result of an uncontrolled desire for self-enrichment at any cost was a common trope in the 1970s police series.

Police work is minimal: in a pattern that was to be continued in later series, conveniently uncovered clues or timely volunteered information are processed behind the scenes by experts in chemistry, ballistics and literary quotations. Like the Chandleresque private eye, whose contact with others is an occasion for moral evaluations that are totally con-trolled by the narrator, McGarrett's presence serves as a scaled indicator of the moral worth of the characters. His vast knowledge of human nature enables him to pierce the armour of the culprit, to form suspicions on the basis of which the police machine can be set in motion. For all the lip service paid to modern scientific methods, it is psychological intuition ('I'm not entirely convinced by his story') that forms the basis of police work. This formal device, made necessary by the serial production of narratives, is facilitated by the fact that viewers are already aware, from the opening sequence, who the criminal is: McGarrett is aligned with the objective, God's-eye-view narration, reinforcing the police as a disinterested locus of social truth, able to judge the foibles of others. This frees the police series to concentrate on the area where ideologically it must work the hardest: the reconciliation of the social fact of endemic crime with individual motive.

Ambition is a catch-all motive, but given that this is expressly encouraged by the American Way of Life, the police series must establish the boundary line past which it becomes unacceptable greed or, alternatively, unrealistic and vain. In 'No Blue Skies' (1968), a nightclub singer, Joey Rand, has become a cat burglar to finance his addiction to poker. He dreams of success: 'two, three, four thousand dollars a week. It's a dream that's going to come true. It happens to people who can't even play the guitar. So why not me?' This is suspect ambition, contaminated by the sins of jealousy and vanity: for McGarrett, Joey's fate is never in doubt ('Guys like Joey, I've seen dozens of them'). In a pointless shoot-out with the police in an underground car park, Joey is mortally wounded. In his dying breath, he achieves a belated lucidity for the benefit of viewers: 'I chose the right place to die, in a hotel basement . . . I was always wide of the mark.' By refusing to accept his place in the local nightclub, by aiming 'wide' at Las Vegas when even the stakes in Honolulu are beyond his means, Joey tragically ends up dying in the 'right place', an apt translation of his social relegation into a criminal class which exists in the 'basement' of society. The metaphor establishes the criminal class, made up of morally weak individuals, as endemic to society in the same way that a basement is a necessary part of a building construction. To continue the metaphor, the majority must be content with their position on the ground floor, without seeking short-cuts to success from below.

This temptation, McGarrett knows only too well, is an unavoidable consequence of the free enterprise system. In 'No Bottles, No Cards, No People' (1971), he is instructed by the Governor to stop the activities of local gangster, Johnny Oporta, who is preparing the way for a Los Angeles-based syndicate responsible for a 'crime wave' on the mainland. The Governor is worried about the uncontrollable consequences of property development and the tourist boom. The syndicate is interested in this tourist money and aims to establish prostitution, gambling and drugs rackets on the island. Like other successful gangsters, Johnny has a respectable business cover for his activities. Paying a visit to the luxurious, high-rise offices of 'Johnny Oporta and Associates: Public Relations', McGarrett sarcastically remarks: 'Nice office, and it's only the beginning, eh, Johnny? If you work hard, you get rich'. The rhetoric of American capitalism is laid bare, realism demanding that legal and illegal business be treated as inextricably connected. The police series is on shaky ground here, and is forced to portray top gangsters taking time off from their business activities to become personally involved in violent crime. The populist association of big business and crime, appealing to the vast American middle classes, was not to the liking of conservatives, who began to complain in the 1980s that television was disproportionately populated by corrupt and murderous businessmen. This argument is best put into perspective by Todd Gitlin: 'If television is unkind to businessmen, it is scarcely unkind to the values of a business civilisation. Capitalism and the consumer society come out largely unscathed.'[7] Unsurprisingly, individual businessmen of deficient personal morality were often used as scapegoats for the reverse side of American capitalism. More importantly, the strategy of social neutrality adopted by the police series in the 1970s precluded it from upholding business interests to the detriment of others.

Having established the political neutrality of the police, *Hawaii Five-O* is able to confront political confrontation directly. In 'Not That Much Different' (1969), McGarrett has the difficult task of investigating the murder of Julian Scott, one of the editors of 'Peace Magazine', during an anti-war demonstration. The victim's fellow peace activists do not take kindly to McGarrett's presence ('We've nothing against you personally, but rather against what you represent'). McGarrett expounds his philosophy, one that sees no major contradiction between enforcing the law and sympathising with youthful idealism:

John F. Kennedy, Robert Kennedy, Martin Luther King and before that Mahatma Gandhi. That reminds you of a basic truth about this world – there are a lot of violent people out there. People like you especially need to be protected against fanatics . . . I hate violence. I believe violence breeds violence. I want peace. I believe that all wars begin with an act of individual violence. I'm working for peace too.

Insistently speaking in his own name and favourably inclined towards 'Peace Magazine', McGarrett resolves the contradiction between individual idealism and service to the state: the police are a public service against a state of endemic violence, a carefully dosed combination of liberalism and authority. At a time of sharp political division, a wedge is driven between the moral and the political: unlike in the 1950s, political difference is admitted to return for observing the moral imperative of the law. An alliance is proposed between those of opposing political viewpoints against a hardened criminal class (against which not even the uncorrupted paradise of Hawaii is immune), an alliance minimally founded on respect for the law and the renunciation of violence. A second wedge is driven between liberal protesters who accept the system and more radical ones who resort to violence.

It is precisely around the question of violence that McGarrett uncovers heated policy divergences among the workers for 'Peace Magazine', divergences that ultimately derive from personality differences. The varying ways in which the anti-war activists react to McGarrett's (neutral) presence betray them to viewers as morally acceptable or unacceptable people. Far from being a policeman, as the protesters claim, Julian Scott's murderer turns out to be Manning, one of their own number whose support for violence hides an incipient fascism and a psychotic jealousy of the widely respected Scott ('And then I saw Julian, in full glory, everything I'd always wanted to be. With Annie beside him . . .') It is the way Manning sets up a kangaroo court, an alternative to the law itself, to try a protester he has falsely accused of the murder, that convinces one of the protesters to alert McGarrett, whose thesis is thus confirmed: the political motive for violence is a cover for personal moral deficiencies which are the real cause of all social violence. Political questions have been directly addressed, only to be conjured away. Within the respect for the law, liberal opponents can be integrated into the American system. This truth, impressed on McGarrett, the activists, and viewers alike, means that McGarrett's foray into the anti-war milieu has been a positive dialogue for all concerned. From his contact with obviously decent protesters, McGarrett can declare, with all the force of his moral authority, that 'this generation are not all bad'.

The foundation of the law on personal morality rather than on political authority is even clearer in 'To Kill or be Killed' (1970), in which the divisions caused by the Vietnam War are openly recognised. Jack Rigney, the son of General Earl Rigney, has fallen to his death from a hotel room (murder? suicide?), after returning from a two-year tour of duty in Vietnam. His brother, Mike, an anti-war protester, has disappeared and is therefore a suspect. In fact, Mike Rigney has absconded because, opposed to the draft, he is faced with the choice between escaping to Canada or going to prison for his convictions.

The Pentagon applies pressure on McGarrett to discontinue the case, arousing his and our suspicions that something is rotten within the federal bureaucracy. McGarrett vigorously affirms his independence: 'I have never taken orders from anyone. I work for the State of Hawaii, not the Army'. General Rigney learns that the phone in his son's room was tapped by the army which informs him that 'there are things in this affair that must never be revealed'. In the episode's parallel plot, Mike Rigney is disillusioned with the escape route to Canada proposed by a group of anti-war radicals, caricaturally portrayed as lank-haired, bearded, marijuana-smoking hippies with a fondness for money. In effect, their escape route is a highly profitable business.

Finally, the truth comes out. Despite pressure from the Pentagon, McGarrett finds a missing tape, Jack Rigney's suicide message, which relates his participation in a My-Lai type massacre of women and children during a 'pacification operation'. Displaying the upright qualities of his military father, Mike Rigney decides to go to prison for his anti-war beliefs. Even General Rigney is now convinced that the war is a mistake.

The episode's anti-war sentiment appears audacious but more accurately reflects the strategy of the police series at an ideologically difficult moment. The neutral upholding of the law is separated from the questionable policies of the military and political authorities, drawing on the traditional populist distrust of federal government. A distinction is made between worthy and unworthy protesters, those who, like Mike Rigney, 'love their country' and are prepared to accept the consequences of the law, and others, whose marijuana smoking betrays an 'un-American' lack of moral hygiene. The crucial issue, in fact, is what it means to be an American at a time of national division. The respectfully portrayed 'Hawaii Draft Resistance Committee' makes strong demands on the patriotism of would-be draft resistors: as an anti-war counsellor tells Mike, pacifism is a noble idea, but if it were followed in every case, 'we'd still be a British colony'. To which Mike Rigney replies: 'I love my country as much as anyone else but this war has nothing to do with patriotism.'

Once its political work had been done, *Hawaii Five-O* settled back into a routine police series in which standard stories of the genre, personal greed leading to crime leading to punishment, were played out in local colours in the same way that its replacement, *Magnum*, was able to use a Hawaiian location and the infrastructure set up for its predecessor to reanimate the private detective format. *Hawaii Five-O* was an important series for several reasons. A new breed of cop was forged in the character of McGarrett: upholding the law, but broad-minded, tolerant and entirely at ease in a multi-racial climate, professionally doing a job but sparing the viewer a sermonising commentary. Second, the location becomes an important part of the assemblage, allowing standardised stories of police procedure to be 'coloured' by the particularity of a city (New York, Los Angeles, Houston, Miami) and the personal relationship between an out-of-towner cop and his local team-mate, united in their cultural and personality differences.

Street credibility

A metropolis somewhere in California, mid-1970s. The dust from the 1960s has settled and left behind an irreducible population of kooks, fruitcakes and psychopaths. New police methods are required, combining street skills, tolerance and courage. *Starsky and Hutch*, one of a number of highly successful series produced by Aaron Spelling and Leonard Goldberg (*Mod Squad, Charlie's Angels, Dynasty*), ran for ninety-four episodes from 1975 to 1979: at the height of the series' popularity in 1976, both leading actors received 20,000 fan letters a month.[8] Its meaning reduced to its constituent elements, *Starsky and Hutch* is totally programmed, establishing the norm for the carefully calculated products that have dominated television in the years since.

Dave Starsky is of New York Jewish street-kid origins, a macho braggart, a back-slapping jock whose life revolves around girls, bars, baseball and driving his Ford Torino. His best buddy, both on the job and off, is Ken 'Hutch' Hutchinson, a quiet, serious, college-educated romantic for whom nirvana is strumming a guitar in the cool night air of his native California. Although they are often at odds, theirs is a strong friendship based on mutual respect for the other's way of being. The two halves of America are reconciled in a new pact against crime and social disorder, requiring greater tolerance of different lifestyles. Reflecting the influence of 1960s liberalism, this tolerance extends to marginals and small-fry delinquents who are seen as useful allies in the fight against an increasingly freakish criminal class, fallout from what was portrayed as the previous decade's excesses. The air has cleared into an ambivalent fatalism in which neither the liberal nor the conservative approach to crime can be confidently upheld: the notion that crime is endemic to modern society is even more pronounced than in *Hawaii Five-O*. This

mutual cancelling-out, calculated to appeal to viewers from both positions, gives the series a curious 'blankness' that was to be even more
accentuated in the later, derivative *Miami Vice*.

Social problems spring into existence by coming to Starsky and
Hutch's attention, not so much as issues to be addressed as a backdrop
against which the duo can be favourably *positioned*. The total lack of any
strategy for dealing with the problems evoked sometimes causes unease.
In an episode involving a battered child, Starsky and Hutch also come
into contact with a young black policewoman who has to deal with such
cases on a daily basis: dedicated beyond endurance, she is close to tears at
the hopelessness of her task. A heap of files are stacked on her desk, the
vast majority of which will remain dead letters for want of sufficient
resources (the time of the ten people working under her is taken up
exclusively with more serious child murder cases). The policewoman
tells Starsky and Hutch that their sympathy is all very well, but when they
(and the viewer) move on to their next (exciting) case, she will still be
saddled with problems beyond her means. To this, Starsky can only reply
that things are bound to get better in the future, a weak, unconvincing
appeal to the traditional American optimism that the episode has done
so much to undermine.

The impression given of two male models, reproducing the dark-
haired/blond haired, extrovert/introvert pairing of *The Man from UNCLE*, is
revealing in that it definitively places the series closer to the advertising
spot than to traditional drama. The same formal device is used as in
advertising: positioning a product by juxtaposing it with a carefully
calculated chain of signifiers. In accordance with the dominant function
of commercial television, assuring an audience for advertisers, each
episode is thought of in terms of a fixed number of 'technical events',
visual or sound effects that break the 'natural rhythm' and segment each
story to allow for advertising breaks. This means that stories have to be
correspondingly simplified. The most notable difference compared to
the earlier drama-based series is that the resolution of fundamental
contradictions is built into the series' design rather than addressed as
such in the stories. Social tensions are overcome by the mere positioning
of the two protagonists in relation to others.

Thus the generation gap and the race question is 'resolved' in the pair's
relationship with Captain Dobey who, despite constant grumbling at
their unorthodox, sometimes illegal methods, is deeply proud of his two
subordinates. For all their pranks, insolence and upbeat lifestyles, Starsky
and Hutch are the best cops he has: allowing them to drive a sports car,

and wear denim and leather on the job, is a small price to pay. The race question is further 'resolved' in their relationship with Huggy Bear, owner of the bar where the duo hang out after hours, and something of a rogue, a huckster: his dubious business ventures almost certainly extend to minor crime. But this is well worth overlooking, for Huggy is a mine of 'hot tips' which usually lead Starsky and Hutch directly to the culprit: even more importantly, Huggy's presence confirms their street credibility. A further designed effect, almost certainly lost on most foreign viewers, is the reconciliation of Eastern ethnic and California cool, an East-side/West-wide appeal to all America. Each story is totally programmed from this assemblage.

In the episode 'The Vampire', (1976) there are no more than twenty set pieces in a limited number of different locations. The viewer knows from the opening scenes who the mysterious 'vampire' is: given that he is the dancing instructor of the three victims, it is only a matter of time before Starsky and Hutch effect a closure. A matter of time . . .; the series has forty-five minutes to kill. Most of the 'time-wasting' set pieces serve no other purpose than to underline the pair's street credibility or tolerance of the strange habits of others. The vampire theme is an occasion for humorous banter playing on Starsky's superstitiousness (wearing garlic around his neck) and Huggy's sly opportunism (attempting to sell a stake and hammer to Starsky): it also sets up an encounter with a greedy, eccentric occultist, otherwise unconnected with the plot.

The 'vampire', René Nadasy, has the unfortunate habit of dressing up in vampire costume and biting the jugular veins of attractive female students from his classical dancing school. The goal of this operation is to collect sacrificial blood so that he can be reunited with his dead wife through the satanic ceremonies organised by Slade, another unfortunate by-product of the 1960s. Manifestly into drugs as well, Slade owns a sleazy nightclub where one of the victims worked as a dancer: rifling through his appartment, Starsky and Hutch come across jars of blood and compromising photos of his ceremonies. 'Some of these people are well known', exclaims Hutch, confirming Nadasy's opinion that 'this city is rotten to the core'. Slade justifies his activity in frankly capitalist terms: 'One has to earn a living. At the bank, they smile when I arrive. I get the red carpet treatment.' The series' ideological blankness makes it easy prey for this type of cynicism. Starsky and Hutch are the only honest white knights left and the Devil calls the tunes.

An air of decadence hangs over the series, positioning Starsky and Hutch's humanist values but also testing them. There is a curious turn-of-the-century feel to the new modernism as if, like the late Victorians, it were aware of its own decline. The uncontrolled breakdown of traditional social discipline has unleashed strange forms of archaism into the City: derivatives (and carbon copies) of the Charles Manson type fanatic abound. After the defeat in Vietnam and the oil shock, key events prefiguring America's relative decline as a world power, nothing is certain any more. Arguing for the possible existence of vampires, Starsky observes: 'We're in the twentieth century. Anything is possible nowadays. We can take pictures on the surface of Mars. Girls form football teams . . .' Far from the technological optimism of the 1960s, Starsky's remark betrays a blustering unease with the social consequences of his own 'tolerance'. The existence of vampires is placed on the same discursive level as the space race and feminism.

In the war of all against all, a brutal cynicism is the name of the game. In one episode, Starsky and Hutch are summoned to the home of the loathsome Amboy, a grossly overweight cocaine king. Over caviar and champagne, the latter proposes a deal:

Amboy: You're individualists and you deserve a break. At least, that's what this country offers.

Starsky: Are you trying to bribe us?

Amboy (indicating his luxurious possessions): All this is a perfect example of the success this country brings . . . I'm just a businessman who sells goods.

Hutch: We don't want your future. It stinks.

Amboy: I'm the one who's got the girls, the wealth and the possessions. If you've got money, you make the law.

The series is in trouble here. Starsky and Hutch's treatment of an unresolvable crime problem on an individual criminal basis is by-passed by the general nature of Amboy's declaration, which baldly calls into question the very essence of the American system. Nothing, either in the episode in question or in the series as a whole, contradicts or inflects the truth of what Amboy says. Positively positioned against this backdrop, Starsky and Hutch have no interest in addressing the crime and corruption of an unregulated free enterprise system as political or even moral issues: betraying the absence of any strategy in relation to urban disorder, the series is content to allow criminals to make truth statements about society. Starsky and Hutch compensates for this curious passivity by directing purely reactive violence against criminals of somewhat psychopathic disposition. Threadbare scenarios are given an almost purient interest by dwelling on the more sordid, 'irrational' features of big-city life. In this respect, the prankish set pieces and the good-natured wind-down in

Huggy's after another vicious kook has been dispatched play an important role in clearing the air, a (feeble) conjuring away of the ambiguities involved in portraying a negative, pessimistic image of America. For ambiguities there are. After virulent criticism of the series' violence, the third and fourth seasons concentrated on field excursions into diverse social latitudes (casinos, cowboys, cruises, pin-up girls, etc.) and soap opera-derived romantic interludes. Criticisms of excessive violence are usually a displacement of a profound ideological unease which cannot be named.

The difficulty in generating narratives from a minimalist assemblage without confronting the social dimension of crime forces Starsky and Hutch's activity into a form of private theatre in which crime is above all a purely personal threat to them or their friends. Often cases are taken up because of a threat to one of the pair's numerous acquaintances from all walks of life: countless others involve frustrated convicts with a personal grudge against the pair. Detective work, where it exists, is at the elementary level of general knowledge: in one episode, Starsky exposes a police colleague as a liar and therefore a criminal by knowing that the fishing season has not opened yet. For all its swagger and squealing of tyres, the series is more at ease in an amateur detective format, preferably with the duo in disguise, showing off the range of their social skills.

An episode involving anonymous threats to Hutch's friend, the country and western singer Sue-Ellen Granger, sets up a occasion for Hutch to demonstrate his singing talent and Starsky to show off his ignorance of a Southern and Western musical form. The brief appearance of the hoarse-voiced villain in a recording studio enables him to be identified as an ex-singer and radio disc-jockey who was stabbed in the throat years before. As he explained it, he loved Sue-Ellen's first record so much that he played it over and over on the bar jukebox until a fed-up fellow drinker stabbed him, putting an end to his singing and his radio career. All because of Sue-Ellen . . . The illegitimate elevation of personal misfortune into social grievance is reminiscent of a Victorian explanation of crime: the plot is an updated version of 'The Phantom of the Opera', and the threat from embittered thespians and other 'losers' was a common trope in the series. Refusing to recognise the social causes of misfortune, the series often constructs stories of failure based on personal weakness: as in most American action series since, criminals are generally portrayed as mad dogs that have to be put down, so avoiding the 'sociological' problems posed by a criminal underclass.

Starsky and Hutch was a very influential series. The formula of the inseparable pair of police officers, united in their differences (of personality, gender, region or ethnic origin), positioning themselves against a background of endemic urban crime, has become a standard aspect of the genre. It is not difficult to see *Hunter, Texas Police* or *Miami Vice* as modern derivatives of this formula.

Reified dirt

In the ghettos of 'South Manhattan', Theodore Kojak and his ethnic team (Greek, Italian, Jewish, WASP) fight a holding operation against a criminal class of sadists, muggers, gangsters and perverts who impose their own law.[9] Unlike *Starsky and Hutch, Kojak* (1973–78) is closer to realist drama, with quite different themes and stories adapted to the basic format. The fundamental element linking these various themes is the character of Kojak, a cynical, hard-as-nails Greek American who knows the street like the back of his hand. More 'realistic' than Starsky and Hutch, Kojak uses crime to fight crime, unorthodox methods which have cost him promotion: in effect, his success depends a great deal on the information supplied by an army of seedy, small-time criminals. In a situation of rampant corruption and social breakdown, there seems to be little point in observing the niceties of the law: the police are fighting an impossible war and know it. It is against this backdrop that Kojak is positioned as an incorruptible, 'human' cop, courageously carrying out a hopeless task and earning the respect of the criminal class if of no one else. At best, like a missionary in a hostile culture, he can save a few individual souls. A melancholy pessimism pervades the series, that of a society facing the end of a dream.

In 'The Godson' (1977), Kojak intervenes to save the soul of his black godson, also named Theo in honour of the rookie cop who found a lodging for a pregnant black woman some eighteen years ago. No longer under Kojak's influence, Theo has become a racketeer: revolted at the misery in the ghetto and contemptuous of blacks who accept to work for a pittance (including his mother), he is tempted by an offer to join the gang of Eddie Gordon, a white who reigns over the ghetto in an ostentatious display of wealth. Torn between Gordon and the renewed influence of Kojak, Theo eventually succumbs to the former's offer, only to discover he is a racist. But it is too late: during a diamonds job that goes wrong, Theo is killed in the crossfire between the police and the gang. As in the police novels of Ed McBain, the objective, reified description of urban alienation is sufficient in itself to explain the existence of crime. Far from being a rudimentary form of social consciousness, the harsh portrayal of social decay becomes a way of evacuating the responsibility of a harsh economic system. In an extraordinary passage, Theo's mother tells Kojak: 'Look at the street. Look how dirty it is. You want the real culprit? Look at those (overturned) garbage cans, there are more crimes in this street than there are garbage cans . . . I know what you tried to do for Theo. But this time, the street has won.'

In an unconvincing closure, Kojak promises to supervise Theo's younger brother who seems destined for better things ('I want to be a fireman') because by nature he is better disposed to Kojak than was his brother. Although Theo's tragic destiny can at least partly be explained by flaws in his nature, Kojak also accepts his share of the blame for having been too busy to visit Theo for the last ten years. This is an uncomfortable combination of sociology and human nature which, as Kojak knows, is not a solution to the existence of a permanent underclass. But the redemption of individuals allows Kojak to position himself against an uncaring system as well as redeeming his own efforts in the impossible war against crime. In one episode, Kojak admits to a young woman whom he has saved from heroin addiction that 'the war can never be won; we can only slow down their operations'. His only reward is 'to save a pretty girl like you, there's no better way of getting back on the rails'. This is a revealing remark. It suggests that Kojak's fight against crime fulfils some private need, even if its social consequences are negligible. The limitations of a humanist approach to crime, operative only within a private theatre in which the social dimension has been evacuated, stand exposed.

The major internal tension of the series is centred around the contra-dictions of humanism itself. A liberal humanism, which extends 'human qualities' to the criminal underclass, tends to spill over into a sociological explanation of crime, one that quickly makes the original humanist premises redundant. Any political translation of this philosophy, involv-ing at least some redistribution of wealth, is way out of line in American public discourse. The other, less appealing strand of humanism reduces social phenomena to the possession of certain human qualities or the lack of them: certain individuals are denied full human status, defined in such a way as to exclude them. Politically influential in calls for a more severe, punitive approach to crime, the latter option has found a ready home in the more simple-minded American police series: all manner of social problems can be conjured away by reducing crime to a private sport between humanised cops and dehumanised psychopaths.

Kojak hesitates between these two options. The latter is readily present in many episodes but in itself tends to undermine the series' pretentions to realist drama, present in the sociological and historical references (a common trope is the dangerously ill-adapted Vietnam veteran). There are several ways out of this dilemma. One is by presenting the police (but crucially not Kojak and his team) in highly ambiguous terms, suggesting that the fight against crime is not a black and white problem (in both senses): in a variant of this position, it is the political class which is corrupt, incompetent and self-seeking. The other is the device of redemption, to use Kojak's immense human qualities to bring souls from the underclass round to his way of thinking, over and above the realistic, 'sociological' backdrop. In one episode, Daniels, a black Vietnam veteran and failed boxer, decent but gullible and none too bright, is shot after a failed hold-up and a pathetic hostage-taking in a church. Before dying, he tells Kojak: 'Go and see my son, make him see I deserved this end.' Kojak is thus in a position to inform the son that 'your father was a total dead loss'. This is both harshly realistic and extremely moralistic. The point is that by the mid-1970s, only someone like Kojak could get away with saying this. The series spends much of its energy conceding the existence of widespread corruption and urban poverty just to allow Kojak to pass this sort of judgement on others.

This meant distancing itself from the bureaucratic, politically tarnished level of law enforcement and several episodes feature Kojak insolently obstructing, or disobeying, the FBI. In 'A Need to Know' (1976), Kojak is ordered by the FBI to release Karl Detro, a child molester who works as a driver for an unnamed Eastern bloc embassy. Kojak is furious to discover that Detro is not even expelled from the country: the FBI is protecting him because he has military secrets for sale. For Kojak, abstract questions of state security are trifling compared to the danger posed to children by Detro's liberation. Needless to say, Kojak's fears are proved to be grounded: the series aligns the interests of the local police with the needs of ordinary citizens, in common alliance against the political bungling of the federal state. Bitterly, Kojak tells the FBI chief: ('Behind your desk) you got that big government badge with a nice-looking eagle. You wanna know what I got behind me? A dirty window sill full of pigeons. . . .' In a society reified as dirt (an impression visually reinforced by the use of grey and blueish hues), the modern, 'clean' offices of the FBI suggest an absence of reality, a corruption that lies just under the surface. In 'Kojak's Days' (1977) the telephone-tapping of the controller of a numbers racket reveals his clients to be a police commissioner and several politicians.

The grime and dust of Kojak's office, the undrinkable coffee and the chronic lack of police resources all establish his right to judge social dirt (whether from above or below his own position) in human, rather than sociological terms.

The city is a concrete jungle that makes heavy demands on its residents: the original, Social–Darwinist metaphor is further metaphorised in a way that places responsibility on urban existence itself rather than a competitive economic system. In 'Life, Liberation and the Pursuit of Death' (1975) Kojak intervenes to save the life of Lorelai Mason, a young advertising executive, caricaturally portrayed as a hyper-anxious, pill-popping workaholic obsessed with professional promotion. In her own words, the advertising profession is 'a real rat race; the only way to succeed is to trample over everyone else': her ambition has led her to divorce her husband 'because he wanted children but I wanted a career'. As fate would have it, during one of her frequent insomniac nights, she witnesses two youths dumping a body into the harbour. Two brilliant students from wealthy backgrounds have murdered their psychology professor for having excluded them from his course. Perverting the logic of operant conditioning experiments, the two students had been electrocuting rats for having made the right choices, with a view to making them insane. Discovering Mason's identity, the two decide to continue their experiment on a 'perfect' human subject: by interfering with the mundane details of her everyday life (changing her clocks, replacing her tranquillisers with placebos, tampering with her refrigerator and television), they reduce the unsuspecting Mason to the point of nervous collapse. Crime is explicitly associated with the alienation produced by personal ambition (and its sub-set, feminism): 'rats' like the two students – the metaphorical connection is spelt out by Kojak – thrive in the 'rat race' which dehumanises the city's inhabitants. In the face of impossible odds, Kojak's romantic postioning resolves the fear of a dehumanised police in a dehumanised society through the use of tough but humane methods to hold the rats at bay.

The hesitation between humanist and sociological explanations of crime, between realism and Kojak's moral judgements, leads to continual tension. The social dimension of crime is intrusive but constantly short-circuited: most episodes begin with a long-shot of the New York skyline before zooming in on a random crime selected for the viewer because it will come to Kojak's attention. The objective and the subjective are united in a closed circle: somewhere in New York City, a crime is committed, somewhere else is Kojak, the criminal's Nemesis, solving crimes by becoming interested in them. Despite pretentions to showing modern police work in all its grimy reality, many of the episodes fall back into the 'murder mystery' mode in which crimes are solved through simple deduction, intuition and attention to fortuitous detail (verbal slips, lies, etc.).

The ambiguous nature of the police and the situating of crime in terms of private life are combined in 'Monkey on a String' (1977), in which Vince, a young Jewish member of Kojak's team, succumbs to corruption through his addiction to gambling and an uncontrollable desire to offer his wife a fur coat, expensive perfume and other material goods. Interestingly, it is in a poker match with Kojak and his team-mates that Vince's gambling habits are revealed. In a long, pitiful soliloquy delivered to his wife, Vince justifies his weakness:

Vince: I lost $230. The dishwasher has broken down, I'm two months late on the car repayments and I've told Kojak not to cash the check until I get paid so I don't go into overdraft. I thought I'd won. I don't know what it is, I'm not a gambler. But the Friday night poker session with my friends, that's just part of life . . . Everything's mounting up, the expenses for dad's funeral, your boutique which is not making any money, if it's not one thing, it's the other. Never any luck! It's as if God has shown you to me and said that's all a man needs to be happy for his entire life; don't come asking me for anything else . . . I wanted to offer you the whole world! . . . You should have seen my father before he had his heart attack. Six foot eight and built like a battleship, but kind, six mouths to feed on a train driver's wages and he never complained. Every Saturday, he came home and Mom was waiting for him with envelopes laid out on the table. One was for the electricity, one for the gas, one for Dr Horowitz – there must have been a dozen of them and Dad would kiss Mom on the cheek and hand over his wages. She had an old coat, worn to threads, almost in pieces. It took him a while but Dad finally convinced her to buy a new one. She chose it at Klein's. I remember it had a fur trimming on the collar, in any case, it looked like fur. She started to save for it little by little each week. Of course, that's not what Dad wanted, he would have preferred her to forget about the bills for once and buy it in one go. He knew he'd never get her to change her mind and that the way things were going, the children would be all married by the time she'd saved enough. So Dad decided to lend a hand. Without her knowledge, he took $5 out of the cake tin and laid it on a two-year-old called Aquaduct. You should've seen the smile on his face when he came back from Klein's with the new coat. But Mom never wore it. Until the day she died, she left it in its box on top of the cupboard in the bedroom. She wanted to punish him, you see. It didn't matter that he'd won: people like us didn't have the right to try our luck, we had to be content with what destiny had given us. That was twelve years before Dad had his attack, but that was the day he died, the day she refused to wear the coat.
Laetitia: I'd have worn it.

That gambling is not an absolute wrong in itself is shown by Kojak's participation in the poker session, and the sympathetic portrayal of Vince and Laetitia, but a more relaxed personal morality requires, as in the case of the street-wise Kojak, an irresolute sense of where the line between right and wrong is drawn. A less than convincing explanation for Vince's gambling problems, the pathetic story of his father nevertheless illustrates the inappropriateness of rigid moral guidelines for an advanced consumer society, without being able to suggest a more appropriate code which can come to terms with the legitimate desire for material goods. In an attempt to cater for both liberal and conservative approaches to law and order, crime is seen to stem from a moral weakness but this weakness is, in turn, explained by the excessive moral strictness – albeit for admirable principles – of Vince's mother, behaviour more suited to an earlier, pre-consumption epoch. Crucially, it also gives a sociological colouring in the relative poverty and material difficulty of Vince and his father, forced to live respectively on a policeman's and train driver's wages. The series' realist options generally forbid the grounding of crime in psychopathic individuals as in *Starsky and Hutch*: rather, each criminal act has its 'human' circumstances which put to the test Kojak's special knowledge of human nature. Characteristic of the increasingly self-doubting American liberalism of the 1970s, the sociological presence of inequality is evoked but not insisted on: the contradiction between conservative and liberal explanations of crime, arising from the need to surround ('humanise') a single criminal act in terms both of social disadvantage and moral lapse, can only be resolved in fatalism, the inability to escape from destiny. Vince and his wife Laetitia are positioned as decent people at heart, but the consequences of a moment of weakness (Vince helping himself to the remaining contents of the safe after a robbery he is investigating) can only be closed by his redemptive death in the line of duty, to save the life of his partner.

The inability to portray police work consistently in terms of a wider social context – which would be fascinating but also deeply disturbing – led the realist police series increasingly on to the terrain of private life. In later series influenced by *Kojak* (*Cagney and Lacey*, *Hill Street Blues*), the effect of realism is obtained by foregrounding private life over police method. In keeping with their integration of formal elements from the soap opera, these series tended towards a serialised form with continuing private dramas juxtaposed against episodic public ones: crime is just one factor among others (relations with colleagues, spouses, etc.) used to highlight differences of character among the protagonists. Strategies for dealing with crime are dissipated among the widely varying personalities of the precinct whose different approaches cancel each other out and nourish interpersonal rivalries. In *Cagney and Lacey*, the treatment of crime in terms of 'women's problems' positions the two policewomen as caring human beings whose qualities – and weaknesses – are confirmed in their (highly sentimental) private lives. The use of both social and personal dramas as plot mechanisms resolves a personal approach to crime in a 'humanist realism' in which police behaviour is also shown to be influenced by private life. In a reversal of the neutral space opened up by *Hawaii-Five-O*, the police can now intervene in public matters because they have private lives: by sharing the personal weaknesses of others, they are in a position to empathise with social problems, even if they can do nothing about them. The social and economic crisis so relevant to the difficulties of policing has been displaced on to the terrain of the personal crisis: crime is something that everyone must live with, just as every individual life is punctuated by personal problems that, never fully resolved, can nevertheless be 'lived with'.

A fallen world

Most of the attention attracted by *Miami Vice* has focused on its style, and there is no denying that its 'tropical' lighting, locations, set design, figure-framing and camera technique all display an overt formal force that seems extravagant in comparison to the traditional television series. Rock music sequences, which interrupt the narrative continuity, establish the series' aesthetic affinity with the music videos shown on the all-clip channel MTV and the idea of MTV cops' is reputed to have been behind the idea of the series. *Miami Vice* was the first series to make use of neurophysiological research on the viewing process: research carried out in the Communication Technology Laboratory of the University of Michigan has shown that (American) viewers tend to become impatient with overly elaborate stories or characterisations. In an attempt to maintain constant visual and sound excitement, the series uses aesthetic devices from the clip (aggressive camera movements, 'unnatural' colour schemes and mood music) to fill out the story rather than resorting to 'irrelevant' complications of plot and dialogue, both reduced to a minimum. Executive producer Michael Mann's motto was said to be 'no earth tones': sienna, ochre, red and brown were eliminated in favour of rose, lime, lemon, aquamarine, turquoise and peach, the sensuous feel of pastel and flourescent colours.

In its self-conscious use of style, Miami Vice is seen as the archetypal 'postmodern' series and it is usually in terms of whether this is seen as a positive or a negative phenomenon that the series, and the MTV aesthetic to which it is related, is evaluated. Todd Gitlin's argument that postmodernism is the 'blank expression and flat appearance come together in a common chord which resounds through contemporary culture like a great dead sound'[10] can be easily dismissed by enthusiasts for the 'postmodern condition' as a form of nostalgia for a time when reality triumphed over artifice. For John Fiske, on the other hand,

MTV is orgasm . . . No ideology, no social control can organise an orgasm. Only freedom can. All orgasms are democratic: all ideology is autocratic. This is the politics of pleasure. The signifiers work through the senses on the body to produce pleasure and freedom: the signifieds produce in the mind for ideology and control.[11]

For Fiske, and other commentators like E. Ann Kaplan, the MTV aesthetic is a potentially disruptive form which, through its anarchic, fragmented use of signs, is 'critical of bourgeois hegemony', thus '(rejecting) the social machine and its power to regulate our lives'.[12] In other words, postmodern style, which Fiske sees incarnated in the MTV aesthetic and in series like Miami Vice, is not only given a residual anti-bourgeois status but elevated to a space beyond ideology, that of pure pleasure.

This discussion of postmodernism in essentialist terms, relayed to simplistic – and seemingly arbitrary – political judgements only obscures the issue. Postmodernism has become a terrain on which the old battles of cultural optimism and cultural pessimism can be fought out once again, where the reactive judgements of an older form of culturalism can be revamped in modern guise. Nowhere is this more evident than in the pretence that postmodern style is somehow beyond ideology: in the 1960s, the conservative sociologist Daniel Bell presented the modern consumer society as an objectified, pragmatic world in which the grounds for major ideological (and political) conflict had disappeared. What Fiske presents as postmodernism's 'liberation from the social' can also be seen as a recasting of the 'end of ideology' thesis, a working out of the strategies from an earlier stage of the consumer society, those of 1960s pop which sought the same death of affect, the same use of style to flatten out the portrayal of social life.

Attempts to discuss a series like Miami Vice in terms of an idealist 'condition' like postmodernism are not so much wrong as unhelpful. Once the series has been categorised within the positive or negative features that make up the master discourse, nothing more can be said: as with all forms of culturalism, discussion is reduced to academic posturing. For all its stylistic force, Miami Vice is no more or no less 'ideological' than any other series; for all its stylishness, it is no more or no less 'styled' than any other series. What needs to be analysed is the way form and content come together in the particular ideological strategy of Miami Vice.

The two major pillars of Reaganian free market ideology have been condensed into its assemblage: law and order, and conspicuous consumption. This is not to say that the series is in any way reducible to Reaganism: as with other series, the manifest political colouring varies from episode to episode and some (but not very many) could conceivably be construed as (vague) criticisms of Reaganian foreign policy, racism or private medicine. But both elements mentioned above are present. The series seeks a terrain on which they can coexist without coming into contradiction, in order to circumvent the claims by political critics of economic liberalism that it is precisely the perverse social effects of the latter which exacerbate an already serious crime problem in late capitalist societies. In the series' generally Reaganian options, endemic crime and economic crisis are the fault of moral weakness (Vice); on the other hand, there is nothing (morally) wrong with conspicuous consumption and the pursuit of private wealth. Crime and poverty are explained in harshly moral, rather than 'sociological', terms while at the same time the state increasingly disinvests itself of responsibility as already meagre public resources are transferred into private hands through radical tax reductions. The resolution of this contradiction is an impossible task which the series does not even attempt: rather, an overwhelming attention to style and the look of things (desperately) tries to avoid confronting the consequences of its assemblage. Yet for all this difficulty, the association of stylistic modernism and political conservatism, in contradistinction to their relation in the 1960s, was a highly successful ideological strategy in the 1980s. The extreme fragmentation of the advanced (consumer) world into the desires of individual bodies, the lack of a mobilising project to give 'direction' to society as a whole, make any attempt critically to relate different aspects of existence seem hopelessly old-fashioned, 'unstylish', in a (perjorative) word, 'political'. Conservatism takes the form of an extreme apoliticism manifested in the rejection of any enlightened action by the state, the cultivation of personal identity alone, the acceptance that 'there is nowhere else to go but to the shops' (Hebdige). In Miami Vice and its down-market cousins like Hunter, the rejection of politics includes the police administration itself as one more bureaucracy: extending the liberalist attack on the state to law and order institutions (foreshadowed in the negative image of the FBI in 1970 police series), the 1980s cop makes a lonely stand in a world in which virtually all social bonding has been torn to shreds by a voracious, cynical individualism, the consequence of the very consumption values the series seeks, on at least one level, to uphold. As we have seen in the case of *The Invaders*, the translation into coherent narratives of an ideological strategy which is already contradictory makes it difficult for the series to avoid turning back on itself and attacking its own premises. The appealingly aesthetic portrayal of an inherently viceful world (to avoid the 'sociological' tendencies of realist police series like *Kojak*), and the corresponding valorisation of its two protagonists as 'style heroes' leads to a central ambiguity which the series is never able to overcome. Style itself becomes a form of vice which destroys the innocent, one-to-one relationship between signs and things that existed in a morally pure society; an advanced consumer society is viceful because consumption is no longer utilitarian and uplifting but extravagant, superfluous, desirous. Like the apple of the Tree of Knowledge in the Garden of Eden, vice, like the commodity, is seductive. Appearance, wrapped in colours, only disguises the true nature of things. In 'The Little Prince' (1985), the beautiful snow-white decor of the mansion of Jorgensen, a fabulously wealthy businessmen, also symbolises the 'filthy' heroin on which his fortune has been built. Jorgensen's son, Mark, a heroin addict himself, murmurs in a drugged daze, 'it's all white here, like a clinic. White is not a colour.' White is no longer necessarily a 'value', a symbol of purity but also the symbol of a national sickness. In a world in which appearances are deceptive, the permeability of the line between Good and Evil, and the schizophrenia of human nature, become obsessive themes.

Sonny Crockett is white, divorced, an ex-alcoholic beach bum of dubious antecedents, who lives in elegant negligence on a houseboat with his pet alligator and drives a Ferrari Daytona. His partner and buddy is Ricardo Tubbs, a 'dude' of mixed, black-Hispanic descent, a charmer with a diamond in his ear, who has moved to Miami after the killing of his policeman brother in a gangland murder. Crockett is tough and down-to-earth; a Vietnam Vet and ex-football star, he represents 'regular-guy', small-town values. Tubbs is romantic, sensitive and intellectual: epicurean and impeccably dressed, he represents New York sophistication. Despite these cultural, racial and personality differences, their friendship, and their loyalty to their taciturn, understanding boss Castillo (a veteran of both the Civil Rights marches and the Vietnam War, an interesting and revealing ideological condensation) and their fellow team-mates, the working-class, Southern white ethnic Switek and Zito (both Elvis fans), and the policewomen, Trudy (black) and Gina (Cuban), are the ultimate values of the series against the all-powerful influence of the Vice. Only in the police is the reduction of social relations to mercantilism and self-interest refused in favour of 'human' values which also include an ideal partnership between men and women based on deep respect (not even compromised by Crockett's unsuccessful love affair with Gina). The only method at the police's disposal in the fight against vice is deception. Both Crockett and Tubbs are forced to live an improbable double existence as Burnett and Cooper, gangsters and drug dealers, in the course of undercover police work: it is their competence in this domain, and the conviction with which they play their parts, that confirms their superiority. Grossly underpaid, fighting against impossible odds in intolerable conditions, the police must 'prove' themselves on the terrain of their enemies (for Trudy and Gina, this involves even more improbable undercover work as prostitutes). The strategy of setting a desperate war against vice against a glamorous backdrop of conspicuous consumption in whose values the police are expert cannot be controlled and spills over into confusion and schizophrenia, an explicit theme through-out the series. In 'Mirror Image' (1988), Crockett becomes amnesiac after narrowly surviving an explosion but retains his former skills which he puts at the service of a local gangster in personally attempting to eliminate his partner, Tubbs. As in the Nicaraguan policy of the Reagan government, 'it takes a guerrilla to clobber a guerrilla',[13] typical of the cynical confusion of values of which Irangate was the most caricatural illustration. Similarly, the condensation of business and (sexual) vice, a constant, obsessive trope in the series which determines most of the incidental subtexts and functions as a concrete translation of the argument that economic decline is the result of a moral weakness, of having succumbed to vice on a national scale, can finally only point to the schizophrenic values of capitalism itself. An untramelled free market system materially rewards and encourages the very forces that are destroying it from within. In 'Honor Among Thieves' (1988), whose plot is lifted straight from Fritz Lang's M, the Miami crime syndicate track down a schizophrenic, psychopathic murderer of teenage girls whom he kills with cocaine injections after raping them. The increased police activity and public awareness of the ravages of drugs is bad for the syndicate's cocaine import activities. The syndicate's leader, Palmo, has taken on the trappings of refined respectability (a personal French chef, classical music, golf), trappings which cannot entirely cover over the modest origins evidenced in his friendship with his uncouth, ill-educated bodyguard, Cyril: in a trenchant, general evaluation of the relation between appearance and reality, Crockett describes Palmo's import business as 'one-tenth Colombian art, nine-tenths Colombian flake'. Palmo's respectability, as is his affirmation that 'we're businessmen, we don't knock off teenagers', is a hypocritical lie, for he and his syndicate are as directly responsible for the deaths of teenage girls as is the sex murderer, albeit in a less spectacular, more detached, and ultimately more insidious, way. In a pointed denouement, Delgado, the sex killer, leaps to his death, killing Palmo in the process. To a policeman first on the scene who asks 'which one is the murderer', Crockett wearily replies, 'take your pick'. Unlike in the earlier *The Untouchables*, which awards a strategic role to the state, the line between good and bad capitalism, between reality and appearance, between Good and Evil can no longer be drawn with any ideological confidence. The dramatic condensation of economic and sexual vice tends to brand the capitalist system itself as immoral, a point we shall return to.

Most viewers doubtless remarked on the discrepancy between Crockett and Tubb's lifestyle and their role as beseiged upholders of the law, between the Ferrari and their absolute incorruptibility. The assemblage is so shaky that a whole episode had to be concocted to explain how a poorly-paid policeman could come into possession of a luxurious sports car (a reward from a wealthy industrialist for saving his daughter's life is used to buy a cocaine dealer's Ferrari which has been impounded by the police). This may not even have been necessary: the series is in a domain similar to that of the advertisement, beyond realism. The modern advertisement is the perfect ideological form, a complex, often 'fantastic' assemblage which, unlike in fiction, need never have to confront the consequence of being set in motion. Like the advertising spot, the series aspires to a state of rest; more than any other series so far, *Miami Vice* makes a self-conscious use of style to refuse narrative, to slow it down to the most minimalist dimension possible. The assemblage in place, the poses adopted, there are few places to go: the rock video sequences, which often accompany purely incidental action, are simple time-wasting devices from a narrative point of view. Many of the set pieces are mere extensions of the assemblage, positioning the pair against a backdrop which allows them to show off their consumer skills and to flirt with vice.

In 'The Great McCarthy' (1984), Crockett and Tubbs pose as

out-of-town coke dealers seeking to buy a shipment from the fabulously wealthy Louis McCarthy: checking through McCarthy's bank accounts (complete with $2,300 restaurant bills), Tubbs exclaims that he 'spends more in a month than I earn in a year'. Although it is patently obvious that McCarthy's clothes boutique alone cannot account for his lifestyle, the police have never been able to catch him red-handed. But for all his worldly success, McCarthy has a chink in his armour: his ravishing black companion Vanessa, who manages his shop, is cheating on him both financially and sexually. Tubbs impresses the flirtatious Vanessa with his cool demeanour and free spending, sufficiently so to secure a lunch invitation with McCarthy who is equally impressed by Crockett and Tubbs's hedonist philosophy ('there's what I want and what I need'), consumer sophistication (talk of wine and gourmet food), wealth (they pretend to be owners of a power-boat) and sports skills (Crockett secures the right to participate in McCarthy's private boat race by beating him in a pool game). It is by participating in the race (and winning) that Crockett and Tubbs discover McCarthy's contraband method – changing identical boats in mid-course, profiting from a detour through a patch of mangrove islands. McCarthy's character is never developed although his sumptuous parties and fawning admirers are presumably meant as a reference to that other symbol of decadence, the Great Gatsby: in a pattern that was to be repeated throughout the series, established narratives (many already processed through *Starsky and Hutch*) are simply re-styled in what is little more than a pretext for *illustrating* the assemblage. Psychological drama is thus merely 'sutured' into most episodes: present in time-filling set pieces, its consequences rarely spill over into the action scenes of the main story line except as a pretext for mood music or incidental dialogue. This is a very strange effect. In a complete reversal of the 1950s and 60s television drama tradition, the psychological dimension is a mere adjunct to style, a mere surface. In 'The Great McCarthy', Tubbs falls in love with Vanessa, only to discover that she is the murderess of her accountant and lover, Gifford (an accountant turned coke addict, turned coke dealer, turned police informer, a truly pathetic but typical downfall). The emotional anguish of arresting one's lover of a few minutes before is evoked but not insisted on: after all, Tubb's affair with Vanessa is entirely incidental to the power-boat race around which the whole episode is constructed. In fact, the very character of Vanessa (like that of Gifford) functions purely as a condensation of economic and sexual vice and confirms that sex, like drug trafficking, is a dangerous game for all alike.

The line between normality and vice, between 'good' and 'bad' consumption is so blurred as to be non-existent at times, fading away before a line of coke; the Ferrari and the cocaine form part of a coherent world of pleasure and the series makes little or no effort to separate them. In a world in which police work demands disguising oneself as a criminal, in a society without clear moral guidelines between right and wrong, it is little wonder that the police themselves are constantly faced with the threat of losing sight of the all-important line. In 'Streetwise' (1985), Vic, a policeman who has been working on an undercover job for eleven months, is arrested in a brothel (the appropriately named Ramrod Motel) in the company of a prostitute in possession of cocaine. Rather than simply transgressing, Vic has truly fallen in love with Carla, the prostitute. Suspended, he explains to Crockett:

> Vic: I know when I'm a cop and when I'm acting. I don't need anyone to tell me where the line between them lies.
> Crockett (to the accompaniment of poignant mood music): You really look like you lost sight of it a long time ago. You crossed it one day to see what it was like on the other side. The problem is that you forgot to come back . . . I've done this sort of thing much longer than you have and I have to look at myself in the mirror every morning and tell myself who I really am . . . I've been through what you're going through now and I know what it's like.

Feebly explained as being due to the lack of sexual contact with his wife as a consequence of her night-shift nursing job, Vic's sin can only be redeemed by death in the line of duty.

In 'The Return of Calderan' (1984), Crockett tells Tubbs: 'I've been playing a part for ten years now. You never get used to it', while in 'The Prodigal Son' (1985), he discusses 'who I am and what I am' with his lover who turns out to be a spy working for a crooked banker: 'It'd be nice if one part of my life was real', he declares and when asked what he is really like, he can only reply, 'that gets a little cloudy sometimes'. Superhuman powers of moral resistance are needed: in the same episode, a female cop, Tubbs's former lover, has fallen in love with the leader of a drug syndicate while on an undercover mission. The greatest danger in entering the empire of vice, in stepping over the line, lies in losing forever one's sense of right and wrong, one's sense of self, one's soul. In a world in which appearances are no longer grounded in stable moral values, who can really know where the line is drawn? As R. L. Rutsky argues: 'beneath appearances lie only more appearances . . . duplicity and vice are pervasive; they infuse and corrupt everything, including the Law'.[14]

Unlike other commentators who cannot see beyond the series'

stylishness, Rutsky brings out its theological dimension, essential if one is to understand the strategy of *Miami Vice*. Superficially, Miami is a paradise, abounding in signifiers of luxury and leisure. At the same time, it is a centre for international drug and arms trafficking and one of the most violent cities in the United States. Miami is a fallen world, one in which the circulation of 'good' and 'bad' commodities merges into a general economy of desire. The exchange value of cocaine irrigates the city's economy, providing the basis for its wealth (which ultimately includes Crockett's Ferrari): in 'The Prodigal Son', a crooked corporate banker explains to Crockett that the entire banking system is dependent on Colombian drug money to pay off the interest on the Colombian national debt and so keep the economic system afloat. Politics and finance have ruined at once the country's moral and economic health: nothing can be humanly done but to wait for the Last Judgement. Like the prefigurations of the Biblical Apocalypse, irreparable moral decay is manifested in so many 'signs'. The empire of Vice is one of fragmented appearances in which all 'natural' connection between use value and exchange value has been lost. Cocaine is the ultimate commodity whose dominance consecrates the values of purely individual pleasure. Consumption is likened to drug addiction in 'The Great McCarthy' when Tubbs jokily (and knowingly) impresses Vanessa in her fashion boutique with the observation that Crockett is 'shaking all over, he hasn't bought anything for three hours now'. One recalls the similar relating of drugs and consumption by William Burroughs: 'Junk is the ideal product . . . No sales talk necessary. The client will crawl through a sewer and beg to buy . . . The junk merchant does not sell his product to the consumer, he sells the consumer to his product . . . He degrades and simplifies the client.'[15]

Rutsky also rightly remarks that the circulation of commodities in *Miami Vice* is international, not limited by borders: thus we have Ferraris, continental fashions, Colombian cocaine and Bahamian banks (a sure 'sign' of vice). Miami itself is characterised by a mixing of languages and cultures. Commodity exchange and Vice circulate freely across national and state lines. As Rutsky points out, 'most of the villains are, in fact, foreigners. But it is not simply their status as foreigners that places them in opposition to the law. Their criminality is more a function of their internationality, of their lack of place. The Law, on the other hand, depends on borders'.[16] In 'The Prodigal Son', questions of jurisdiction crop up continually as the action moves between Colombia ('It's their world, man'), Miami and New York where the police initially refuse to co-operate because the pair are 'way out of your jurisdiction'. In 'The Return of Calderan', Crockett and Tubbs are given explicit instructions to respect the jurisdiction of the Bahamian police when on Bahamian territory, although this becomes impossible when they learn that the local police chief is in the pay of Calderan. Evil moves with ease across national borders. In the same episode, Calderan's hired killer is said to be 'known by Interpol, no name. The prints take us back to 1974, the killing of the former ambassador of Chile in Mexico City, 1975, the Turkish military attaché in Rio de Janeiro, 1977, a cultural attaché, 1980, the Palestinian spokesman in Central Park and the list goes on . . . They think he's Argentine.' The foundations of free enterprise, the free flow of commodities and people, have created conditions in which international crime can flourish on American soil. The geographical limitations of police jurisdiction are formally mirrored in the 'liberal' political and philosophical safeguards that protect the criminal: as a city official declares in 'Honor among Thieves' after the decreeing of a curfew, 'there (is) a disease in our city and you don't fight a disease with warnings and Miranda warrants'.[17]

It is here, in the parallel unequal confrontation between the law and trans-border commodity flows, between the police and the rest of society, that the series' unwillingness to distinguish between good and bad consumption, good and bad capitalism, can begin to be understood. For no longer can fundamental American values be equated with those of free enterprise, nor can the police play their 1970s role of mediators and social workers. The uncontrollable ravages of drugs have produced the 'ultimate American nightmare' ('Honor among Thieves'): in 'Welcome Home' (1986), Crockett remarks of a former army buddy, 'he even sells himself, that's the American dream, Tubbs'. The very free enterprise system on which American society is founded has produced a twin, foreign menace; a junk capitalism from the Third World (especially Colombia) which dumps worthless, destructive commodities on the American market, feeding a never-ceasing demand for the Vice which is destroying society from within; and a more advanced capitalism from Japan and Europe whose commodities have outperformed the Americans at their own game. *Miami Vice* is littered with offhand references to European (the Ferrari, the Lamborghini, the designer clothes) and Japanese (television sets, videos) commodities. In a 1986 episode the series' resident pair of police informers offer to sell, 2,000 black-market Japanese television sets: 'Flat screen, beautiful finish, superb quality, best possible price . . . Our warehouse is on 35th Street, we've got half of Tokyo there.' In 'The Genius who Came in from the Cold' (1988), three Japanese industrialists come to Miami to buy up a revolutionary cryogenics procedure that has been used on a Jamaican reggae star, a condensation of the twin threat into a single narrative. In 'Italy' (1986), the friendly father and son rivalry between two racing pilots, Frank Tepper (a sexual pervert who has murdered the prostitute Florence Italy) and Danny Tepper (a decent young man whose wife has just given birth to a son) is the foregrounded, displaced opposition between American and foreign capitalism. A racing grand prix, sponsored by Löwenbrau, symbolically takes on the dimension of a course between American (Camel, Pepsi, Goodyear, Farm Stores) and foreign (Bosch, Nissan, Scandanavian Sun, etc.) sponsors. It is Danny, sponsored by Löwenbrau, who wins ahead of Frank, sponsored by Farm Stores. Frank's sexual perversion is weakly psychologised by the explanation that Danny is not his real son, Frank's wife having 'slept around a lot'. This is an interesting aside for several reasons. It suggests that vice has a temporal origin: judging by Danny's age, it was in the early 1960s that he was born, an era ushering in an unprecedented consumer society. This is an important clue in that it gives a prior, causal relationship to the condensation of vice and economic decline. The latter is located in moral decline which is in turn located in the 1960s; it is by succumbing to (sexual) vice that the American way of life has gone bad. In this respect, the sadistic murder of the prostitute Florence Italy is a condensation of sexual vice and economic weakness: the name also refers to the country which produces the Ferrari and the Lamborghini. The longing for expensive foreign commodities feeds on America's moral decline. A minor vignette from the same episode completes the intrinsic link between moral and economic decline. To a café owner whose business is disturbed by prostitutes hustling on the pavement outside, a transvestite caricaturally replies in empty 1960s rhetoric: 'We're in America, it's a free country, we're living in an epoch of sexual liberation.' It is left to a corrupt Captain in 'Welcome Home' (appropriately played by G. Gordon Liddy of Watergate fame), who has made a fortune from importing heroin from Southeast Asia, to underline – however hypocritically – the suffering caused by an immoral economic system: 'In this country, we don't understand pain very well. What we understand is money. Everyone expects to have as much money as they want; without pain, what a joke.'

No distinction can be made between good and bad domestic capitalism. In 'The Little Prince' (1984) the financier Mark Jorgensen, who has invested in the heroin traffic, is described as 'the guy who buys and sells companies as if they were used cars . . . when he sneezes, Wall Street catches a cold'. In 'The Pirates' (1986), the importing of Colombian cocaine is preyed upon by pirates in a regression to the buccaneering period of primitive capital accumulation: 'the Chamber of Commerce won't be too happy about that', remarks Tubbs cynically. On a mission in New York in 'The Prodigal Son', Tubbs observes (once again, ironically) that 'here we're in the cradle of civilisation'. To which Crockett shoots back: 'it's also its biggest garbage tip'.

At times, the series' neo-populist sneering at the worlds of finance and politics veers towards a sociological explanation of crime. In 'The Little Prince' Tubbs recalls his New York upbringing: 'In the Bronx and other places like that, I saw kids doing themselves in with drugs. They had a thousand reasons for wanting to escape from their environment.' But this thesis, although acknowledged, is finally not upheld. Tubbs continues: 'but what's sad is when it happens to people with a good life ahead of them which they ruin.' In a 1985 episode, Tubbs recognises a dead bandit as Lieutenant Jones from the Crime Squad and explains his descent into crime with the formula 'nine times out of ten, it's for money'. 'No', corrects Lieutenant Castillo, 'ten times out of ten', as the backing intones 'it's the lure of easy money'. The series is full of basically decent people succumbing to temptation, doing a little dealing or trafficking for some easy money, unaware of the danger they are running for themselves and for society. In one episode, a pretty young air hostess whom Crockett is keen on dies in agony after the cocaine samples in her stomach have burst. The vice has literally penetrated into her system and in this, as in most cases, the wages of sin is death: all for a derisory sum so that she can buy a BMW, a foreign car at that. In an irredeemably fallen world, positive, non-mercantile values exist only in the beleaguered fortress of the law and even there, only among the battle-hardened warriors of Lieutenant Castillo, those who, against all odds and aided by their exceptional worldliness and experience, know (roughly) where the line between right and wrong is drawn.

Vice, then, is a force that few can resist. In an episode from 1986, Crockett and Tubbs arrest Archie Ellis, a black high-school student, for delivering cocaine. Heartbroken, Archie explains that he did it as a one-off chance of earning some money to buy a pair of football boots; a football and track star, Archie has staked everything on an athletics scholarship from which a drugs conviction would automatically debar him. Convinced of Archie's basic goodness, Crockett persuades the district attorney to drop the charges, after Archie has saved his life, much to the delight of the black social worker who believes that Archie can be saved from the ghetto. For Archie alone has the chance of getting out. The ghetto is controlled by a fifteen-year-old black Fauntleroy who styles himself 'Count' Walker to underline the brutish, feudal nature of the ghetto. The immensely wealthy, cruel and petulant Walker dominates the ghetto with his chauffered limousine: his drug business represents the only realistic hope of wealth for its inhabitants. In a key image from a clip sequence, two ghetto children stare bug-eyed, mouths agape in admiration, as Walker showers them with money. Anxiety over the integration of the rising generation, a major theme in police series, has given way to a renunciation of hope. No future . . . Walker refuses to deal with anyone over eighteen because 'they represent death'. The consumer paradise is a jungle, a reified form of vegetable existence, something Walker understands only too well: as he tells Crockett and Tubbs, 'it's a real jungle here, full of plants. They all need sun and I'm here to supply it, as much as they need'.

Archie's soul seems to be saved. Crockett offers him money for football boots and a football, promising to follow his career. Archie is back on the track of real American values. But following the killing by Walker's gang (with a grenade launcher) of a carload of opposing gang members (among whom is Ramirez, a promising young undercover cop), and public outcry against the open drug dealing and racketing in schools, Bill Pepin, the district attorney, goes back on his word and maintains the charges against Archie unless he acts as bait (carrying microphones hidden on his body) to trap Walker whose cocaine is causing too many overdoses for the D. A.'s liking. Despite a heartbroken Crockett's insistence that he has one chance in a million of trapping Walker and a high chance of sending Archie to his death, Pepin remains unmoved: we later learn that his major concern is the television news and his reelection prospects. Crockett and the social worker McKee try to persuade Archie to refuse Pepin's plan but the football scholarship means too much to him; furthermore, as he tells Crockett in a moment of remorse, no one forced him to deliver the cocaine. McKee (whose activities in the ghetto are couched in missionary terms) implores Archie with the series' ultimate argument: 'You're wrong, Archie, don't you see that you're selling something else – your soul.' Against all odds, Archie traps Walker, but the wages of sin is death: Walker discovers the microphone and shoots Archie at point-blank range. In the bleakest of all possible worlds, there is no road to redemption, not even for Archie, who wants so much to atone for his sins ('I did something I should never have done ... Nobody forced me to do it'). The cynical, hard-hearted Pepin can now go before the television cameras but Crockett can barely contain his disgust and rage at the sacrifice of an individual for a gang leader who will be replaced within days. Mortified, Crockett offers his condolences to McKee who refuses to invite him inside: Archie's grandmother returns the football which, in a final, loaded gesture, Crockett dumps into a garbage can. The values of sport and education, patiently constructed in 1970s police series as an alternative to crime for the black underclass (Ironside's bodyguard is an ex-delinquent who has turned to law studies), are unceremoniously discarded. As in most episodes, the explanation for a rampant drug problem hovers uncertainly between a generalised inner weakness on the part of individuals and external, sociological factors (the black ghetto, the 'soft' treatment of juvenile delinquents) before scuttling the dilemma altogether in sheer fatalism. The poverty of the ghetto derives from a godless existence in which its inhabitants, having lost their souls, have been reduced to the state of plants or animals. In a telling vignette, Trudy redirects a fat, drunken black on the point of urinating against her car: 'there are trees for that'.

The relentless theological undertow of the series rules out any political solutions to the extent that Crocket and Tubbs are fighting as much with corrupt politicians and lax judges as with criminals. Here the series is often both reactionary and gratuitous in its casual, knowing asides on a judicial system which heavily favours the criminal against the efforts of the police. In an episode in which Crockett goes to jail to protect the identity of an informer from an (old-woman) judge who has strong principles about the rights of the defence, we are informed that one of the gangster Alvarado's go-betweens works for the mayor's office, although this passing remark is never integrated into the plot. Crockett also goes to prison for the same reason in 'Travesty of Justice' (1987), which shows how easily a gangster is able to pervert the course of justice by paying a juror. Similarly, in 'The Return of Calderan', the master trafficker Calderan contemptuously declares to Crockett: 'What do you make? $300 a week? For two miserable dollars, the cops will eat out of my hand ... You wanna know the only time when I get near a judge? It's when I play golf with him at the club. $42 million without tax. That's what I call a free country.' But the series is unable and unwilling to explore the consequences of its repeated, offhand slurs against politicians, judges and university professors (the liberal Establishment) who are made scapegoats for the police's lack of success. An almost wilful sense of failure permeates the series, positioning Crockett and

Tubbs as cynical, worldly, sensitive heroes and suggesting that there is nothing human to be done in a fallen world. 'If we can't help (Carla) start a new life, then what's the point?' asks Tubbs in 'Streetwise', a rhetorical question that the final images of Carla plying her charms in the street answer for him. *Miami Vice* continually draws back from drawing radical political conclusions from the corruption, breakdown and disorder it describes: the rejection of political solutions, the religiously-grounded resignation and the lack of any positive strategy for dealing with crime in a purposeful and coherent way make it difficult to programme meaningful stories from the assemblage without also making a radical critique of the American political and economic system. Religion absorbs a political vacuum and distrust of 'politics' extends to both left-wing and right-wing revolutionaries from Latin America, culpable of exporting political problems (and the threat of a new Vietnam situation) as well as junk commodities.

In 'An Eye too Many', Tubbs penetrates an arms syndicate dealing in ground-to-air missiles stolen from the army to Caribbean and South American terrorists. The boss of the syndicate is the unspeakably vicious Tony Amato who thrashes his wife for daring to consult a lawyer about a divorce. Whereas the FBI are content just to recover the missiles, Crockett and Tubbs, fired by Amato's mistreatment of his wife, will settle for nothing less than his imprisonment. Although Amato is caught red-handed, his political influence is sufficiently strong to secure his instant release. 'Who are you guys working for?', an indignant Tubbs asks Amato's lawyers, 'the FBI? The CIA?' Beyond the reach of the law, Amato cannot escape his divine comeuppance: as he leaves the courthouse, he is shot dead by his long-suffering wife. That the hand of Destiny intervenes over and above the efforts of Crockett and Tubbs testifies to the importance of stylistic and emotional posturing over rational police procedure. The use of poignant musical colouring transfixes the poses into a pervasive fatalism, a world resigned, buffeted by uncontrollable events. Miami's palm trees and neon lights are a reified backdrop against which the tragedy of human existence, placed under the sign of Vice, can be played out. The music often seems to be directing, puppet-like, the movements of the protagonists while song lyrics provide an oblique commentary on the action from a higher sphere.

Public activity is just a pretext for the display of private sentiments which fill out the narrative without inflecting it. In 'The Return to Calderan', Tubbs falls in love with Angelina, whom he takes to be Calderan's mistress before discovering that she is his daughter and is unaware of her father's criminal activities: this allows for much soul-searching about having 'to play a part' and a rueful ending when Angelina rejects Tubbs for having caused the death of her father. In 'Evan' (1985), the need to work with a service secret agent Evan Freed who has infiltrated an arms syndicate is a sounding board for a private drama that occurred 'centuries ago' when Crockett, Freed and Mike O'Gill were an inseparable team. Freed's malicious taunting of O'Gill's homosexuality led the latter to suicidally charge a lone gunman. The consequence of a past drama fills out the story with soul-searching on all sides, reviving Crockett's guilt for being unable to help his friend, putting to the test his relationship with Tubbs and enabling Evan to seek redemption (the word is used) from Crockett before dying in the same circumstances as O'Gill. In 'The Little Prince', the police investigation of the corrupt fiancier Jorgensen is a pretex for illustrating the psychological problems of his son Mark, driven to heroin addiction by resisting an 'unnatural' upbringing based on the idea of his family's genetic superiority. The father and son motif, in which the son rebels against the father's vice, is an obsessive theme which confronts one of the series' major anxieties – is vice a natural element of the human condition, genetically transmitted, or is it the result of external evil? In its direct appeal to the younger generation, the trope reflects uncertainty over the ability of family values (as dispensed by the 1960s generation) to resist the spread of vice.

For the police, any attempt to mix normally in society is necessarily to cross the all-important line between morality and vice. In a 1985 episode, 'tired of living alone', Trudy renews with her old boyfriend David in despair after killing in self-defence, a trauma which is aggravated by the insensitive attitude of the police bureaucracy who are wholeheartedly on the side of the 'victim'. Accompanying David to a rock concert where a decadent Mick Jagger lookalike prances about and sings 'I'm the King of Babylon', Trudy is revolted by the Vice that is rampant among the cocaine-sniffing fans: 'I'd like to arrest everyone here.' The biblical reference here (Babylon being the code word for Rome in *Revelation*) draws a parallel with the decline of ancient Rome through, as the myth has it, sheer decadence. Trudy later confides to Gina: 'David and I have been together for a week and already I'm beginning to consider all his friends as suspects. Being a cop prevents you from having normal relationships.' Her love affair with David cannot withstand the arrest of one of David's cocaine dealer friends through Trudy's police work. Representing the 'normal' voice of society, David, who is not a criminal, tells her: 'You are a woman without heart and without honour.' Single-handedly fighting vice to society's indifference or hostility leads, despite the bravado and swagger, to the portrayal of the police in self-pitying terms, sometimes caricaturally so. In 'The Return of Calderan', the constant and dangerous contact with the 'scum of society' is evoked by Crockett's wife's lawyer as an argument for depriving Crockett of access to his own son.

The persistent cataloguing of a decadent, fallen world necessarily leads to an equally persistent, but repressed question: what is the cause of all of this vice? One answer, as we have seen, is the sexual and moral licence of the 1960s. Another, more profound, is given by the episode 'An Old Friend' (1986). Crockett meets up with an old Vietnam army buddy Robert Kahn who asks him to be the godfather of his newborn son. Kahn has become the manager of a nightclub in financial association with two gangsters (one of whom, we learn is Kahn's father) who are under investigation by the police for the attempted murder of a dancer who knows too much about their activities. Crockett confronts Kahn with the criminality of his father and financial backer:

> Kahn: For the first time since my return (from Vietnam), I feel like a man. I've got a wife, a child and a job. I can walk in the street with my head high.
> Crockett: So that's what being a man is, standing by with your arms crossed while a young mother is murdered, just so you can live in a good neighborhood! What's gotten into you? You've lost all sense of right and wrong . . . The only duty you have is to yourself, if you can look at yourself in the mirror every morning and be proud of what you are, then you've done your duty. Otherwise, you're not worth very much, not to your wife, your child, or to yourself.
> Kahn: . . . You brought me back half-dead from an ambush in the heart of Vietnam, but it's my family, my blood. I can't separate myself from them. (Holds pistol to head). It's like that corporal in Danang, the one who blew his brains out . . . I wonder whether he looked at himself in the mirror before he did it.
> Crockett: The friend I knew always did what he had to do, badly, but he did it, that's what got us out of the jungle without going crazy. We never had a massacre in our unit. You and I refused to throw prisoners out of the helicopter, too bad what the lieutenant said. We did what had to be done, that's what being a man is and nothing else.

The tension between a religious and a sociological explanation for the Vice has given way here to a historical explanation for what is, meta-phorically, a second Fall, the decline of the United States as a world power. In Vietnam, and in the 1960s more generally, America was confronted with a test of its historic destiny and failed 'to do what it had to do'. A macabre image from 'Welcome Home' (1986) bears out this interpretation. A flashback to the evacuation of Saigon, April 1975; The Doors sing 'Strange Days' over newsreel clips of an ignominious, panic-stricken retreat . . . Stone, a journalist friend of the young Corporal Crockett, shows him a grisly discovery: the corpses of American soldiers are being used to smuggle heroin back into the United States: 'You go to the end of the world, you fight for your country, you get killed and you end up in a body bag with filth that kills others in turn.' The self-pity of the police, their sense of betrayal, draws its polemical force from the way the liberal Establishment has shamefully turned on the Vietnam veterans as scapegoats for humiliation and decline. Caught in Vietnam, the vice is a virus from a less civilised country: untreated at the time, it has spread out of control in America itself. In an oblique reference to AIDS, vice is metaphorised into a contagious disease. Speaking of a series of cocaine sex killings, the D.A. in 'Honor among Thieves' declares, 'the City of Miami has the equivalent of a plague on its hands'. In 'Welcome Home', Crockett reminisces with Stone:

It was in Cambodia, we were all scared . . . it was night, there were dark shadows everywhere on the field, we could hear faint noises, we had sentries everywhere, one of them found a guy with his throat cut so he started screaming insults, Charlie was all around and he was there screaming. I woke up . . . I saw this kid, a young corporal and he was going to destroy all the superb dogs we had on patrol . . 'got to kill them all,' he said, 'they've been too well trained, it'd be too dangerous to bring them back home.' I've often thought about it. Maybe we should have shot him too for the same reason.

In the face of what is, in part, a self-inflicted wound, a culpable negligence, the first reflex of Americans is to shoot the guard dogs, to blame the police themselves. Despised by all, even by judges and the police administration, the cop must fall back on a very private sense of honour, to be able to look at oneself in the mirror without flinching. This, along with the line between right and wrong, is a recurring image in the series. The first line of defence against vice lies with the individual: it is by looking at oneself in the mirror that one comes face to face with *the cleanliness of one's soul*. The secret reward of the cop is to be able to live with himself, to have a name, to be 'a man', a morally responsible subject and not an object like the decomposed prostitutes fished out of Miami harbour or those who have sold their souls for material wealth, who have sold themselves, like Burrough's drug addict, as pure commodities. This includes the rock stars on which the series depends. In a revealing, throwaway aside, an informant in 'Italy' declares, 'everyone's got a name except Madonna and Sting.'

Personal honour demands a samurai-like loyalty to the clan in what can be interpreted as a nod to the superior discipline of the Japanese. (In an episode relating a tale of duty and honour dating from Vietnam, Lieutenant Castillo is explicitly cast in samurai terms, both figuratively and allegorically: helping the son and widow of his dead friend escape from the KGB and CIA, Castillo tells their story in allegorical terms as 'the tale of the Shogun and the samurai' and kills the KGB agents with a samurai sword). The samurai ethic of the cop involves a stoic solitude, the abnegation of a 'normal' life in the dreamworld of suburban videoland. In a 1985 episode, Crockett's love affair with a wealthly professional woman interferes with his work (and his relationship with Tubbs, who sees no good in her designer furniture), and is broken off for this reason. Similarly, it is the demands of police work that cause the breakdown of Crockett's marriage, and a machine-gun attack on his family in his own home that destroys a brief reconciliation in 'The Return of Calderan'. The only reward that comes from contact with reality is a form of superior self-knowledge and sensibility that distances the police from the rest of society. Unable to use their street credibility and understanding of human nature in a mediating, social worker role, Castillo's clan use the cleanliness of their souls to play the role of priests or missionaries for the cause of good: to carry out this duty, they must forswear the joys of family life, and sexual contact with others invariably sets up a conflict of interest with their police obligations. Their real mission is not to rid society of crime – an impossible task – but to minister to the souls of others. In the closing minutes of 'An Old Friend', Robbie finally puts the interests of a young woman and her child before those of his father and his own comfort. In the process of saving them from his father's hired thugs, he is mortally wounded. Kneeling over the dying Robbie, Crockett tells him that 'he did the right thing'. Most episodes are organised so that police procedure concords with the real mission of saving souls.

Undoubtedly the most ambiguous series of all time, Miami Vice no doubt began as a cynical attempt to juxtapose two police 'style heroes' against a glamorous vice backdrop ('MTV cops'), in an extension of the formula of Starsky and Hutch: the ambiguity of the title (Miami Vice Squad or Miami's vice?) and the content of the early episodes where Crockett and Tubbs are constantly flirting with vice tends to suggest this. But finally, the underlying anxiety over American economic decline and moral breakdown pushed the series away from its initial (Reaganian) project of celebrating consumer wealth and style in a law and order setting into one of showing that economic and moral decline are intrinsically linked. The two strategies are contradictory, which some-times produces a curious effect. The foreign sports car, for example, is an ambiguous symbol, reflecting unease about consumption itself: on the one hand, the Ferrari valorises Crockett and allows him to show off his driving skills, but in one episode involving poor white dwellers of the Everglades, his car is criticised for being 'foreign'. Similarly, the flashy imagery and up-to-the-minute rock music accompany religiously-based, 1950s style moral injunctions, and scenes of rock concerts are at once celebrations and condemnations of 'sex and drugs and rock and roll', as is the glamour casting of rock stars in villain roles. As a bulwark against the danger of a simple regression to the past in its renewal of traditional moralising, the 1980s police series strategically calls on a new strain of feminism, concerned with the dangers to women of pornography and vice, and harnesses it to a conservative and generally authoritarian world view. The female cop is as tough and resourceful as her male colleague: in *Hunter*, in which cops stalk the city on semi-private missions of vengeance, she is an equal partner and close buddy in a non-sexual relationship; in *Texas Police*, she is the lieutenant for two male cops. The determined use of women (along with racial and ethnic minorities) in the fight against vice, the extension of the 'buddy system' to women in what are portrayed as virtual combat conditions, is a guarantee that society has changed in at least one positive way since the 1950s: it also serves to detach feminism from its more radical 1960s context. Yet this 'feminism' is skin-deep and hypocritical, reflecting the overall ambiguity of the series. Women are given responsibilities in the war against crime but their undercover work as prostitutes enables them to be portrayed in the crudest sex-symbol terms. Furthermore, the policewoman can expect to be raped, or forced to have sex against her will, in the line of duty: in a prurient appeal to the viewer's indignation, Gina, disguised as a call girl, is fucked (over) – no other word is appropriate – by a fat-gutted, coarse-featured hood, thus setting up a situation in which 'rough justice' can later be applied by the victim herself with the greatest possible legitimacy. The series likes this scenario so much that it uses it at least three times.

   Miami Vice represents perhaps a limit-point of the series. In the ultimate consumer world, the social is merely a backdrop for individual postu-ring. The inability to propose new forms of dramatic tension between the social and personal levels of existence – other than their sutured juxtaposition – means that the very form of the series is in crisis. One option, as we have seen, lies in filtering public activity through a serialised retreat into private life, a move away from the classic series form into a modernised soap opera that extends beyond a female audience. In retrospect, we may well see the aesthetic innovations of *Miami Vice* as the last-ditch combination of two dead or dying forms – episodic series and rock music. In an increasingly fragmented television market, which is seeing the gradual decline of mass, network audiences, there is less need to anchor narratives in a social consensus: the 'youth' market of *Miami Vice* can be catered to at the design and marketing level, although as the less than resounding commercial success of music channels indicates, the transformation of the series into loosely-organised clip sequences and star routines held together by a minimal narrative of convenience has every chance of foundering on the rock of audience indifference. If the television series becomes more of a mobile soundscape to be half-watched, just as commercial radio is half-listened to, it may deservedly fall victim to its own blankness and irrelevance: only a perhaps outdated commercial logic (regular audiences and syndication rights) lies behind the exploitation of a single assemblage to the point of exhaustion. What lies at stake in the years ahead is the very autonomy of television fiction as a cultural form independent of commercial packaging. As Simon Frith argues:

The use of video techniques across the media (represents) . . . a further confusion of entertainment and packaging . . . It is not surprising that video techniques have been absorbed most easily by TV commercials (where many of them came from in the first place), or that the TV use of video to promote rock has also meant the TV use of rock to promote everything else.[18]

The remaking (with modern packaging) of old series like *Star Trek* and *Mission: Impossible* adds to the impression of a dead time, a cultural form that has come to the end of the road.

Notes

Chapter 1

1 In the field of television fiction, most work has been done on the serial and sitcom form: the focus on the family and personal relations between the sexes (and its predominantly female audience) makes this form of particular interest to feminist critics. The tendency to read television fiction in terms of the way it 'actively' raises social issues also makes the 'adventure' series less amenable to academic discussion. For a very thorough, but non-synthetic, review of existing work on various genres of television fiction, see John Fiske, *Television culture* (London: Methuen, 1987). (See also John Fiske and John Hartley, *Reading television* (London and New York: Methuen, 1978.) Two collections of essays have been organised around production companies. *MTM, 'quality television'* (ed. Jane Feuer, Paul Kerr and Tise Vahimagi, London: BFI, 1984) contains analyses of *The Mary Tyler Moore Show*, *Lou Grant* and *Hill Street Blues* while *Made for television: Euston films Limited* (ed. Manuel Alvarado and John Stewart, London: BFI, 1985) includes readings of British series like *The Sweeney* and *Minder*. For an article-length discussion of British police series, see Geoffrey Hurd, 'The television presentation of the police', in Tony Bennett, Susan Boyd-Bowman, Colin Mercer and Janet Woollacott, eds., *Popular television and film* (London: BFI, 1981). Also recommended is the historical overview of different genres in Brian G. Rose, ed., *TV genres: a handbook and reference guide* (Westport, Conn. and London: Greenwood Press, 1985).

2 Max Horkheimer and Theodor W. Adorno, 'The industrial production of cultural commodities', in *Dialectic of enlightenment* (New York, Herder & Herder, 1972).

3 Walter Benjamin, 'The work of art in the age of mechanical reproduction', in *Illuminations* (London: Fontana, 1973).

4 McLuhan divided media into 'hot' (radio, cinema) and 'cold' (television, comics) categories by virtue of their technical ability to extend a single sense (hot) or many senses (cold). In McLuhan's argument, 'cold' media like television required greater interaction from the audience to 'fill in' the medium's low definition, and this participatory quality was more important than the content of message: 'the medium is the message'. Few take McLuhan's arbitrary distinctions seriously today, but his influence can still be felt in celebrations of the 'active viewer' and in public relations arguments for the democratising, 'interactive' virtues of new media in the computer age (I am thinking in particular here of crusaders like Alvin Toffler). See Marshall McLuhan, *Understanding media* (New York: McGraw-Hill, 1964); Alvin Toffler, *The third wave* (New York: William Morrow, 1980).

5 Greil Marcus, *Rock and roll will stand* (Boston: Beacon, 1969).

6 For a discussion of the impact of McLuhan on rock music and the counter-culture, see David Buxton, *Le Rock: star système et société de consommation* (Grenoble: La Pensée Sauvage, 1985), pp. 111–26.

7 For an example of the interactionist approach, see Paul Hirsch, 'Sociological approaches to the pop music phenomenon', *American Behavioural Scientist*, 14 (1971).

8 The stress on the 'active' nature of popular culture and the cultural creativity of (working-class) subcultures was an important element in the emergence of cultural studies as a legitimate academic discipline in the 1960s, largely through the pioneering efforts of the Birmingham Centre for Contemporary Cultural Studies. For a representative sample of the 'Birmingham School', see Stuart Hall and Tony Jefferson, eds., *Resistance through rituals*

(London: Hutchinson, 1975). The political thrust of this project, a determined romantici-sation of working-class and youth culture which veered towards populism, often trans-lated the active/passive opposition into class terms (working class/middle class) within popular culture. Needless to say, these categories were ill-suited to popular television, accounting for a blind-spot in the British cultural studies tradition. (In all fairness, it should be pointed out that the French intellectual tradition, with its literary–philosophi-cal bias, has practically ignored the question of the media and popular culture).

9 Ralph Gleason, 'Rock: a world bold as love', *Rolling Stone*, 65, (3 September 1970), p. 46.
10 Charles Reich, *The greening of America* (New York: Random House, 1970), pp. 145, 244.
11 'Sex, dope and the revolution', *IT*, 107, (1 July 1971), pp. 15–16.
12 Fiske, *Television culture*, pp. 313, 324.
13 The circularity of the viewer-centred approach can also be seen in Ien Ang, *Watching Dallas: soap opera and the melodramatic imagination* (London: Methuen, 1985). Ang placed an advertisement in a women's magazine stating: 'I like watching the TV serial *Dallas* but often get strange reactions to it. Would anyone like to write and tell me why you like watching it too, or dislike it?' (p. 10). The very terms of the question are an invitation to particularly motivated *Dallas* viewers to rationalise their viewing habits, to produce 'personalised' evaluations that can only participate in the wider ideology of the *Dallas* phenomenon. In Ang's book, a very limited sample of – to my mind – trivial viewer comments on a single moment of television (*Dallas*, early 1980s) are academically 'processed' to illustrate the existence of a general 'melodramatic imagination'. I fail to see the interest of this style of media sociology, which simply displaces the problem of the ideal viewer in demystifi-cation approaches on to another level – of what or whom is the sample of 'ideal (active) viewers' representative, if not of the writer's own options? – without any correspond-ing gain to offset the abandonment of textual analysis (see also n. 41 below).
14 Roland Barthes, *Mythologies* (St Albans: Paladin, 1973).
15 Jean Mitry, *La Sémiologie en question: langage et cinéma* (Paris: Les Editions du Cerf, 1987), p. 30.
16 Noel Burch, *Une praxis du cinéma* (Paris: Gallimard, 1986), pp. 12–13.
17 Ibid., p. 13.
18 Fiske, *Television culture*, p. 132.
19 Umberto Eco, 'Narrative structures in Fleming', in O. Del Buono and U. Eco, eds., *The Bond affair* (London: Macdonald, 1966).
20 Vladimir Propp, *Morphology of the folk tale* (Austin: University of Texas Press, 1968).
21 Eco, 'Narrative Structures'.
22 Claude Lévi-Strauss, 'Structure and form', in *Structural anthropology*, Vol. 2, (Harmonds-worth: Penguin, 1978).
23 Fredric Jameson, *The political unconscious* (London: Methuen, 1986), p. 121.
24 Fiske, *Television culture*, p. 137.
25 Todd Gitlin, *Inside prime time* (New York: Pantheon, 1983).
26 Quoted in ibid., p. 81.
27 Quoted in ibid., p. 150.
28 Claude Lévi-Strauss, 'The structural study of myth', in *Structural Anthropology*, Vol. 1 (Har-mondsworth: Penguin, 1972), pp. 206–31.
29 Ibid., p. 216.
30 Claude Lévi-Strauss, *The savage mind* (London: Weidenfeld & Nicolson, 1966).
31 Jean-Pierre Vernant, 'Oedipe sans complexe', in J. -P. Vernant and P. Vidal-Naquet, *Mythe et tragédie en Grèce ancienne* (Paris: Maspero, 1973), pp. 80–1. (English translation: *Myth and tragedy in Ancient Greece* (New York: Zone Press, 1989).)
32 These Freudian terms are not, of course, used by Lévi-Strauss himself. Here, I would simply remark on the formal similarity between the ideological structure of the narrative and the transhistorical unconscious. The danger of any over-hasty synthesis is to repeat the tendency of classic structuralism to rewrite all narratives in terms of some simplified, ahistorical Ur-narrative.

33 Pierre Macherey, *Pour une théorie de la production littéraire*, (Paris: Maspero, 1966), p. 177. (English translation: *A theory of literary production* (London: Routledge & Kegan Paul, 1978).)
34 *Ibid.*, pp. 183–266.
35 Raymond Williams, *Marxism and literature* (Oxford: Oxford University Press, 1977), pp. 83–9.
36 The concept 'ideologeme', forged by analogy with Lévi-Strauss's 'mytheme', was used by Julia Kristeva in her *Semeiotikè* (Paris: Seuil, 1969) to describe the 'materialisations' of 'intertextual functions' throughout a text, giving it its 'historical and social coordinates' (p. 114). For another definition of the same term as at once an abstract concept and a (political) protonarrative, see Jameson, *The political unconscious*, p. 87.
37 'An interview with Pierre Macherey', *Red Letters*, 5 (summer 1977), p. 5.
38 For a definitive analysis of the American television system, see Gitlin, *Inside prime time*. Other essential references here are Kaarle Nordenstreng and Tapio Varis, *Television traffic – a one-way street?* (Paris: UNESCO, 1974); Nicholas Garnham, *Structures of television* (London: BFI, 1973); A. Mattelart, X. Delcourt and M. Mattelart, *International image markets* (London: Comedia, 1984).
39 The criticism of popular television forms is all the more important in view of the fact that, because of their apparent popular consent, they have become a social space immune to critical analysis, a state of affairs that a humanist, viewer-oriented approach, forced to 'apologise' for existing viewer choices, can only perpetuate. Particularly deadly (and influential) is the response typified by American television writer Roy Huggins:

> Every person of common sense knows that people of superior mental constitutions are bound to find much of television intellectually beneath them. If such innately fortunate people cannot realise this gently and with good manners, if in their hearts they despise popular pleasure and interest, then, of course, they will be angrily dissatisfied with television. But it is not really television with which they are dissatisfied. It is with people.

Quoted by Armand Mattelart in the 'introduction' to *Communication and class struggle, Vol. 1* (ed. A. Mattelart and S. Siegelaub (New York, Bagnolet: International General, 1979)), p. 42. The strength of an ideologically grounded analysis is that it completely circumvents such arguments.
40 David Buckingham, 'Television literacy: a critique', *Radical Philosophy*, 51 (spring 1989), p. 23.
41 Fiske, *Television culture*. I have singled out Fiske as being representative of the new populist strain in British cultural studies, typified by an incoherent blend of different schools-thinkers (each served up to students as a 'revelation' rather than being used in specific arguments) with empirical, 'vox-pop' studies of audiences. For a trenchant, superbly argued critique (which I came across after completing the manuscript and endorse wholeheartedly), see Meaghan Morris, 'Banality in cultural studies', *Block*, 14 (autumn 1988). Morris argues that in Fiske's 'ethnographic' approach,

> the people have no necessary defining characteristics – except an indomitable capacity to 'negotiate' readings, generate new interpretations, and remake the materials of culture. This is also, of course, the function of cultural studies itself . . . So against the hegemonic force of the dominant classes, 'the people' represent the most creative energies and functions of critical reading. In the end, they are not simply the cultural student's object of study and his native informants. The people are also the textually delegated, allegorical emblem of the critic's own activity. Their *ethnos* may be constructed as other, but is used as the ethnographer's mask. Once 'the people' are both a source of authority for a text and a figure of its own critical activity, the populist enterprise is not only circular but (like most empirical sociology) narcissistic in structure. (p. 20)

42 Jameson, *The political unconscious*, p. 289.
43 I should also like to acknowledge the influence of Judith Williamson's film criticism in

the defunct *New Statesman*.

44 The series analysed in this book have been watched on French television over a three-year period in, of course, their dubbed French versions. This means that the snatches of dialogue quoted throughout have been translated from the French and will not, therefore, correspond exactly to the original scripts. The dialogues have, however, been carefully transcribed from recorded video-cassettes and I have no reason to suspect that the original English would differ markedly from the versions given here (for a small number of episodes, I have had access to the English version). In any case, my analysis is concerned with ideological content and does not depend on a close linguistic reading. I can only ask for the reader's indulgence on this point and hope that the quoted dialogues are nevertheless helpful to the analysis. For the author, a French citizen of New Zealand origin, working from the French versions was a condition of the book's very existence.

Two less defensive justifications can also be given. These 'international' series do not exist only in their English versions: for those in non-English-speaking countries, dubbed versions constitute the 'original' (for a good many of the series discussed here, I have only ever seen the French version). Second, probably only in France could the viewing of such a wide historical range in a relatively short time have been possible: for economic reasons, the new French private channels have served up a constant, repetitive diet of old series.

Chapter 2

1 Most of the following details are taken from Erik Barnouw, *Tube of plenty* (Oxford: Oxford University Press, 1975).

2 See George McKenna's introduction, 'Populism: the American ideology', to his edited collection *American populism* (New York: Putnam's Sons, 1974). The writings and speeches contained in this book illustrate different historical strains of populism in its rural and urban, left-wing and right-wing, versions. The religious dimension of populism is crucial. About 97 per cent of Americans affirm some belief in the existence of God, a figure that has remained fairly constant this century. In a campaign speech in the 1950s, General Eisenhower declared, 'Without God, there could be no American form of government, nor an American way of life. Recognition of the Supreme Being is the first and most basic expression of Americanism' (quoted by Malise Ruthven in *The Times Literary Supplement* (9–15 June 1989), p. 629).

3 For a discussion of Turner's thesis, presented in a speech to the American History Association in 1893, see Jean-Louis Leutrat, *Le Western* (Paris: Armand Colin, 1973), pp. 145–7.

4 André Glucksmann, 'Les aventures de la tragédie', in Raymond Bellour, ed., *Le Western: sources, mythes, auteurs, acteurs, filmographies* (Paris: Editions 10/18, 1966), pp. 71–89.

5 Quoted in Jean-Louis Rieupeyrout's definitive history of the Western, *La Grande Aventure du Western: du Far West à Hollywood* (1894–1963), (Paris: Editions du Cerf, 1971), p. 118.

6 Daniel Bell, 'Modernity and mass society: diversity of cultural experiences', quoted in Armand Mattelart's introduction to A. Mattelart and S. Siegelaub, *Communication and class struggle*, 2 (New York, Bagnolet: International General, 1983), p. 52. The reference given for Bell's text here is to an anthology on communication in Spanish.

7 Quoted in Rita Parks, *The Western hero in film and television* (Ann Arbor, Michigan: UMI Research Press, 1982), p. 141.

8 Ibid., pp. 159–61, 130.

9 Quoted in ibid., p. 151.

10 Quoted in ibid., p. 163.

11 Ibid.

12 From 'The high cost of hoodlums', an article written by John Gunther for the October 1929 issue of *Harper's Monthly Magazine*, reprinted in George C. Mowry, ed., *The twenties: Fords,*

flappers and fanatics (Englewood Cliffs, NJ: Prentice Hall, 1963), pp. 114–20.

13 Thus the voice-cover conclusion to 'Star Witness' informs us that 'two days before the execution of McOriss, the wholesale price (of fish) dropped by 50 per cent'.

14 Two post-war statements of America's 'manifest destiny': 'American experience', exulted Henry Luce of *Time* magazine, 'is the key to the future . . . America must be the elder brother of nations in the brotherhood of man.' The wartime Secretary of State and one of the founders of the United Nations, Cordell Hull: 'All these principles and policies (free trade, democracy, self-help, free enterprise) are so beneficial and appealing to the sense of justice, of right and of the well-being of free peoples everywhere.' Both quotations from Paul Kennedy, *The rise and fall of the great powers* (London: Fontana, 1988), pp. 464–5.

15 Quoted in Gary Geranni and Paul Schulman, *Fantastic television* (New York: Harmony Books, 1977). I have taken this quotation from Georges-Albert Astre, 'USA, films, téléfilms . . . renouveau?', in *Cinéma* (Paris), 241 (January 1979), p. 23, and re-translated it into English.

16 It is perhaps worth noting here that the creator of *The Invaders*, Larry Cohen, later went on to make a series of 'schlock' horror movies which self-consciously combined monstrous beings with religious allegories of puritanism and guilt.

17 For an analysis of organicism in relation to Conrad, see Avrom Fleishman, *Conrad's politics: community and anarchy in the fiction of Joseph Conrad* (Baltimore, Md.: Johns Hopkins University Press, 1967). Also of interest here is Robert Kiely, *Robert Louis Stevenson and the fiction of adventure* (Cambridge, Mass: Harvard University Press, 1965). I should also signal a book-length academic study of *Star Trek* (all too rare in the case of series): Karin Blair, *Meaning in Star Trek*, (Chambersburg, Pa.: Anima Books, 1977) which unfortunately I have been unable to consult.

The displaced justification of the Vietnam War as being necessary to American power and the conquest of space, but without resorting to crude McCarthyist attacks on protesters, can be seen in the episode 'The City on the Edge of Forever' (1967), written by Harlan Ellison. Time-travelling to the earth of the 1930s, Kirk falls in love with Edith Keller, a progressive, dedicated social worker and pacifist. Computer projection shows that the Earth has two possible futures: either her life will be tragically cut short in a car accident or else she will go on to lead a (misguided) pacifist movement which will delay America's entry into the war sufficiently to allow a Nazi victory. In order for history to resume its 'normal' course, she must die, regardless of the emotional cost to Kirk. For a synopsis of all the *Star Trek* episodes, see Alan Asherman, *The Star Trek compendium* (London: Titan, 1987).

18 Under the influence of Ernst Dichter's 'motivation research', advertisers from the 1950s on adopted a quasi-Jungian conception of a universal symbolism based on a fundamentally constant human nature. See Gérard Lagneau, *La Sociologie de la publicité*, (Paris: Presses Universitaires de France (Que sais-je?, 1977).

Chapter 3

1 For a more detailed analysis, see Henri Van Lier, 'Culture et industrie: le design', *Critique* (Paris), 246 (November 1967).

2 See Dick Hebdige, *Hiding in the light: on images and things* (London, New York: Routledge, 1988), pp. 45–77.

3 For a powerful analysis of the supercession of 'needs' by a 'logic of social differentiation' in which demand becomes virtually infinite on a symbolic level, see Jean Baudrillard, *La Société de consommation* (Paris: Gallimard, 1970).

4 Norman Mailer, 'The white negro', in *Advertisements for myself* (London: Panther, 1968), p. 271.

5 *TV Times* 281 (26 May 1961), p. 3.

6 Quoted in Alan Levy, *Operation Elvis* (London: André Deutsch, 1960), p. 111.

7 Quoted in Tony Palmer, *All you need is love* (London: Futura, 1977), p. 217.

8 *TV Times* (14 October 1962), pp. 14–15.

9 Richard Hamilton, *Collected words* (London: Thames & Hudson, 1982), p. 28.

10 For an analysis of the Mods and pop, see Hebdige, *Hiding in the Light*, pp. 77–147; George Melly, *Revolt into style* (Harmondsworth: Penguin, 1970); Simon Frith and Howard Horne, *Art into pop* (London and New York: Methuen, 1987).

11 G. Murdock and R. McCron, 'Consciousness of class and consciousness of generation', in Hall and Jefferson, eds., *Resistance through ritual*.

12 Len Deighton, *The Ipcress file* (London: Hodder & Stoughton, 1962).

13 Michael Denning, *Cover stories: narrative and ideology in the British spy thriller* (London and New York: Routledge & Kegan Paul, 1987). See also Tony Bennett and Janet Woollacott, *Bond and beyond: the political career of a popular hero* (London: Macmillan, 1987).

14 John Buchan, *Mr Standfast* (Harmondsworth: Penguin, 1988 (1919), pp. 221–2.

15 *Playboy*, November 1965, p. 76.

16 *TV Times* (9 September 1960), pp. 8–9.

17 *Ibid.* The actor Patrick Magoohan was constantly presented by the *TV Times* in highly moral and socially uplifting terms, perhaps to compensate for the anxiety aroused by the secret agent's individualism:

> McGoohan's character, prejudices and beliefs have done much to stage the *Danger Man* format. He does not like cheap sex or unnecessary violence and he wrote a clause into his contract to ensure such matters were excluded from the series . . . 'I don't like violence. I mean take away from Bond his women and his expertise with a menu and there is not much left.' (*TV Times* (26 September 1965), pp. 2–3)

> He dislikes the patronising attitude of people who think they know what kind of entertainment 'the workers' ought to have. He takes active responsibility for what is put on his shows when anyone could be watching from granny to the baby . . . 'You know I fear by 2000 AD we'll all have numbers, no names . . . I don't like people who intrude on my privacy, or anyone else's.' (*TV Times*, (28 November 1965), p. 5)

18 *TV Times* (28 October 1960), p. 3.

19 G. K. Chesterton, *The man who was Thursday* (Harmondsworth: Penguin, 1962 (1908), p. 129.

20 Peter O'Donnell, *Modesty Blaise* (London: Pan, 1966), p. 187.

21 Producer Aaron Spelling, quoted in *TV Times* (12 January 1964), p. 6.

22 Hebdige, *Hiding in the light*, p. 136.

23 Quoted in *ibid.*, p. 135.

24 Review of the episode 'Conspiracy of Silence' on the BBC Radio Home Service, 10 March 1963, transcribed in *Stay tuned* (*The Avengers* fan club magazine), n.d. (1986?) contains the script of the episode 'The Warlock'). A sample of other critical comments: 'I pity any actors who have to cope with lines like . . . "scruples are fine, but ask yourself are they being worn this year" ' (Eric Proust); 'I think sometimes the speed was almost too fast' (Janet Adam Smith); 'To me, there is something very strange about brilliant technique put on trivial content' (Harry Craig), pp. 15–17.

25 *TV Times* (9–15 February 1964), p. 7.

26 *TV Times* (10 March 1961), p. 11.

27 Sydney Newman, Head of Drama, ABC Television, quoted in Dave Rogers, *The Avengers* (London: ITV Books, 1983), p. 13.

28 *TV Times* (10 March 1961), p. 11.

29 Quoted in Rogers, *The Avengers*, p. 29. Pop's idea of 'feminism' was to give heroines technical skills as well as sexual appeal. (Modesty Blaise is a more pronounced example of the fantasy of the 'active woman' whose love-making ability matches her courage and professionalism.)

   Social democratic options are evident in the following portrayal of Cathy Gale as a woman of 'unshakable moral principle': 'When Fidel Castro of Cuba was leading a democratic rebellion against dictatorship, she fought in the hills with him. But as soon as Dr Castro achieved power, he deported her because of her opposition to certain aspects of his regime.' These principles are married with the individualistic, pleasure values of the old upper class combined with a (slight) disrespect for tradition. '(Steed) had all the advantages of being the younger son of a younger son, a scion of a noble family. But he is the black sheep . . . he was sent to Eton but spent most of his time in amateur theatricals.' After being given life royalties from two oil wells after a spell as economic adviser to the Middle Eastern sheik, he 'lived the life to which he has accustomed himself – rare wines, fancy waistcoats, pretty girls and polo' (*TV Times* (20 September 1963), p. 4). Importantly, Steed's source of wealth has been derived from his professional skills rather than his class position.

30 Steven Chibnall, 'Avenging the past', *New Society* (28 March 1985), p. 476. The dialogues from 'Death at Bargain Prices' and 'The Cybernauts' have been taken from Chibnall's article. I am grateful to John Stewart of the British Film Institute for arranging a private screening of 'The House that Jack Built'. I was also able to view three early episodes in the BFI's vault: 'The Little Wonders'; 'Mandrake' and 'The Secrets Broker'.

31 Daniel Bell, *The end of ideology* (New York: Collier, 1962, 2nd revised edn). See also his *Cultural contradictions of capitalism* (New York: Basic Books, 1976).

32 For a classic analysis of camp, see Susan Sontag, 'Notes on camp', in *The Susan Sontag reader* (Harmondsworth: Penguin, 1985).

33 A typical pop joke was to advance plausible, straight-faced and naive alibis for 'daring', 'naughty' and ambiguous sexual references that only the 'sophisticated' could understand. NBC initially objected to the name THRUSH on the (unconvincing) legal grounds that it sounded too much like SMERSH. Eventually THRUSH was upheld (as opposed to SMEAR, THRUST, MAGGOT, BRUTE, SCOURGE, WASP and a host of other names) because 'it seemed unique, conveyed the proper note of a quiet threat and had a sinister ring' (John Heitland, *The Man from UNCLE book* (London: Titan, 1988), pp. 32–3).

Chapter 4

1 Stephen Knight, *Form and ideology in crime fiction* (London: Macmillan, 1980), p. 169. I should like to acknowledge my debt, both to the spirit and the content, of this book.

2 *TV Times* (23 September 1955), p. 21.

3 *Radio Times* 22 August 1968), p. 25.

4 *Ibid.*

5 *Radio Times* (11 January 1968), p. 31.

6 *Radio Times* (22 February 1968) p. 35.

7 Gitlin, *Inside prime time*, p. 269.

8 Mentioned in François Julien, *La Loi des séries* (Paris: Barrault, (1987), p. 160. The success of this series among younger viewers in France, where it ran continuously until 1988, long after it had disappeared from American screens, can be explained by a free adaptation which added in an irreverent tone to many of the more 'flat' original dialogues (Julien, p. 161). In general, the average American cop series is not 'psychological' enough for adult French taste.

9 For an illustration of the generic similarity of populist responses over and above national contexts, consider the following monologue by Inspector Jack Regan in the British series *The Sweeney*, from the same epoch:

I sometimes hate this bastard place (London). It's a bloody holiday camp for thieves and wierdos . . . all the rubbish. You age prematurely trying to sort some of them out. You try and protect the public and all they do is call you fascist. You nail a villain and some ponced-up, pin-striped amateur barrister screws you up like an old fag packet on a point of procedure, then pops off for a game of squash and a glass of Madeira. He's taking home thirty grand a year and we can just about afford ten days in Eastbourne and a second-hand car. ('The Abduction')

Quoted in the excellent analysis of James Donald, 'Anxious moments: *The Sweeney* in 1975', in Alvarado and Stewart, eds.: *Made for television*, pp. 121–2. Because of the heightened political sensibilities surrounding police activity in France, a local version of the rule-breaking 'rogue cop' like Regan and Kojak has never been a viable ideological option. A French version of the liberal-minded, individualist, social-worker cop appeared in the mid-1970s in the *Commissaire Moulin* series of ninety-minute téléfilms.

10 Todd Gitlin, 'We build excitement' in Gitlin, ed., *Watching TV* (New York: Pantheon, 1987), p. 157.

11 John Fiske, 'MTV: post structural post modern', *Journal of Communication Inquiry*, 10, 1 (winter 1986), p. 75.

12 E. Ann Kaplan, *Rocking around the clock* (London: Methuen, 1987); Fiske, *Television culture*, especially pp. 254–5.

13 Gitlin, 'We build excitement', p. 159.

14 R. L. Rutsky, 'Visible sins, vicarious pleasures: style and vice in *Miami Vice*', *SubStance*, 55 (1988), p. 78. For an analysis centred on *Miami Vice*'s representation of masculinity, see Andrew Ross, '*Miami Vice*: selling in', *Communication*, 9 (3–4) (1987).

15 William Burroughs, 'Introduction' to *Naked lunch* (New York: Grove Press, 1982 (1959)), p. xxxix.

16 Rutsky, 'Visible Sins', p. 79.

17 In *Miranda v. Arizona* (1966), the Supreme Court overturned the rape–kidnapping convictions of Ernesto Miranda on the grounds that he had not been given a full and effective warning of his right to remain silent during questioning and have an attorney present. The due process clause of the Constitution was interpreted to require that the police issue standard warnings of the accused's legal rights at the time of arrest. In *Miami Vice*, the Miranda warnings are often given contemptuously to underline the extent to which they hamper the war on criminality.

18 Simon Frith, 'Afterword – making sense of video: pop into the nineties', in *Music for pleasure* (Oxford: Polity Press, 1988), p. 214.